"Moving from Canada to the United States is a daunting task when you consider the reams of required paperwork and tax hurdles. Despite this, more than 20,000 made this move in 2012, often with little or no appreciation of the complexities involved. All of which makes the long-awaited third edition of Brian Wruk's *The Canadian in America* most welcome indeed."

— Jonathan Chevreau, Founder of FinancialIndependenceHub.com

"There are very few people who understand the world of cross-border financial planning like Brian Wruk. This book is a wonderful testament to that. Anyone considering a move across the Canada–U.S. border should have a copy of this book!"

— Tim Cestnick, Managing Director, Advanced Wealth Planning, Scotiabank

"Every Canadian estate planner, lawyer, attorney, and advisor needs to be familiar with U.S. tax and investment matters and Brian's book is a necessary and welcome addition to the library of knowledge in this area."

— Roy Klassen, Estate Planning Attorney

"Dealing with U.S. immigration and tax rules can quickly create a gigantic headache. This easy to understand book offers a gigantic dose of aspirin."

— Bruce Cohen, Author of *The Pension Puzzle* and *The Money Advisor*

"Brian Wruk has put together the most complete resource book covering all areas of relevance for both Canadians and Americans heading south over the 49th parallel. A must-read and resource document for any practitioner serious about dealing with clients relocating south."

— Doug Macdonald, MBA, RFP, Macdonald, Shymko & Company, Fee Only Financial Advisors

"This is the best book I've seen on the myriad of financial and legal issues involved in moving to the U.S."

— Ian McGugan, Editor, *MoneySense* magazine

"*The Canadian in America* is an excellent one-stop resource for Canadians living in the U.S. I will certainly recommend it to our clients."

— Geoffrey D. Leibl, Immigration Attorney, Leibl & Kirkwood

The Canadian in America

Real-Life Tax and Financial Insights
into Moving to and Living in the U.S.

REVISED 3rd Edition

Brian D. Wruk

ecw press

Published by ECW Press
665 Gerrard Street East, Toronto, Ontario, Canada M4M 1Y2
416-694-3348 / info@ecwpress.com

Library and Archives Canada Cataloguing in Publication

Wruk, Brian D., author
The Canadian in America : real-life tax and financial insights into
moving to and living in the U.S. / Brian D. Wruk. — Revised 3rd edition.

Includes bibliographical references and index.
Issued in print and electronic formats.
ISBN 978-1-77041-088-6 (paperback)
978-1-77090-745-4 (pdf)
978-1-77090-746-1 (epub)

1. Canadians—United States—Finance, Personal. 2. Canadians—
Taxation—Law and legislation—United States. 3. Canadians—Legal status,
laws, etc.—United States. 4. Canada—Emigration and immigration.
5. United States—Emigration and immigration. I. Title.

HG179.W78 2015   332.024008911073   C2015-902823-X
C2015-902824-8

Cover design: Tania Craan
Cover images: Suitcase © Coprid/iStockphoto;
U.S. flag © hazimsn/iStockphoto; tag © alexl/iStockphoto
Printed and bound in Canada at Friesens   5   4   3   2   1

ECW Press acknowledges the financial support of the Government of Canada
through the Canada Book Fund for our publishing activities.

I dedicate this book to my grandparents, who have gone home to be with their Savior in heaven. They pursued their own dreams and left Europe to homestead in Canada, creating the next generation of Canadians.

Wilhelm and Louisa Wruk

Edward and Ottilie Hiller

Deuteronomy 2:7
The Lord your God has blessed you
in all the work of your hands. He has
watched over your journey.

In memoriam to J. Pierre Lacroix, my very first manager and mentor. You took this newly minted university graduate and taught me how to write. Thank you for making me the author I am today.

CONTENTS

ACKNOWLEDGMENTS

Given the vast complexities and issues surrounding any move to the U.S., we are unashamed to say that we don't know everything! However, we view ourselves as the quarterback of a team of people to effectively coordinate your move. To that end, our firm relies on a large network of trusted, competent professionals to assist with the variety of issues our clients have. We view our knowledge as being a mile wide and a foot deep, but we have experts in all areas whose knowledge is a foot wide but a mile deep. We have drawn upon these experts to review various parts of this book, and want to thank them individually for their assistance in making this large undertaking possible.

Richard Brunton, a fabulous Canada-U.S. tax accountant in Boca Raton, Florida. Thank you for your encouragement of this project and for imparting your wisdom and knowledge whenever needed.

Brent Gunderson, an excellent attorney in Mesa, Arizona, offering the unique combination of estate planning and immigration to our Canadian-American clients. Thanks for your counsel in these highly technical areas.

Mitch Marenus, our chief investment officer, my partner, my friend. Thank you for helping me through the difficult times and keeping our clients and my investment strategies focused on the long term.

Eva Sunderlin, our Canada-U.S. paraplanner and a cherished associate. Thank you for all the work you did to make this book possible. Thanks for all you do for our clients (and us!).

Jorge Alonso, our Canada-U.S. investment associate and a cherished associate. Thank you for all you do to implement our unique investment approach.

Our clients in Canada and the United States, without whom our firm would not exist. We enjoy the relationships we have with you and appreciate your excitement about this project.

Our friends, in Canada and the U.S., who have pushed us over the years and helped us overcome many obstacles. Thanks also to Isaacs for your edits and Canadian perspective.

My family, especially Dad and Mom. Thanks for all you have done for me over the years and your support of whatever I did (including moving to the U.S., which I know caused you worry). I appreciate the home cooking, your prayers, and the wisdom you imparted. And finally, to my wife, Kathy, and our daughters, Corrine and Emily (my little Canadians) ... I love you and thank you for your support in this endeavor. Again, I apologize for underestimating the time I would be away from you during the revision of this book.

And to our readers, thank you for buying the second edition of this book and our other book — *The American in Canada* (2nd edition) — as well. We trust that those of you who are already "Canadians in America" will find it a useful reference, as will those beginning, undertaking, and completing a move to the U.S. Our hope is this book will save you more time, money, and frustration than we experienced in our Canada-U.S. moves. If you have any questions, comments, edits, or things you'd like to see in later editions, please email us at book@transitionfinancial.com and tell us what is on your mind. For more information or to chat with us live, please visit our website at transitionfinancial.com.

INTRODUCTION

I want to start by thanking all of you who made the first and second editions of this book such a success. I knew there was a need for this information, but I am truly overwhelmed by your kind comments and great suggestions. I have incorporated many of them, along with all the law changes that have occurred (including the host of new disclosure and tax regulations as a result of FATCA and the new IRS PFIC rules on most Canadian investments — including all mutual funds and ETFs), to continue making this book the definitive resource available for those in Canada considering, moving, or already located in the U.S. The complexities associated with moving to the U.S. are astounding, yet according to the Association for Canadian Studies, over 20,000 people moved from Canada to the U.S. in 2012. The question is: how many moved with little or no idea of these complexities? Interestingly enough, Citizenship and Immigration Canada approved 34,185 visas for U.S. residents in 2011, just short of the record in 2010 of 35,060. What causes people to move to another country without understanding the financial impact or opportunity a move presents? We believe it is the similarities in culture, currency, language, and goods consumed between Canada and the U.S. that lead people to think their situation is "simple." In fact, the differences in taxation, investing, health care, wills, and estates are profound. The complexities I encountered when I moved down to the U.S. in 1990 as a single man (poor student), and moved back up to Canada in 1992 with my American-born wife, before moving back to the U.S. permanently in 1996 were mind-boggling, as the following story illustrates.

MY STORY

My fascination with the U.S. started in high school when I took a bus trip to Portland to participate in a school band competition. I became interested in U.S. culture, geography, and so on. Then I took another bus trip with Campus Life that went through Montana, Idaho, Utah, and Las Vegas to Los Angeles. There I experienced Disneyland, Knott's Berry Farm, Magic Mountain, and Universal Studios. These experiences, combined with the oceans, beaches, and warm weather, had me hooked. From that point on, I decided I would eventually live in the U.S. My goal was to get a green card and have the ability to move, live, and work anywhere in Canada and the U.S.

In 1990, I decided a master of business administration degree would help my telephone career, so with the support of my employer I began applying to business schools across the U.S. and Canada. I maintained that, if I was accepted at any of the U.S. schools I applied to, I was going to the U.S. Fortunately, I was accepted by two programs and responded to the invitation from the MBA program at the University of Arizona. As I neared graduation, I began the application process and was getting interest from prospective employers when I gained the affection of a young lady while in Tucson. After graduating, Kathy and I got married, and we decided to move to Calgary to resume my telephone career while she began training as a nurse. To this day, I am not sure why we did that other than to recommence my career. It wasn't until four years later that I realized I was "waking up next to a green card" every morning and that escape from the cold winters and punishing taxes was just an application form away. I applied and obtained a green card through the sponsorship of Kathy, and in April of 1996 I was finally able to realize my lifelong dream of residing in the U.S. I became a naturalized U.S. citizen three years later, as soon as I was eligible in May of 1999.

My migrations between Canada and the U.S. came with much frustration and complexity even though I thought my financial situation was simple. The following examples illustrate how the simple situation of a single, poor student became incredibly complex when moving back and forth across the border.

- Applying for and receiving a student visa required a lot of paperwork and coordination with the University of Arizona.
- I received an assistantship from the university that caused no end of grief in figuring out the payroll and income tax implications in both Canada and the U.S. because there was so little information to be found on the subject.
- Getting married in the U.S. and moving to Canada created untold difficulties with the Canada Border Services Agency when we brought our car, personal effects, and wedding gifts across the border.
- Clearing Canadian immigration with my wife, despite months of paperwork and phone calls beforehand, was onerous — we were told we had broken five immigration laws when our plane landed. Thankfully, immigration officials issued a minister's permit to allow Kathy into the country until we figured out our mess.
- We had to file U.S. income tax returns for my U.S.-citizen wife each year we lived in Canada.
- We had to go through the green card application process when we decided to move to the U.S. and had to make at least two trips to Vancouver (now it's Montreal only) and wait in unbelievably long lines to get fingerprinted, complete the medical (including x-rays), and be interviewed.
- We had to complete paperwork to expedite U.S. Customs and Border Protection processing with our automobile and combined personal effects.
- We had to figure out what income to declare on which tax return and when to file in the year we left Canada and took up residency in the U.S. (including the tax implications of our RRSPs).

- We had to collapse our RRSPs, endure the terrible currency exchange at the time, suffer the Canadian government's withholding tax, and move our money to the U.S.
- Finally, we had to apply for a Social Security card, write the test to get our Arizona driver's licenses, and coordinate our health-care coverage during our move.

Now, let me be clear: I will always be Canadian, will always love Canada, and will always visit as long as God gives me the health and strength to do so. However, I have settled in the U.S., have become a dual citizen, and love the U.S. and what it has to offer. In particular, the weather of Arizona is much better for my health than Canada's winters, and I find I can remain active year round in biking, swimming, and golfing.

And that's the starting point for any move to the U.S.: the desired lifestyle you are trying to achieve. You should never consider a move for monetary or tax reasons alone. Many times have I witnessed a couple with young kids move to the U.S. because one spouse has a great job opportunity and will make incredible money. It doesn't take long for the other spouse to become disenchanted when there is no family nearby, no friends, no support structure, and the working spouse is at the office or traveling all the time in the new career. Good planning should help you to document your desired lifestyle, see the pros and cons of your move, and consider more than just the financial rewards or lower taxes.

• • •

I have written this third edition of *The Canadian in America: Real-life Tax and Financial Insights into Moving to and Living in the U.S.* to equip you with the up-to-date information you need to consider when making the transition to life in the U.S. However, people have questioned why this book is not a step-by-step guide for those who do not want to spend money on good advice, or why they cannot prepare their own tax returns with this book. A step-by-step book on this topic is impossible to write because each person has an individualized fact pattern that requires individualized advice, so no "how to" guide could specifically apply to each circumstance. It is akin to writing a procedural manual for taking out your own appendix — it just can't be done. For example, "How much anesthesia is needed for a person your size? Do you have other medical issues that need to be taken into account? Do you have allergies to certain medications?" The information here is general enough for you to become aware of what applies to your situation. Further, many CRA and IRS forms that are required to be filed have detailed instructions on their respective websites. Finally, this is why I started Transition Financial Advisors — to provide you with an experienced helper to assist you in making this transition or sorting out the issues. Our goal is to ensure our clients have a smooth transition to the U.S. from Canada versus an abrupt move and all the connotations that come with it. The constantly changing rules and their application to your unique financial situation require the right professional help. Plus, your finances are a critical component of your move and deserve the attention they are due. If you had a brain tumor, would you go to the closest doctor (or dentist) to you? Or would you find the absolute best neuro-oncologist you could in Canada or the U.S.?

AMERICAN 1
ASPIRATIONS

A simple man believes anything,
but a prudent man gives thought to his steps.
— PROVERBS 14:15

So, you've decided to move to the U.S. (or maybe you are already there?). It may be because of a great job offer, a spouse, or returning to your roots, but you have decided to leave Canada and move to the U.S. How do you prepare for such a major transition? Or maybe you are already living in the U.S. and are concerned about assets like RRSPs or RRIFs remaining in Canada or how to leave your estate to your heirs remaining in Canada.

You have entered our world . . . the world of Canada-U.S. transition planning. With the laws and regulations of two countries such as Canada and the U.S., such planning quickly becomes complex. This unique niche has been termed "cross-border" planning by some, but we prefer to call it Canada-U.S. transition planning. We caution you now that you shouldn't proceed with your move to the U.S. without allowing yourself enough time to understand all the nuances of your unique situation and then taking enough time to complete all the necessary actions before leaving Canada. If you are reading this book, you are off to a good start.

WHAT IS TRANSITION PLANNING?

You have your stuff packed and the moving company selected, but suddenly you think, "How do I move my financial affairs to the U.S.?"

Financial planning is the core of transition planning, but we clearly define which border we are talking about and, in particular, how to smoothly transition your finances from Canada to the U.S. while saving you time, aggravation, professional fees, and every tax dollar you possibly can.

According to the College of Financial Planning, comprehensive financial planning is "the process in which coordinated, comprehensive strategies are developed and implemented for the achievement of the client's financial goals and objectives." According to the Financial Planning Standards Council (the licensing organization for the Certified Financial Planner™ designation in Canada), financial planning consists of the following six distinct steps.

1. Establish the client-planner relationship.

2. Gather client data and determine the client's goals and objectives.

3. Clarify the client's current financial situation and identify any problem areas or opportunities.

4. Develop and document the financial plan and present it to the client.

5. Assist the client with implementing the plan.

6. Monitor and update the financial plan.

You will notice that financial planning is a process, not a transaction or an end in itself. The same applies to transition planning. Since the financial planning industry is only about 40 years old, a brief history might help. The industry started as a transaction-based business with life insurance agents selling policies over the kitchen table or mutual fund salespeople coming to your door. It has since evolved to a technically based business where people manage an investment portfolio, analyze your insurance needs, or provide tax advice. Today the industry has realized that you can't make decisions with a person's money and ignore the person — the two are integrated. As a result, the industry is rapidly moving toward a relationship-based model where "money is a means to an end, not an end in itself."

Comprehensive financial planning begins by understanding what you are trying to achieve in terms of lifestyle now, and in the future. This is driven by your values and beliefs about money and what you have observed during your lifetime. It is akin to taking off in an airplane with a flight plan in hand. Once our firm knows where you are trying to go (documented goals and objectives), we can develop a specific plan to test the feasibility of your goals and objectives. Then, we figure out how to get you to your destination. Other factors constantly affect your ability to achieve your goals, such as changes in the tax and estate laws, your income and expenses, death, disability, and investment performance. Therefore, our firm views transition planning as a lifelong process, not an event or a transaction. Without a flight plan, how do you know which direction to go when you take off from the airport?

It is important to note the difference between a goal and an objective. A goal is a desired end state, such as "I want to simplify my life" or "I want a better understanding of my financial situation." Only you will know whether you have accomplished that goal or not. An objective is clearly measurable, and everyone knows whether it has been achieved or not. For example, "I want to move to the U.S. by December 31st of this year." Once in place, your plan provides the overall context in which to place the individual, day-to-day decisions. When people struggle with individual financial decisions, it is usually because they do not have a plan. They are stuck in the individual decisions and have lost the overall perspective in which to place each decision. For example, a popular question we field is, "Should we withdraw our RRSPs?" The answer is, "What are you trying to achieve?" The tax implications are one small part of the answer. Why do you want to take them out? When do you need the funds? What will you do with the funds when available? Will you move the funds to the U.S.? How? Do you understand the pros and cons of doing so? Will you invest them? If so, how? For what purpose or objective?

TABLE 1.1

LIVING DESIRED LIFESTYLE

Values, Beliefs, Goals, Objectives			
Client (Spouse, Children, Family, Relatives, Friends)			
Transition Financial Advisors Group			
Comprehensive Overview			
Cash Management Planning	Income Tax Planning	Independence/ Education Planning	Risk Management
• Mortgage broker	• U.S. accountant	• Pension plan	• Insurance agents:
• Banker	(CPA)	administrator	- Property/Casualty
• Currency	• Cdn accountant	• Actuary	- Disability
exchange firm	(CPA)	• RRSP, LIRA,	- Long-term care
• Realtor	• Enrolled agent	RRIF, IRA, 401(k)	- Health
• Auto dealer	• Bookkeeper	• Social Security	- Life
	• Tax attorney	Administration	• Social Security
	(Cdn, U.S.)	• Human Resources	Administration
	• Canada Revenue	Development	(Medicare)
	Agency	Canada (Canada	• Provincial health-
	• Provincial taxing	Pension Plan/Old	care provider
	authority	Age Security)	
	• Internal Revenue	• College savings	
	Service/U.S. Dept.	plan administrator	
	of Treasury	• RESP custodian	
	• State taxing		
	authority		

Table 1.1 depicts the elements of Canada-U.S. transition planning. Based on this table, our firm's transition planning includes the comprehensive analysis of eight specific areas in any Canada-U.S. move.

1. **Customs planning** addresses issues in relocating your physical assets to the U.S. The transportation of items such as pets,

Values, Beliefs, Goals, Objectives			
Client (Spouse, Children, Family, Relatives, Friends)			
Transition Financial Advisors Group			
Comprehensive Overview			
Estate/Charitable Planning	Investment Planning	Immigration Planning	Customs Planning
• Estate planning attorney • Charities • Trust administrator • Estate/gift/trust tax accountant • Custodian • Trustee • STEP member	• Stock broker • Mutual fund manager/company • Brokerage firm • Investment manager • Securities and Exchange Commission • Provincial/state regulator	• Immigration attorney • Immigration & Naturalization Services	• U.S. Customs • Canada Customs • Moving company

guns, cars, or a wine collection across the border has unique issues that need to be dealt with in advance.

2. **Immigration planning** looks at the legal ways of moving to, working in, and residing in the U.S. either temporarily or permanently. You need some legal means of entering the U.S.

because, despite popular opinion, the U.S. is another country, not another province of Canada!

3. **Cash management planning** includes the development and review of your net worth statement and a review of your cash inflows/outflows during your move. From there, our firm can analyze the ownership of your assets between spouses and between Canada and the U.S. (for estate tax issues), and we can calculate various financial ratios to determine if any opportunities or issues exist. The net worth statement serves as a benchmark to evaluate the effects of your move over time. We also address the movement of cash from Canada to the U.S. and how to simplify your life prior to your move.

4. **Income tax planning** is a comprehensive review of your current and projected tax situation with an eye for opportunities to reduce your current and future tax liability both before and after your U.S. move. It is important to note the difference between tax preparation and tax planning. Tax preparation is a purely historical perspective and simply takes what has happened (your tax slips) and records it on a tax form for the Canadian and U.S. governments. At that point, whatever tax liability or refund results is what you must adhere to. Tax planning, on the other hand, tries to optimize your tax situation by reviewing any tax avoidance techniques that may apply to your situation in advance of any tax preparation. There is nothing illegal about proper tax planning or tax avoidance, but it must be differentiated from tax evasion, which is the intentional defrauding of government authorities of the tax dollars they are due.

5. **Independence/education planning** develops detailed projections out to age 100 using current assets, income, and expenses to determine the feasibility of your financial independence and lifestyle objectives in the U.S. Alternative scenarios and sensitivity analysis are conducted to provide

insights into which actions, if any, may be necessary to achieve your goals. For example, do you need to save more and be more aggressive with your portfolio, or can a more conservative approach be taken? Education planning determines how much is required, at what point in time, and what you need to do to fund these future education liabilities. It also provides a review of your education saving options in the U.S. and what to do with your education savings in Canada before moving.

6. **Risk management** examines your current situation for risk exposures and determines the best course of action in addressing them. For example, illness, fire, theft, accident, disability, death, lawsuit, etc. are potential catastrophic events that could devastate what has taken a lifetime to accumulate. There are many differences in managing risk between Canada and the U.S. that need to be addressed to ensure you are fully covered.

7. **Estate/charitable planning** helps you to arrange your affairs so you can (1) continue to control your property while alive, (2) provide for the needs of loved ones in the event of disability, and (3) give what you have to whom you want, when you want, the way you want, at the lowest overall cost. The focus is on control first and on saving tax dollars, professional fees, and court costs second.

8. **Investment planning** determines your investment objectives as derived from your financial plan and then designs an investment portfolio to achieve your required rate of return while managing your portfolio in context with your tax situation, estate planning, and financial independence goals. Ongoing monitoring, reporting, and rebalancing of your portfolio in both Canada and the U.S. are required over the long term to ensure that it achieves your goals and meets your risk tolerance.

BEFORE YOU GO!

The two items you must have thought out and in place before you even consider a transition to the U.S. are adequate health-care coverage and a legal means of residing in the U.S. (valid immigration status).

1. Health-Care Coverage
    You may not be aware, but your provincial coverage will be of little or no use to you when you move to the U.S. The rules are different for each province, but generally, if you are out of your province for six months or more, you are at risk of losing your provincial health coverage. Once you have lost your coverage, you may not be able to get it back immediately, depending on your province (Alberta allows you to have it back immediately, for example, while Ontario has a three-month waiting period). As a result, you must have some form of U.S. medical insurance to cover yourself in the event of illness or injury in the U.S. because there isn't universal government coverage like there is in Canada. This coverage is best secured just before you make the transition to the U.S. There are several options to cover you and your family that are discussed in more detail, along with items such as life, auto, and homeowner insurance, in Chapter 2, "Cover Your Assets."

2. Residing in the U.S.
    Despite popular opinion, you must have a legal means (i.e., valid immigrant or nonimmigrant status or U.S. citizenship) of entering and remaining in the U.S. for any period of time. To work there requires the appropriate authorization as well. No matter what, you have to fit into one of the immigrant or nonimmigrant "boxes" as outlined by the U.S. Citizenship and Immigration Services (USCIS). Unfortunately, many Canadians go to the U.S. on a "visitor's visa" (good for six months) and mistakenly believe they can work in the U.S. because they have been "let in," just like they can in any province. This misconception comes in part because a B-1 (visitor for business) or B-2

(visitor for pleasure) visa is not physically issued when you cross the border (you may get a stamp in your passport, but that is it). This leads some to believe they can stay or work as long as they want. In fact, if you are caught working in the U.S. without a valid work visa, you will be considered an illegal immigrant and could face deportation and the prospect of lifetime banishment from the U.S. There are numerous legal options you can use to enter the U.S., and you can review your possible visa options in Chapter 3, "A Pledge of Allegiance." Once you have these two essentials in place, the following must also be considered.

CUSTOMS

This is where most people spend the bulk of their time, to the jeopardy of most everything else. No doubt the movement of your physical assets to the U.S. is time consuming. You have to make travel plans for yourself, your spouse, and your children whether you are going to fly or drive. There is also coordination of the visa applications for your spouse and your children that can cause havoc at the border if not done correctly. Then there is the packing of your household goods, selecting a moving company, filling out all the requisite forms for U.S. Customs and Border Protection, and so on. When you get down to your final destination, you have to coordinate the arrival of your moving truck with the closing on your house. Then there is unpacking and putting everything away. We offer some considerations in Chapter 4, "Moving Your Stuff."

INCOME TAXES

UNITED STATES

There is much work to be done in optimizing your tax situation before taking up tax residency in the U.S. If you choose not to do it, you can face unnecessary taxes and compliance issues that can be punishing. The Canada-U.S. Tax Treaty and the relevant provisions in the U.S. Internal Revenue Code and Canadian Income Tax Act are your protection from double (and triple) taxation in both countries. Obviously, a thorough understanding of these rules and their application to your situation is the key.

An analogy may help. Imagine you are the owner of a dinner theater, and the Internal Revenue Service (IRS) is sitting in the audience. You have one chance to "set the stage" before the curtains open and the IRS has full view of your "financial stage." As soon as you become a tax resident of the U.S., you open your entire "financial stage" for the IRS to see. At that point, you can no longer set the "stage" to present your financial situation in the best light possible to minimize your tax liability. Interestingly enough, you can be a resident for income tax purposes in the U.S. yet be considered an illegal alien for immigration purposes. Alternatively, you can become an income tax resident of both Canada and the U.S. and have to look to the Canada-U.S. Tax Treaty to avoid double taxation and determine to which country you belong for tax purposes. All of this is explored in greater detail in Chapter 5, "Double Taxes, Double Trouble." As a side note, U.S. citizens, derivative citizens, and green card holders living in Canada must file U.S. income tax returns annually!

Social Security number/individual taxpayer identification number (SSN/ITIN): to work or live in the U.S., everyone in your family must have an SSN (for those working) or an ITIN. The SSN will be required by your employer and is needed to file a tax return or open a bank account. The ITIN is required for those who are not eligible to work in the U.S. but allows you to reduce your taxes by claiming your spouse and children as dependents. See Chapter 5 for further details on obtaining an SSN or an ITIN.

CANADA

Based on popular opinion, many people just stop filing Canadian tax returns when they leave Canada for the U.S. The rationale is usually, "I don't live there anymore, so I don't have to file taxes there anymore." In fact, there are final filing requirements with CRA that could increase your tax bill significantly due to the imposition of the "departure" tax when you leave Canada. In addition, if you don't sever your ties properly prior to and after your move, CRA could come back and "deem" you a resident of Canada, causing you a lot of inconvenience and the potential of additional income tax. Alternatively, the rules state that, if you are considered a treaty resident of the U.S., you are automatically deemed a non-resident of Canada and forced into the departure tax. You need to ensure you do the requisite planning before you leave Canada to understand and quantify the departure tax, know how to correctly sever your ties with Canada, and know how to mitigate the income taxes in your unique financial situation.

The bottom line: if you haven't done the prerequisite planning prior to your move, many planning opportunities may be lost forever, and you will find yourself in a situation where you have to pay many financial professionals on both sides of the border to get yourself back in compliance with both taxing authorities, in addition to paying higher taxes.

CURRENCY EXCHANGE

Along with moving yourself, your spouse, your children, and your physical goods, you have to move some, or all, of your financial assets to the U.S. Doing so can be confusing, and most folks are unsure about how to tackle it. There are many misconceptions about currency exchange, and often people will leave assets in Canada because they believe they will "lose" money by moving them to the U.S., but other risks can be incurred by leaving everything in Canada. These myths and facts are addressed in Chapter 6, "Show Me the Money."

ESTATE PLANNING

In our experience, the area most often neglected is wills and estates. Unfortunately, many Canadians go to their attorney to "update" their Canadian last will and testament before moving to the U.S. to make sure they have it in order. What they don't realize is that it may be a complete waste of time and money because their Canadian estate planning attorney typically doesn't know the U.S. rules for noncitizens living in the U.S. Further, you can have a valid will in Canada, but the provisions contained in the document may not be executable in the U.S. (i.e., domestic laws, disinheriting heirs, etc.) The complexities of estate planning for noncitizens residing in the U.S. are considered in Chapter 7, "Till Death Do Us Part."

INDEPENDENCE PLANNING

Our firm does not use the term "retirement" because it conjures up images of an unscheduled, unproductive life pursuing leisure activities. In our experience, this pursuit of leisure is short lived, and it doesn't take long before people look for more meaning in life, including returning to work! As a result, our firm prefers the term "financial independence" because it prompts the question, "Independent to do what?" Associated with becoming financially independent are the issues of saving for the future with company pensions, U.S. Social Security (SS), Canada Pension Plan (CPP), Old Age Security (OAS), etc. Typically, a move to the U.S. means the start of a new phase in your life. But now that you live in the U.S., it may not make sense to invest in an RRSP or TFSA, so you need to understand the alternatives for saving in the U.S. These issues are dealt with in Chapter 8, "Financial Freedom."

EDUCATION PLANNING

Once people have left Canada for the U.S., many wonder how they will be able to save for their children's education and what happens to the savings they have accrued so far in Canada. Can these savings be used at a U.S. educational institution? If you save for education in the U.S., can the funds be used at a Canadian educational institution? There are some landmines to be aware of here, and these issues are addressed in Chapter 9, "Smarten Up!"

INVESTMENT PLANNING

Many people have established a nest egg for their financial independence, but how do you manage this in the U.S.? Can you move your current investments and RRSPs there? If so, how? Can they remain in Canada? How do you invest in the U.S.? Which financial institutions or mutual funds should you use? How are the various types of investment income taxed in the U.S.? It is a whole new ball game in the U.S., and there are several things of which to be aware. They are addressed in Chapter 10, "Money Doesn't Grow on Trees."

BUSINESS ENTITY PLANNING

If you have a small business in Canada, it can afford you some unique opportunities in your move to the U.S. Business entities can be used to get you a green card in the U.S., help you qualify for free U.S. Medicare, establish a Social Security retirement benefit, and allow you to get disability coverage. There are many planning opportunities available and potential landmines to contend with for small-business owners, which are discussed in Chapter 11, "The Business of Business."

OWNING A SECOND HOME

For some, living in Canada but escaping the cold winter months is appealing. To that end, these "snowbirds" prefer owning a second home in the U.S. for recreation, vacation, or investment purposes. There are many tax and estate-planning issues that arise with owning property in the U.S. while remaining a resident of Canada, and they are highlighted in Chapter 12, "Escaping the Endless Winter."

SELECTING THE RIGHT PROFESSIONALS

When it comes to planning your move, we don't recommend you do it yourself, even in the "simplest" of situations (which are rare). Trust me, I tried with my simple situation, and it didn't go well. That is why I started this firm! To us, it's like giving yourself a haircut — you might do fine on your front bangs because you can see them in the mirror, but what about the sides and the back? The complexities associated with a Canada-U.S. transition are far too complex, and, based on our experiences, it is in your best interests to pay for the right assistance. When you look at your time, aggravation, lost opportunities, and costly mistakes, it should be an easy justification to hire someone to provide the information you need, when you need it, to make informed decisions. The key benefit of doing so is that you get an outside, unbiased understanding of your entire financial situation and the obstacles and opportunities it presents when moving to the U.S. That is the benefit of good advice! With that in mind, Chapter 13, "Mayday, Mayday," presents some of the things you should look for in any qualified Canada-U.S. transition planner.

SIMPLIFY YOUR LIFE

This is probably one of the most neglected areas in making the transition to the U.S. Before you move, take the opportunity to consolidate all of your investment, RRSP, RRIF, LIRA, and TFSA retirement accounts with one brokerage firm. Also, maintain only one checking account and one savings account in Canada where possible. Once you are in the U.S., the management of your financial affairs in Canada will be greatly simplified (i.e., one call to manage all of your accounts, one checking account to deal with, etc.). If you are a small-business owner, it is typically best to sell or wind up your entity prior to moving to the U.S., but it depends on your individual circumstances and how your business entity might be used for immigration purposes, qualifying for U.S. Medicare, etc. Either way, you should try to set up your affairs so that you are not required to manage the day-to-day operations of the entity from another country. There are also many cultural differences, and variations in the postal system, of which you should be aware. There is a brief overview of some of the major differences in Chapter 14, "Realizing the Dream."

COVER YOUR 2 ASSETS

Therefore, a man cannot
discover anything about his future.
— ECCLESIASTES 7:14

There are many risks in everyday life that can have devastating effects on what has taken you a lifetime to accumulate. Unfortunate events such as a sudden illness, the death of a working spouse, an auto accident, or the disability of the primary breadwinner can cause severe problems. These risk exposures must be reviewed in light of your transition to the U.S. to ensure your current risk-management strategies remain appropriate and new strategies are selected as required. Consider the following questions.

- When making the transition to the U.S., what coverage will your provincial health-care insurance provide?
- Are you currently eligible for U.S. Medicare coverage? If not, how can you qualify?
- Which alternatives exist for health-care coverage in the U.S. if you have a "preexisting" condition?
- You may have sufficient life-insurance coverage in Canada; however, if your death benefits pay in Canadian dollars, what effect will the exchange rates have on how much benefit you receive in the U.S.? Are your life insurance needs higher or lower in the U.S. than in Canada?
- Have you considered the same issues with your disability insurance? Will your policy still pay in the U.S.?

- Will your Canadian auto and homeowner insurance cover you in the U.S.? What differences in homeowner and auto insurance need to be considered if you get U.S. policies?
- The U.S. is a more litigious society than Canada. How can you protect yourself in the event of a lawsuit?
- What do you do in the U.S. if you can no longer perform some of the activities of daily living and require skilled nursing care around the clock?

As these questions illustrate, there is the potential of creating new risk exposures when making the transition to the U.S. that were previously covered. The following attempts to establish the facts and dispel some of the myths surrounding the major risk exposures when moving to the U.S.

MEDICAL COVERAGE IN THE U.S.

There are a number of rumors and opinions about the health-care systems in both Canada and the U.S. In our opinion, both health-care systems offer some of the best care in the world, but there is a greater availability of services in the U.S. There is more flexibility in scheduling various tests and in getting elective, nonemergency procedures, and there are more professionals available in a particular specialty. The main reason is that the medical system in the U.S. is primarily "for profit." This means there is competition for patients and group health insurance contracts that leads to a clearer "customer/patient" service orientation. This is particularly acute now that "Obamacare" (see below) has passed and "health insurance exchanges" have been set up to compete for your health insurance business, and private individual policies cannot deny you for a preexisting condition. The Canadian medical system has been criticized for being a good medical diagnosis system but not a good treatment system. We often hear from clients who have been placed on a waiting list for treatment that may come many months later. I have personally experienced hospitalization and medical treatment on both sides of the border. In my experience, the hospitals and physicians in Canada take the view that you are there for them to practice medicine on, while in the U.S. the view is that they are there to get you better to live your life again. The drawback of the U.S. system compared with Canada's health-care system is the lack of universal coverage. We have seen several people come into our practice for pro-bono budget counseling whose finances have been depleted because of high medical costs, co-pays, and prescription costs. It is interesting to note that approximately 62% of all bankruptcies in the U.S. in 2007 were due to medical expenses (2009 Harvard study published in the *American Journal of Medicine*). In Canada, "socialized medicine" means everyone pays (through higher taxes), and as a result no individual's health-care problems can leave them bankrupt. According to the Canada Health Act (1984), "The primary objective of the Canadian health-care policy is to protect, promote, and restore the physical and mental well-being of residents of Canada and to facilitate reasonable access to health services without financial or other barriers." Unfortunately, that is not the case in the U.S., and it is not uncommon to see a bucket at a local retailer's cash register asking for donations to help an employee who was in an accident or needs a heart transplant because they can't keep up with the out-of-pocket medical expenses. I am curious to see if these disappear with the advent of Obamacare, under which everyone can get health insurance. In 2008, the World Health Organization came out with the results of a three-year study that showed major inequalities in health and life expectancy continue worldwide. Its recommendation? Universal health care worldwide.

Despite popular opinion, the medical system in the U.S. will not leave you dying in the gutter outside the hospital because you don't have a health insurance card in your wallet. This would be against the law, and the wrongful death lawsuits would be flying if such incidents occurred. There are countless undocumented workers from South America that are rescued from the desert heat trying to cross into the U.S. and receive medical care at no personal cost before being deported. My wife, Kathy (who is a nurse manager), has seen several illegal immigrants with no health insurance come into the emergency room for dialysis treatment, get admitted, and stay for a few days before being discharged at no charge! Sure enough, two weeks later when they are really sick again, they go back to the emergency room and the cycle starts all over again. Rest assured, they are given an itemized bill for all of their services but it is obviously difficult to collect. Further, the Health Insurance Portability and Accountability Act (HIPAA) of 1996 prevents the hospital from revealing anything about their patients to U.S. Citizenship and Immigration Services or the Border Patrol. There are county hospitals available to the general public, and if you are a U.S. veteran (Veteran Administration or VA), hospitals are available that are funded by the state and federal governments. There is even medical insurance available through your local state for those who cannot afford coverage on their own. For example, in Arizona, AHCCCS (Arizona Health Care Cost Containment System, a scary name) is medical insurance for those who cannot afford it on their own. In all cases, someone has to pay for those without insurance, and this cost, coupled with the rising medical costs, is causing insurance premiums to skyrocket and people in the U.S. to shoulder more of the expenses individually. As a result, the federal government has passed Obamacare, which aims to alleviate many of these issues.

OBAMACARE

In 2010, the federal government passed sweeping legislation called the Patient Protection Affordable Care Act (PPACA). This Act affects Medicare, Medicaid, and private/group health insurance but, probably most importantly, mandates the availability of affordable health insurance to all Americans, beginning in 2014, with no underwriting. The PPACA mandates "health insurance exchanges" and private individual health-care insurance (through healthcare.gov) that will offer U.S. citizens *and* legal residents affordable health-care options regardless of preexisting conditions! These policies have government-mandated "essential health benefits" that provide a comprehensive set of health-care services that must cover a minimum of 60% of health-care costs. There will be four plans: Bronze (covers 60% of health-care costs), Silver, Gold, and Platinum (covers 90%) with maximum out-of-pocket amounts estimated at around $6,000+ for individuals and $12,000+ for families. The premiums for the Bronze plan are approximately $200 per month for a 40-year-old ($450 for a 60-year-old) and depend in which county you reside. Regardless, all health insurance companies will have their policies on "the exchange" or offered privately and will be competing with one another for your business, which should keep premiums competitive. Currently, there are 111 health insurance plans available on the exchange for Maricopa County (Phoenix metropolitan area). This variety is one of the key ways that PPACA seeks to reduce the costs for health care — both in the system of hospitals and providers and to the end consumer. For lower-income participants, there are tax credits to reduce the cost of the premiums, making health-insurance coverage even more affordable (hence the name). You should note that if you do not sign up for health insurance on an exchange, a group plan, or a private individual plan in 2015, you will be subject to a penalty of greater than $325 per person per year or 2% of household income, $695 or 2.5% in 2016, increasing with inflation or 2.5% per year after that. The intent behind the penalty is to get everyone paying into the "pool" so the insurance risk goes down. You must now check a box on your tax return, under penalties of perjury, that you had health insurance all year. As you can see, the penalties can be stiff!

This Act will eliminate all state "high risk pools" (relieving the cash-strapped states), but private individual health insurance policies will remain in place. What is even better is there is no underwriting, and all insurance companies must provide insurance to anyone who applies, even those with preexisting conditions. This is wonderful for Canadians moving to the U.S., as a huge barrier has been removed and affordable health insurance is now available for all, even those that have existing health problems! If you are unable to get health-care coverage through any of the means listed earlier, this will be your final stop. It is expected that 30 million Americans/residents will be entering the health-care system in the U.S. as a result of this legislation. It is unclear at this juncture what this influx will do to service times and access to specialists, tests, and procedures. At the time of this writing, 10 million people have signed up for health care.

Canada appears to be moving toward a private, "pay as you go" system so that those who can afford it can shoulder more of the costs, while the U.S. is moving towards more universal coverage, particularly with the advent of Obamacare. One change we would like to see in Canada is providing each discharged patient with an itemized list of all the charges incurred during a particular visit so people realize that medical coverage isn't "free." Further, Dr. Jacques Chaoulli and his patient, George Zeliotis, successfully sued the Province of Quebec in 2005 in the Supreme Court of Canada. Quebec's health-care regulations were an infringement of individual rights under the Quebec Charter. "Access to a waiting list is not access to health care," the court proclaimed in its decision. The court went on to say that, as long as the government was unable to provide effective health services, it could not prevent its citizens from obtaining these services elsewhere (private health care). This has led to laws in Quebec that permit health-care payments from the government to be paid to private health-care providers. In fact, Dr. Chaoulli has now set up a private health-care clinic in Quebec and charges patients directly to see a physician. Similar lawsuits in Ontario, BC, and Alberta are before the courts but Alberta's case for a two-tier system recently went down in defeat. In some cases, patients want to be reimbursed by their provincial health care for procedures paid out of pocket in the U.S. and England. It will be interesting to see how it all plays out and who is going to pay for it all in Canada or the U.S. It is hard to deny that there is much better access to health care in the U.S. given the number of Canadians crossing the border to pay for an MRI and even "elective" surgeries. This has led a lot of U.S. hospitals along the border to begin offering services and packages to Canadians for elective surgeries with no wait times! Port Huron Hospital in Michigan, for example, is one such hospital doing this. It offers package deals for weight-loss surgery, joint replacement, MRI tests, and wound care. Given where we live and practice, we have occasion to visit with Canadians who specifically come to Arizona to seek and pay for their health-care treatment at the Mayo Clinic in Scottsdale. Once they have experienced the level of care available at the clinic and the beauty of Arizona, it's not uncommon for these folks to contact our firm to look at the opportunities to move to Arizona, particularly since the MD Anderson Cancer Center has expanded to Mesa, AZ.

In my opinion, a combination of the Canadian universal and U.S. private medical systems is probably the ideal scenario. The U.S. seems to be moving toward universal coverage on a more formalized basis with the passing of Obamacare so that individuals and families are no longer devastated financially, while Canada appears to be moving toward a private "pay-as-you-go" or "co-pay" system so that those who can afford it can shoulder more of the costs and get treatment right away. This approach is evident in the private eye clinics and MRI machines popping up all over the place (particularly in Alberta). As both countries continue with increasing austerity measures to deal with the ballooning debt, health care will be a topic hotly debated and likely tinkered with given the amount of money it costs annually.

PROVINCIAL COVERAGE

Your provincial health-care coverage may be good for up to six months after you leave Canada, depending on your province of residence (some terminate it sooner). There are several problems in continuing your provincial coverage in the U.S. that make it of virtually no use to you. First, your provincial health care will only pay "table" rates. For example, the table rate for a hernia operation in Canada may be C$4,000 . . . that is all that will be paid. If you need a hernia operation while residing in the U.S. and it currently costs U$4,990, your provincial health care will pay only C$4,000, and you will be billed by the U.S. hospital for the balance. Second, there are limits on the daily rate paid for hospitalization; this rate covers a very small portion of what is required (Alberta pays C$100 per day, for example) and includes the room, bandages, food, medicines, etc. In the U.S., however, there is one fee for the room, another for the physician, another for the nurse, and each bandage, pill, and syringe is tracked separately. Needless to say, this system leaves you with the balance to pay personally. Third, you will have to prove to the provincial health authorities that your intent was to remain in Canada and not move to the U.S. It stands to reason that, if you are taking advantage of the Canadian health-care system, you should continue to pay into it. As a result, this could be viewed as a "tax tie" to Canada, and you could face continued taxation from Canada as well as the U.S.

Travel insurance can assist you on a temporary basis (usually up to six months) for any balance owing, but if you have a "preexisting" condition, you may not be able to get insurance coverage for it. Likewise, the travel insurance company may attempt to attribute any illness to the preexisting condition so it doesn't have to pay benefits. We have worked with a couple of clients who qualify for U.S. medical benefits as part of their Canadian employer's retiree benefits. Also, some Canadian federal government retiree medical benefits provide coverage in the U.S. Each situation is unique and must be examined individually for the opportunities or risk exposures that exist. Typically, these benefits offer some coverage but should not be relied upon to cover everything in the U.S. Obtaining U.S. health-care coverage is your best alternative in the U.S., and using your Canadian retiree medical benefits for coverage when you are "sunbirds" in Canada may be a viable solution to achieve your Canada-U.S. lifestyle (see our companion book *The American in Canada*). The new health-care insurance exchanges and guaranteed issue brought in through Obamacare offer a wonderful solution for Canadians looking to move to the U.S. and obtain health-care coverage right away.

U.S. EMPLOYERS

Approximately 60% of people in the U.S. get their health care covered through their employer under a group health insurance program. For those making the transition to the U.S. for employment purposes, the best coverage available is usually the group health-care plan through your U.S. employer. Typically, the larger the employer, the better the health plan choices you have. However, as with almost any health-care plan in the U.S., be prepared for a "co-pay" by cash, check, or credit card for any doctor, lab, x-ray, etc. My family of four is on a group health insurance policy with my wife's employer (Kathy is an RN manager at a local hospital). Since she is a part-time employee, my family shares more of the cost each month. To obtain full health-care coverage, dental, and prescription benefits, we pay approximately U$600 per month, which comes off her paycheck before taxes. As a comparison, British Columbia health-care costs C$1,662 annually in 2014 for a family of three or more if your income exceeds C$30,000, whereas in Alberta, there are no premiums for health care.

For those hoping to retire before age 65, you must be cognizant of the fact that you'll be without health insurance once you leave your U.S. employer, unless you have been employed long enough to qualify for retiree medical benefits (which most employers are discontinuing with the passing of Obamacare). Typically, this means you have some combined total of age and years of service that equals 75 to 85. The situation is not the same as in Canada, where you automatically qualify for provincial health-care coverage when you leave your employer — provided you make the monthly premium payments (depending on province of residency). There is a federal law (called the Consolidated Omnibus Budget Reconciliation Act or COBRA) that allows you to take your employer health insurance benefits with you for up to 18 months (36 months in some circumstances) after you leave as long as you take over the premium payments, but this coverage tends to be very expensive. If you are not eligible for retiree medical benefits, you'll have to obtain an individual health insurance policy, go through the health insurance exchange, or consider working part time at a place that offers medical benefits to part-time workers. For example, most hospitals and even Starbucks offer medical benefits to part-time workers (but generally not their families). However, it is expected that most part-time workers will no longer be insured through a group plan; rather, they'd more likely be provided some funds to put towards a private policy or an individual health insurance policy on the health insurance exchange.

U.S. MEDICARE

Canadians living legally in the U.S. for at least five years become eligible to pay for U.S. Medicare starting at age 65. U.S. citizens (naturalized, derivative, or physically born in the U.S.) and their spouses (noncitizens included) are generally automatically eligible at their own age 65, provided the qualifying spouse reaches 65 (newlyweds have to be married for one year to their U.S. citizen/resident spouse before the Canadian spouse is eligible for Medicare through the U.S. spouse and only at the Canadian's age 65). Medicare is currently made up of four parts: Part A, Part B, Part C, and Part D. Part A is hospital insurance and helps to pay the cost for care while in a hospital. Part B is medical insurance and helps to pay for the doctors, outpatient hospital care, and a variety of other medical services not covered by Part A. Part C is a Medicare Advantage plan that combines Parts A, B, and D and is offered by private insurers through a Health Maintenance Organization (HMO) or Preferred Provider Organization (PPO) plan, but Obamacare is likely to eliminate these plans. Part D is the drug prescription plan.

In 2015, Part A costs U$407 per month (U$4,884 annually) per person. However, to qualify for free Medicare Part A at age 65 (whether a U.S. citizen or not), you must have "earned" income that you paid Social Security taxes on in excess of the required amount (U$4,880 in 2015) for at least 10 years (terrific planning opportunity). Once you have established the required 40 quarters of Medicare-eligible earnings, you qualify for free Medicare Part A coverage. Another important aspect of qualifying for U.S. Medicare is the disability benefits you can receive (see section on disability insurance later in this chapter). Once 30 quarters have been established, the premium for Part A drops 45% to U$224 per month (U$2,688 annually). Canadian spouses who have not paid one nickel into the U.S. Social Security system do not qualify for free Medicare Part A coverage under the qualifying spouse unless they have reached age 65 and lived in the U.S. for at least five years or have qualified under their own earnings record. Another wrinkle that has been added is, if you don't qualify for free Part A and don't enroll in it as soon as you are eligible at age 65, your monthly premium increases 10% for twice the number of years you should have had Part A but didn't sign up. It is important to understand your benefits and sign up as soon as you are eligible, or it could be costly. At times, Medicare planning can make or break your finances and bring into question your pending transition to the U.S. There are many strategies to get you qualified for free Medicare Part A, but it depends on what stage of life you are in, your unique financial situation, and your individual goals and objectives.

Part B coverage for doctors and outpatient hospital care costs U$104.90 per month in 2015 (U$1,258.80 annually) per person, and everyone pays it no matter how many quarters of eligibility you have. The monthly premium for Part B is now "means tested," which means the more you make, the more you pay, and is broken down in the following table. To determine your premium, Medicare uses your income tax return from two years earlier, and your premium is automatically deducted from your Social Security payments.

TABLE 2.1

MEDICARE PART B PREMIUMS, 2015

If Your Yearly Income in 2013 Was . . .			
You Pay (U$)	**Single**	**Filing Married**	**Filing Separate**
104.90	85,000 or less	170,000 or less	85,000 or less
146.90	107,000 or less	214,000 or less	
209.80	160,000 or less	320,000 or less	
272.70	214,000 or less	428,000 or less	129,000 or less
335.70	above 214,000	above 428,000	above 129,000

Similar to Part A, you must enroll in Part B as soon as you are eligible at age 65, or your monthly premium increases 10% for twice the number of years you should have had Part B but didn't sign up. The intent of Congress with this policy, passed with Obamacare, is to get everyone medical coverage as soon as they are eligible. Further, they don't want people eligible for Medicare remaining on the private health insurance policies available through the "Health Insurance Marketplace."

The Part C "Medicare Advantage Plans" are offered by a variety of private health insurance companies in all different states. These plans tend to be less expensive than Medicare with a supplement, but they tend to be more restrictive in terms of which doctors, hospitals, and other facilities you use (must be in network). They are generally all-inclusive plans that include drug coverage (see below), so they can be quite economical. However, with the passing of Obamacare in 2010, the future of Medicare Advantage Plans is unknown because the payments to these types of plans are gradually being reduced to be more in line with average fee-for-service payments. These payment reductions started in 2012 and will reach the full amount in 2016. As a result of these reductions, it is conceivable that Part C plans may go the way of the dodo bird.

The Part D drug coverage can cost as little as six to eight dollars per month in some states and goes up from there (depending on which state you reside in and which plan you select). In addition, Part D is now "means tested" as well, as outlined in the following table.

TABLE 2.2

MEDICARE PART D PREMIUMS, 2015

If Your Yearly Income in 2013 Was . . .			
You Pay (U$)	**Single**	**Filing Married**	**Filing Separate**
Plan premium	85,000 or less	170,000 or less	85,000 or less
+12.30	107,000 or less	214,000 or less	
+51.30	214,000 or less	428,000 or less	129,000 or less
+70.80	above 214,000	above 428,000	above 129,000

Everyone eligible for the drug plan must enroll as soon as they are eligible at age 65, or penalties are added on a permanent basis in the amount of 1% per month of the national base beneficiary premium (which was $33.13 in 2015). There is a U$320 deductible in 2015, and then annual prescription expenses from U$325.01 to U$2,960 are shared through a co-insurance plan specific to which plan you subscribe to. After that, you enter the Part D "donut hole," where you pay 45% for brand-name drugs and 65% for generic drugs. Once you have spent $4,700 out-of-pocket for the year, you are out of the "donut hole," and "catastrophic" coverage automatically kicks in. With the passing of Obamacare, discounts and other benefits begin to kick in within the donut hole, and there are provisions that will gradually eliminate the "donut hole" by 2020, at which time the costs of all drugs will simply be 25% of the total drug cost.

While Medicare provides good base coverage, it cannot be relied on to cover all of your medical expenses. In addition to the premiums listed above for Part A, there is a deductible in 2015 of U$1,260 that must be paid for a hospital stay from 1 to 60 days (U$0), U$315 per day for days 61–90, and U$630 per day for days 91–150, while hospital stays greater than 150 days are not covered at all! For Part B, there is a deductible of U$147 per year in 2015, plus you pay 20% of the Medicare-approved amount after that. You'll need to purchase a Medicare Supplement policy to cover the expenses not covered by Medicare. These Supplements have 10 government-defined types of policies, ranging from basic (A) to comprehensive (J). They are all the same no matter who provides them, so it becomes a matter of price. Your Medicare Supplement does require underwriting, but it is very lenient, and we have not heard of an instance of anyone being turned down. Medicare Supplements cost approximately $1,500 per year per person.

LIFE INSURANCE IN THE U.S.

Another area often overlooked when making the transition to the U.S. is the appropriate amount of life insurance to cover the risk exposure if the primary breadwinner dies prematurely. All of your policies should be reviewed with an experienced eye to ensure you have the right type and amount of coverage while avoiding potential U.S. income/estate tax issues (see Chapter 7, "Till Death Do Us Part," for more details). For example, your life insurance coverage could drop significantly as soon as you take up residency in the U.S. How? If you need C$500,000 in Canada to cover your needs and you move to the U.S. and have a need for U$500,000, you could be underinsured because, at an 85¢ exchange rate, you have only U$425,000 in coverage! This amount will leave you underinsured by U$75,000 in covering your risk exposure in the U.S. Another important aspect is to reevaluate your life insurance needs in the U.S. to see if you need more, the same, or less insurance than you did in Canada based on the change in your financial circumstances. For example, if your lifestyle goes up and you now need U$650,000 in life insurance in the U.S., relying on your Canadian life insurance policy alone could leave you underinsured by U$125,000. If you decide to collapse your life insurance policies in Canada and take out the cash value (you have been reporting this as a foreign account, haven't you?), you'll be subject to tax in both Canada and the U.S. As you can see, the complexities surrounding a simple item such as life insurance are often overlooked.

DISABILITY INSURANCE

If you are under the age of 40, statistics say you have a higher probability of becoming disabled than dying. For young, high-income workers, becoming disabled and no longer being able to earn the income you are accustomed to can be devastating to your finances. In addition to losing the high earning potential for the balance of your life, your medical expenses tend to increase dramatically at the same time because you are temporarily or permanently disabled and need additional nursing care, medical equipment, etc. To cover this risk exposure, a disability insurance policy can be invaluable in insuring your future income.

There are generally two types of disability insurance: Own Occupation ("Own Occ") and Any Occupation ("Any Occ"). With Own Occ, the policy pays benefits if you are unable to return to the occupation held prior to your disability. This means if you were a brain surgeon prior to your disability and you are unable to return to your occupation as a brain surgeon, the policy will pay you benefits (generally up to 60–66% of your salary). With Any Occ, the policy pays benefits only if you are unable to return to any occupation. If you were a brain surgeon prior to your disability and you are able to return to a different job (e.g., "Welcome to WalMart! How can I assist you today?"), the policy will not pay any benefits. Obviously, any Own Occ policy will be more expensive than an Any Occ policy.

Generally, if you have worked for five of the past ten years in the U.S. (establishing 20 credits), you are eligible for a disability benefit through the Social Security Administration. If you fail to meet these requirements, the Canada-U.S. Totalization Agreement can be used to get you qualified for disability benefits. The agreement allows your time in Canada to be used by the U.S. to qualify for partial disability benefits. There is usually a one-year waiting period before benefits are paid, and they are based on your Social Security earnings record. To understand what your disability benefit is, you should log on to your Social Security Administration account and view your statement at least annually. These payments can continue up to age 65 until you qualify for Social Security payments. As with any government benefits, it is difficult to qualify because you must prove you are unable to perform any type of work at all ("Any Occ" policy). You should check to see if your Canadian policy pays benefits when residing in the U.S. — but understand the policy pays in Canadian loonies so you introduce currency exchange risk into your situation if you have to collect benefits to support a U.S.-dollar lifestyle.

In the U.S. and Canada, most major employers will have a group disability insurance policy, and you are well advised to get the most disability insurance possible through them. If you own an individual policy in Canada and move to the U.S., it is likely your insurance company will continue to pay benefits based on your employment time in Canada, but you should confirm the details before paying any more premiums. If you have no group policy benefits available through your employer, you should seriously consider obtaining an individual disability insurance policy provided you are insurable. Whether you secure a Canadian or U.S. policy depends on where you are going to live in the longer term and whether you need the policy to be portable and follow you to employment in the U.S., where you will need to insure a U.S.-dollar income.

Disability insurance policies can be issued for short-term disability (generally six months) and long-term disability (anything over six months up to age 65). Obviously, long-term disability carries the biggest risk exposure, as short-term disability needs can be covered with saved-up vacation time and savings. One tax note: you need to understand if you are paying for your disability insurance premiums or if your employer is paying for them, as it can make a dramatic difference to your benefits. If your employer pays your premiums, any benefits the policy pays will be fully taxable to you, giving you a significant haircut in the benefits available for your care. However, if you pay your premiums with after-tax dollars, your benefits will not be taxable to you.

LONG-TERM CARE INSURANCE

One of the largest issues facing the federal governments in both Canada and the U.S. is providing long-term care to the aging boomers and baby boomers. Long-term care consists of home care, assisted living, or skilled nursing care in a qualified facility for those who are unable to maintain the activities of daily living (dressing, eating, continence, transferring, and bathing). With today's medical advances, people are living longer but generally sicker (Alzheimer's, dementia), and as a result these costs can quickly become very expensive. The average cost across the U.S. for a private room in a nursing home is U$230 per day. These costs will be higher in Hawaii, Alaska, and New York but less in Wyoming. In Canada, the government subsidizes long-term care costs in government subsidized nursing homes (residential facilities) as part of its socialized medical system, so the average out-of-pocket co-payment amount across the country for a private room in a nursing home is about C$76, but it is "means tested," so you may pay less depending on your after-tax income. As in the U.S., this may be higher in places such as Nova Scotia and New Brunswick and lower in places such as Alberta. The government-subsidized facilities can have unusually long waiting lists, and the quality is not as good as in some of the private facilities, which you will pay more for out-of-pocket. Despite popular opinion, health insurance does not cover these costs, and U.S. Medicare coverage is virtually nonexistent. However, two recent federal court rulings have left open the possibility that Medicare may have to cover long-term care expenses in certain situations. There are state government benefits available, but to qualify for free state government long-term care you have to be virtually impoverished with nothing left to pay for it. The long-term care insurance industry is more developed in the U.S. than it is in Canada; obtaining this insurance may be a good alternative if you can get underwritten, considering you share the risk exposure with an insurance company. If you are unable to qualify, you have a risk exposure that needs to be taken into account in your plan.

OTHER INSURANCE: AUTO, HOME, LIABILITY

AUTO INSURANCE

Private companies run all auto insurance in the U.S., while in Canada some provinces have government-run auto insurance. One difference you will notice is that auto insurance is quoted on a six-month basis in the U.S. versus annual premiums in Canada. Furthermore, auto insurance tends to be more expensive in the U.S. You will also see under-insured- and uninsured-motorist coverage in the U.S. along with towing and rental-car coverage. Uninsured/underinsured-motorist coverage is used if a driver who doesn't have insurance — or doesn't have enough insurance — hits you. This coverage pays for medical costs and loss of income for you, family members, and your passengers. California estimates over 10% of drivers in the state don't have car insurance, but many experts believe the actual number is much higher. In the event your car is no longer functioning, your insurance will pay for it to be towed and pay for a rental car while your vehicle is being fixed or replaced. Liability limits are typically U$100,000–$300,000 versus C$1 million in Canada, and your state of residence will dictate the minimum amount of coverage you are required to carry. As you can see, there are a number of new terms and limits with which you will have to become familiar.

HOMEOWNER/CONDOMINIUM INSURANCE

Just like in Canada, in the U.S. you are required to have homeowner insurance if you have a mortgage on your home (the bank wants to protect its investment!). This coverage is fairly standard, and it is best to consolidate your auto and homeowner policies with the same firm since you can usually save on premiums. Ensure you get coverage to protect yourself in the event that someone slips on your driveway or falls into your pool, as outlined in the liability section below. But beware . . . if you are running a small business out of your home, your homeowner insurance typically won't provide the coverage you need.

LIABILITY

The U.S. is a much more litigious society than Canada because the laws are more liberal in permitting lawsuits, and the case law has proven that big payouts are possible. As a result, there are countless attorneys in the phone book and on TV and radio advertising to those who may have been injured in a car accident or medical malpractice. Tort reform is being called for in the U.S., but it is uncertain when anything will be done by Congress to address it. Make sure you protect yourself with an excess liability (umbrella) insurance policy. This policy, when correctly coordinated with your auto and homeowners policies, can provide you with a team of defense lawyers and protection of your assets should a legitimate or nuisance lawsuit be filed against you. We never recommend you retain your Canadian property and casualty insurance policies when making the transition to the U.S. (unless you retain the asset) — they just don't provide the coverage you need as a resident there, and may suggest a tax residency tie back to Canada.

3 A PLEDGE OF ALLEGIANCE

I pledge allegiance to the flag of the
United States of America . . .
— FRANCIS BELLAMY

For some Canadians, quoting these words in a U.S. citizenship ceremony someday is the ultimate dream, while for others seeing their kids come home from school quoting it from heart is the deciding factor in returning to Canada. It is a personal issue that each person must wrestle with and come to a conclusion on. The issue of immigration to, and citizenship in, the U.S. can be confusing, and this chapter aims to provide you with a basic understanding of the options you have for living and working in the U.S. on a long-term basis. However, it is not a substitute for a good immigration attorney. To live year-round or work at any time in the U.S., you must have the appropriate nonimmigrant or immigrant status, or be a citizen of the U.S. If you are not a U.S. citizen, your long-term objectives should determine whether you pursue a nonimmigrant visa with or without employment authorization, a green card, or citizenship, because there are tax implications, health care, cost of living, and lifestyle issues to consider with each option. Again, a thorough analysis of your unique situation is required to determine the best immigration strategy for you and how to best achieve your goals. For example, if you hope to move to the U.S. and remain there for the balance of your life, you need to ask your immigration attorney for the road map to get you from where you are now (Canadian citizen) to where you want to be (dual Canadian-U.S. citizen). Likewise, if you want to move to the U.S. for a short-term job opportunity and then return to Canada, a different road map is required.

A lack of planning in this area can result in some negative consequences. One scenario we often see is one spouse gets a job offer and sponsorship for a temporary visa from a U.S. employer, while an immigration strategy for the dependent spouse is not addressed. Once in the U.S., one spouse is working, and the other is left at home in a strange city because they cannot work, and there is no family or support structure in place. This situation tends to raise tensions in the nonworking spouse and create a longing to go back to Canada. Other issues can arise if a child is in the U.S., with a temporary visa issued, as a dependent with their parents.

REAL-LIFE EXAMPLES

Few people realize that when their child turns 21, that child is forced to leave the U.S. unless they can obtain their own immigration status. In one situation, a family we counseled moved down from Canada with minor children to open up a small business on an E-2 Treaty Investor visa. Their oldest son, who was actively involved in the business, turned 21 and was forced to leave the U.S. He had reached the age of majority, was no longer considered a dependent, and had no legal immigration standing to remain in the U.S.. This caused a lot of hardship on the parents because the son was integral to managing and staffing the store. Eventually, the whole family was forced to move back to Canada as the small business failed.

The Trade NAFTA (TN) visa has caused some U.S. immigrants unforeseen difficulties as well. People often forget that this is a temporary visa. As a result, staying in the U.S. is entirely dependent on whether your employer will sponsor the renewal of your visa. We have witnessed poorly conceived immigration strategies where people have moved to the U.S. with a TN visa intending to stay permanently. In one example, we worked with a scientist who faced a return to Canada because the company he worked with fell on difficult financial times, and a layoff was imminent. The scientist had six months to find another company to hire him in his field of expertise to continue sponsorship of the TN visa. Needless to say, this was a very stressful situation that could have been avoided with a well-thought-out immigration strategy, better negotiations with his employer upfront, and a plan for contingencies.

Another situation we have witnessed is becoming a naturalized U.S. citizen or holding a green card for a long time when you plan on returning to Canada. In both situations, you typically have to continue filing U.S. tax returns even if you live in Canada because the IRS taxes its citizens and permanent resident green card holders on their worldwide income regardless of where they are living at the time (see Chapter 5, "Double Taxes, Double Trouble"). We encourage you to start this part of your transition early by meeting with a competent immigration lawyer who can assist you in designing your U.S. immigration strategy from start to finish and achieving your goal of temporary or permanent residence or citizenship if that is your desire.

U.S. IMMIGRATION VISAS

Despite the close relationship between Canada and the U.S., anytime you cross the border you mustn't forget you are crossing into another country. Therefore, you must have the proper documentation to prove your origin and identity. All travelers entering the U.S. must have a passport . . . period. The biometric identifiers in a passport and the documentation supporting it allow the USCIS to better track and confirm whom they are allowing into the country.

We have stated many times that 9/11 changed/will change many things between Canada and the U.S. To that end, The U.S. and Canada issued on December 7, 2011, an agreement to a Joint Border Action Plan "designed to speed up legitimate trade and travel, improve security in North America, and align regulatory approaches between the two countries." One key initiative coming out of this plan is that "entry-exit verification will be put in place so that both countries can count people coming in and going out to enforce immigration and other programs." On June 30, 2014, this initiative became a reality. In fact, you can now go online and obtain your travel history at https://i94.cbp.dhs.gov/I94/request.html.

There are two ways of obtaining legal status in the U.S.: through a business/professional relationship, or through a primary family member sponsoring you (including a same-sex marriage). The age of maturity to be considered for a visa based on a parent's status is 21; over that age, you must apply independently under a sponsoring parent, other qualifying relative, or business/professional relationship. Despite thoughts to the contrary, if you don't fit into one of the immigration categories outlined below and have not secured the appropriate visa, don't even think of moving to and remaining in the U.S. Unfortunately, very few "special circumstances" are permitted.

TEMPORARY BUSINESS/PROFESSIONAL VISAS

The decision about which visa to pursue depends on what you are trying to accomplish and on understanding the pros and cons of each alternative. The most common visas Canadians use for making the transition to the U.S. on a temporary or permanent basis are the B-1, B-2, E-1, E-2, F-1, H-1B, K-1, K-3, L-1, L-2, and TN visas (see Table 3.1).

TABLE 3.1
NONIMMIGRANT VISAS

A-1 Diplomats: for traveling ambassadors, public ministers, career diplomats, or consular officers.

A-2 Accompanying support: for other foreign government officials or the staff of A-1 visa holders.

A-3 Accompanying party: for an attendant, servant, personal employee, or immediate family member of an A-1 visa holder.

B-1 Visitor for business: this visa is what you receive when you attend a conference or visit a branch office or subsidiary company in the U.S.
- No application is required.
- No physical visa is typically issued.
- You don't typically receive a passport stamp.
- It is only good for six months.
- You are not eligible to work (earn a wage) in the U.S.

B-2 Visitor for pleasure: this visa is what you receive when you visit family or "snowbird" in the U.S. (See our companion book *The Canadian Snowbird in America* for more details.)

- No application is required.
- No physical visa is typically issued.
- You don't typically receive a passport stamp.
- It is only good for six months.
- You are not eligible to work in the U.S.

C-1 Continuous transit: for aliens in transit passing through the U.S.

- No application is required.
- It is good for a maximum of 29 days.

C-2 United Nations diplomats: for those traveling to UN meetings in New York.

C-3 Foreign Government Official: family members or personal assistants.

C-4 See TWOV

D Crew member: for sea or air crew members.

E-1 Treaty trader (importer/exporter): for a person who works for a Canadian-owned/controlled firm in the U.S., and the position involves abilities essential to operation of the U.S. firm.

- It is generally issued for two years.
- It is renewable for as long as you continue to qualify.
- It does not lead directly to a green card (nonimmigrant visa).
- You typically file U.S. tax returns annually.
- It may include a spouse and/or child.

E-2 Treaty investor: for Canadians citizens with a substantial investment in a business to create U.S. jobs.

- It is generally issued for two years.
- It is renewable for as long as you continue to qualify.
- It does not lead directly to a green card.

- You typically file U.S. tax returns annually.
- It may include a spouse and/or child.

F-1/OPT Student: for students seeking an education in the U.S.
- You must prove you have sufficient funds to support yourself and your family for the duration of your studies.
- It is issued for each year of study; once studies are completed, you must return to your home country.
- It does not lead directly to a green card.
- You are able to work in certain positions on campus without additional express permission of the United States Citizenship and Immigration Services (USCIS) and off campus in certain circumstances.
- You typically don't file U.S. tax returns.

Optional practical training: allows you to work and live in the U.S. on a temporary basis for training purposes only.
- It is an extension of the F-1 visa.
- Your work must be related to your field of study.
- It is issued for an additional 12 months after the F-1.
- It does not lead directly to a green card.
- You typically file U.S. tax returns annually.

F-2 Dependent: for the spouse and dependent children of an F-1 student visa holder.
- No work in the U.S. is permitted.

G-1 International organizations: for principal resident representatives of a recognized foreign government to an international organization (such as NATO).

G-2 International organizations: for other representatives of a recognized foreign member government to an international organization.

G-3 International organizations: for representatives of a nonrecognized foreign nonmember government to an international organization.

G-4 International organizations: for international organization officers or employees.

H-1B Specialty workers: typically for professionals who have a degree (or equivalent experience) and a job that requires that degree.
- It is typically issued for three years initially.
- It is renewable once for a total six-year stay.
- It is typically pursued when you can't qualify for a green card, but it does lead directly to a green card if the employer can demonstrate to the U.S. Department of Labor, in a separate and additional application process, that there are no U.S. citizens or permanent residents qualified and willing to do the job.
- There is an annual quota of 65,000 that starts each October 1 (and are gone just as fast as tickets to a U2 concert).
- You typically file U.S. tax returns annually.

H-2A Seasonal farm workers: for a temporary worker performing agricultural services unavailable in the U.S.
- Labor certification is required to confirm there is a short supply.
- It is issued for one year.
- It is renewable for two additional terms (maximum of three years).
- It is expensive and rarely used.

H-2B Unskilled labor: for a temporary worker performing other services (nonfarm workers) unavailable in the U.S.
- Labor certification is required to confirm there is a short supply.
- It is issued for one year.
- It is renewable for two additional terms (maximum of three years).
- It is expensive and rarely used (except in some special circumstances by some hockey players).

H-3 Trainees: intended for those going to the U.S. to get on-the-job training and then return to their foreign countries.
- It is issued for one year (maximum).
- An extension is possible for two more years (maximum of three years).

H-4 Dependents: for the spouse or dependent child of any H visa holder.
- Can legally work in the U.S.

I Media: for foreign media correspondents, representatives, employees, and their families (a popular visa during the World Trade Center tragedy).

J-1 Exchange visitor: for those in an approved exchange program for education, culture, or employment.
- It is used primarily by doctors, professors, or scientists studying in the U.S.
- It is issued for the term of the program (predefined).
- You don't typically file U.S. tax returns.
- It does not lead to a green card.
- You may have to return home for two years before being eligible to change to another status.

J-2 Dependents: for the spouse and dependent children of a J-1 exchange visitor visa holder.
- No work is permitted unless separate authorization is obtained.

K-1 Fiancés/ées: for those about to move to the U.S. and wed a U.S. citizen within 90 days of entry (including same-sex marriages).

K-2 Dependents: for unmarried children under age 21 of K-1 fiancé/ée visa holders.

K-3 Spouses: for those moving to the U.S. with a U.S. citizen spouse while waiting for their immigrant visa to be processed (including same-sex spouses).
- This category was created in 2001 to deal with the eligible spouses of U.S. citizens who were forced to live apart from their U.S. spouses while their visas were being processed.
- It is issued for two years only.
- Work authorization is granted for two years only.
- You must continue the I-130 petition process or change of status application filed and active with USCIS.
- It precedes an application for a green card.
- It is a temporary solution to the large backlog at USCIS.

K-4 Dependents: for unmarried children under age 21 accompanying a K-3 spousal visa holder.

L-1 Intracompany transfer: for companies in both Canada and the U.S. that need to transfer executives, managers, or those with specialized knowledge between certain related companies in both countries.
- You must have worked in a country besides the U.S. for at least one of the past three years.
- It is typically issued for two years only but can be renewed for a total of seven years.
- It is considered a "shortcut" to a green card for executives and managers only (specialized knowledge excluded).
- You typically file U.S. tax returns annually.

L-2 Dependents: for the spouse and dependent children of an L-1 intracompany transfer visa holder.
- Work is permitted.
- You typically file U.S. tax returns with the L-1 visa holder.

M-1 Vocational/nondegree students: for those studying in the U.S., but not in a program leading to a degree.
- It is typically issued for one year, with annual extensions.
- One month of work for each four months of study is allowed after studies are completed.
- You typically don't file U.S. tax returns.

M-2 Dependents: for the spouse and children of an M-1 visa holder.

N Special immigrants: for the parents and children of certain special immigrants.

NATO representatives: there are NATO-1 through 7 visas for all representatives, staff, experts, support staff, and dependents related to NATO.

O-1 Extraordinary ability: for those with sustained national or international acclaim for displaying extraordinary ability in art, science, business, or athletics.

- It is typically issued for three years initially and then renewable for one year, or the period of the event, whichever is less.
- It is used by well-known professional athletes coming from Canada to play in the U.S.
- There is an annual quota on this visa.
- You typically file U.S. tax returns annually.

O-2 Accompanying support: for support staff vital to O-1 visa holders.
- You typically file U.S. tax returns annually.

O-3 Dependents: for the spouse and dependent children of an O-1 visa holder.
- No work is permitted.
- You are typically included on O-2 U.S. tax returns.

P-1 Performing entertainers and athletes: for those with less acclaim than O-1 visa holders, but still internationally recognized.
- It can be issued for up to five years and can be extended to ten years.
- There is a quota of 25,000 visas annually for all P categories.
- You typically file U.S. tax returns annually.

P-2 Exchange program: for those artists and entertainers in a reciprocal exchange program with a foreign country.
- You typically don't file U.S. tax returns.

P-3 Unique abilities: for artists and entertainers who are culturally unique.
- You typically don't file U.S. tax returns.

P-4 Dependents: for the spouse and dependent children of a P visa holder.
- No work is permitted.

Q-1 Cultural exchange visitor: for a participant in an international cultural employment exchange program run by the USCIS.
- You must be engaged in business for at least two years.
- You must employ at least five people.

Q-3 Dependents: for the spouse or child of a Q-2 visa holder.

R-1 Religious workers: for workers within a religious organization.
- You must be part of the same religious denomination for at least two preceding years.
- It can be issued for a maximum of five years.
- Generally file U.S. tax returns

R-2 Dependents: for the spouse or child of an R-1 visa holder.

S-5 International informants: for certain aliens supplying critical information relating to a criminal organization or enterprise.

S-6 International informants: for certain aliens supplying critical information relating to terrorism.

S-7 Dependents: for qualified family members of S-5 or S-6 visa holders.

T-1 to -4: for victims (and their families) of a severe form of trafficking in persons.

TN/Trade NAFTA visa: a unique category based on the North American Free Trade Agreement (NAFTA) between the U.S., Canada, and Mexico.
- It includes a specific list of professions that are eligible (including medical professionals, scientists, engineers, computer professionals, architects, accountants, and consultants).
- You must have a degree (unless a management consultant).
- It is renewable every three years for an unlimited period of time.
- It does not lead directly to a green card.
- You typically file U.S. tax returns annually.

TD Dependents: for the spouse or child of a TN/Trade NAFTA visa holder.

TWOV: Transit without visa.

U-1 to -4: For victims (and their families) of certain crimes.

V-1 Dependents: for the spouses of lawful permanent residents of the U.S. waiting for more than three years for immigrant visas.

- This category was created in 2001 to deal with the eligible spouses of U.S. citizens and permanent residents who were forced to live apart from their U.S. spouses while their visas were being processed.
- You are able to work.

V-2 Dependents: for the children (under 21) of lawful permanent residents of the U.S. waiting for more than three years for immigrant visas.
- You are able to work.

V-3 Dependents: for the children (under 21) of the spouses of lawful permanent residents of the U.S. waiting for more than three years for immigrant visas.
- You are able to work.

FACTS AND MYTHS

There are both facts and myths surrounding immigration to and remaining in the U.S. for an extended period of time. Here are some common ones we have dealt with.

MYTH: SPECIAL CIRCUMSTANCES APPLY

As a general rule, you are required to apply for a temporary visa, work permit, or permanent resident visa before coming to the U.S. While there are options for exceptional circumstances, you shouldn't rely on them, and you should consult with an immigration attorney in advance. A relatively straightforward application can become seriously delayed, or fail altogether, if you are simply unaware or ignore immigration requirements. Although Canadians can travel as visitors to the U.S., there are still restrictions on what you can do and how long you can stay in the U.S.

Despite popular opinion, you can't remain in the U.S. unless you have a valid immigration status to do so, even if a visa wasn't given to you at the border nor your passport stamped. In one case, we talked to someone in California who had been in the U.S. for years on a visitor's visa (only good for six months), had assumed an actor's name for acting pursuits, and ran a small business paying only California sales tax. The person simply stopped filing Canadian tax returns and has never filed a U.S. income tax return. The person has even gone back to Canada on occasion to visit family and bring back furniture! Regardless, it is a game of roulette that will quickly come to an end as border crossings are more closely monitored with the events of 9/11.

Some immigration policies aren't so flagrantly broken. We have witnessed well-intended children bring an ill parent to the U.S. to live with them for an extended period of time because there was no other family in Canada. Unfortunately, the parent is still considered an illegal alien despite the good intentions of the family. Further, provincial and travel health insurance policies have finite time limits and limited coverage, leaving the ill parent stuck with a huge medical bill that could devastate what has taken a lifetime to accumulate.

MYTH: RETIRE IN THE U.S.

There has been media coverage and much misinformation about a "Retirement visa" that permits Canadians over the age of 55 to retire to the U.S., as long as they will refrain from working, buy a $500,000 home, and maintain a residence in Canada. First, everything is proposed at this point, nothing has been signed into law. Second, neither political party in the U.S. has much to gain politically by leaving this in a bigger bill, which would still need to be negotiated within the larger context of immigration reform gaining momentum in the U.S. Third, you currently can only stay up to six months in the U.S. on a B-2 visitor's visa (see Chapter 5 for more details). At this point, then, there is no retirement visa to the U.S. for Canadians — but stay tuned, as Congress is committed to immigration reform and this circumstance may end up being included in some form.

MYTH: BUY A RENTAL PROPERTY

Many folks have asked us if they can buy a home in the U.S. to live in and another home to rent out to obtain a U.S. visa. The visa they are pursuing with this strategy is an E-2 treaty investor. This strategy is rarely successful because it has come under severe scrutiny in past years. To begin with, this is not considered a "material, bona fide" investment (in time, effort, and money) to justify the issuance of an E-2 visa. However, if you own a couple of apartment buildings or are going to purchase substantial real estate, your chances increase. The investment for prospective purchases and development needs to be irrevocable (held in escrow), but a lot of it depends on the mood of the adjudicator that day and whether he believes you are meeting the issued guidelines for a "substantial" investment through "material participation" in the management of the real estate holdings. This is where an experienced immigration attorney should be brought onto the team to provide insights into what types and numbers of properties qualify, and to help you meet the definition of material participation.

FACT: YOU WILL GET CAUGHT

Some people, with little regard for the laws of the land, have asked, "How will the government know?" or, "How will I get caught?" Scrutiny in this area has increased significantly since the unfortunate events of 9/11 and reached its culmination when Canada and the U.S. announced the Beyond the Border: A Shared Vision for Perimeter Security and Economic Competitiveness initiative on February 4, 2011. Since the U.S. and Canada are the largest trading partners in the world, the U.S. has been working with Canada on a policy of "secure borders, open doors." On December 12, 2012, officials from Canada and the U.S. signed the U.S.-Canada Visa and Immigration Information-Sharing Agreement. The main purpose of this agreement is to enable a systematic and automated means of sharing immigration and visa information between the two countries on third-country nationals applying for a visa or citizenship. This means the other country will automatically be consulted to see if this same person has any history or has applied for entry into the other nation. No information is being shared about citizens or permanent residents in both countries at this time, in accordance with Canadian and U.S. laws, but the information is being captured in a database, and government officials with a "need to know" have access to it. In addition, a coordinated Entry/Exit Information System has been developed, and despite assurances to handle information on travelers "responsibly," both governments are now tracking and sharing information about who enters and exits either country.

With Canada and the IRS cracking down on international tax cheats and the IRS going after U.S. citizens living abroad, it makes sense that the countries' entry/exit databases have become integrated. With the economic downturn in the U.S., there have been documented cases of Canadian citizens living in the U.S. going to Canada, applying for unemployment insurance benefits using a Canadian address, and then going back to their home in the U.S. (you are ineligible for most Canadian benefits, including UIC, if you are a non-resident of Canada). To stop this abuse, it appears the Canada Border Services Agency is comparing the border entry/exit dates (on at least their side of the border) to catch the perpetrators.

Overall, "beyond the border" policies are intended to build systems to expedite the passage of legitimate travelers but make it much more difficult for illegitimate travelers (i.e., those whose stated purpose may not be consistent with their travel and behavioral patterns) to cross the border. To achieve these goals, both countries are creating, maintaining, and sharing a database of biometric identifiers using the latest in technology to identify the wrong people and prohibit them from entering the U.S. or overstaying their visas, while enhancing traffic flow for those crossing the border for legitimate purposes. All visitors will have their two index fingers scanned and a digital photograph taken to verify identity at the port of entry. Further, the IRS (part of the Department of the Treasury) and the U.S. Citizenship and Immigration Services (USCIS, part of the Department of Homeland Security) appear to be working more closely together, similarly to Canada Revenue Agency and Citizenship and Immigration Canada. It appears they are combining tax slips with visa records to ferret out tax evaders and illegal aliens. Whatever you do, don't enter the U.S. illegally or overstay the temporary period of time that has been granted to you on your passport or your work/visitor/student permit. The likelihood of getting caught increases with each passing day. Besides, for anyone who is not an American citizen, entering the U.S. is a privilege, not a right. To that end, respect the laws of the land.

MYTH: CANADA-U.S. MARRIAGE IMMEDIATELY GRANTS THE SPOUSE THE RIGHT TO LIVE IN THE U.S.

With the advent of the internet and increased Canada-U.S. travel, many Canadians are finding love in the U.S. Our firm has seen a large increase in inquiries (and horror stories) from Canadians getting married to U.S. citizens (same-sex marriages included). Many of these brides-to-be are in tears when they realize their wedding plans are in jeopardy due to the unanticipated long immigration processing times. The difficulty starts when deciding where to get married. If you are getting married in Canada, the U.S. resident approaches the Canadian Border Services officer, who asks, "The purpose of your visit?" If you reply, "To get married," you will be asked for your permanent residence card under the Family Sponsorship category. If you can't produce it, your entry into Canada will be up to the discretion of the border official and whether he or she will grant you temporary residence so you can get married. Likewise, if you are getting married in the U.S., the Canadian resident approaches the USCIS officer, who asks, "The purpose of your visit?" If you reply, "To get married," you will be asked for your K-1 fiancé/ée visa. If you can't produce one, you will likely be denied entry into the U.S. because your intention is to get married and remain in the U.S. — you won't be allowed into the U.S. under a B-2 visitor's visa (intending to visit). It is important to be truthful since the agent may document the conversation, and if you are caught lying you could be banned from entering the U.S. for five years or more.

At the heart of the confusion is the concept of "dual intent." It has been fought successfully in the courts and, with this option, you can have two reasons for entering the U.S. but share only one of them if the agent doesn't ask enough questions to expose the other. For example, if you are legitimately going to the U.S. to visit family and to get married, you are truthful in all aspects about your visit with family (staying at their house, length of stay, etc.), and you get married to your fiancé/ée on the same trip, you can enter with a B-2 visitor's visa, get married, and remain in the U.S. while you file for a change of status to a green card. If the agent doesn't ask you if you have a fiancé/ée in the U.S., or whether you have any other intentions for your trip, you can achieve your immigration goals through dual intent. Again, it is important that you stay in the U.S. while your green card is being processed, which means you won't be able to return to Canada for a few months unless your attorney files for a traveling exemption (I-131 — Application for Travel Document) as well.

Canadian immigration laws and policies allow for officers to exercise a bit more discretion when encountering situations of dual intent. Officers are permitted to allow someone to enter as a temporary visitor if they are satisfied that the individual will, in fact, leave Canada at the end of the term of authorized temporary stay. American immigration laws regarding dual intent are much stricter and more straightforward in their wording and application, and most USCIS officers will require a significant amount of evidence on the intending immigrant of his/her ability and intention to leave the U.S. after a temporary stay before admitting them as visitors into the country.

If you are married and want to join your spouse in the U.S. (including same-sex marriages), you have two choices to emigrate to the U.S.: a green card or K-3 spouse's visa. The K-3 visa was introduced in 2001 to shorten the processing times because USCIS was taking so long to process green cards. The problem today is that K-3 and green cards are taking about the same time to process (8–10 months depending which USCIS office is processing your application). When you receive a K-3, you can emigrate to the U.S., begin working, and file a change of status for your green card. The problem is that, once you file for your K-3 visa or green card, you must stay in your country of residence until the processing is completed. If you want to be together as newlyweds, the U.S. citizen has to stay in Canada and risk becoming a Canadian resident for tax purposes. Alternatively, the U.S. citizen has to return to the U.S. and wait for the Canadian's K-3 or green card to be processed before they can be together again. The bottom line is you should be prepared to spend some time apart . . . not something newlyweds want to hear.

As you can see, the right immigration planning — well in advance of your planned nuptials — can help to make your dreams come true. Otherwise, you could be stuck in the kind of nightmare we have seen many times.

IMMIGRANT VISAS: GREEN CARDS

The technical term for a green card is "lawful permanent resident status." The term "green card" is derived from the original color of the card provided when you obtained lawful permanent resident status in the past.

In fact, the card has gone through a myriad of colors because the USCIS changes it slightly every year to stem false duplication. The latest green card is now actually green in color and design pattern. USCIS now also requires biometric identifiers (a fingerprint of your index finger and a photo) to ensure the validity of the cardholder. Today there are about 2.5 million green cards issued annually, and the card contains your picture, an expiration date, your fingerprint, and other pertinent details, as illustrated in Figure 3.1.

Once you have held a green card for five years (three years if married to a U.S. citizen), you are eligible to apply for U.S. citizenship. At my citizenship ceremony, I handed in my green card, and it was replaced with my Certificate of Naturalization. Any Certificate of Naturalization is a very valuable document and should be stored in a safe deposit box.

FIGURE 3.1

THE U.S. "GREEN CARD"

When you apply for a passport, you will be required to provide your Certificate of Naturalization, but contrary to popular opinion you will receive it back when your passport is issued.

Many people are unaware of the regulations, duties, and responsibilities surrounding their green card until they go to the border and it is seized. Green cards used to be issued with no expiration date, which meant they were permanent. That is no longer the case. Green cards are issued for a 10-year time period, after which they need to be renewed. This is the government's attempt to enforce the "intent to abandon" rules. Since holding a green card is considered lawful permanent residence, you must demonstrate to the USCIS that you are actively using the right granted to you, or the "intent to abandon" rules may apply. Some of these duties include using your green card by living in the U.S. and filing U.S. tax returns annually. Leaving the U.S. for an extended period of time has been deemed abandonment of your green card. Many people are unaware of these regulations and are simply living in Canada with a green card in their pocket, totally unaware that a USCIS officer might deem them to have "abandoned" their green card on their next visit to the U.S. (See our companion book *The American in Canada* for more details.) This is typically determined too late, when the green card holder attempts to reenter the U.S. If you have a U.S. green card and you are residing in Canada, you need to "use it or lose it." If you lose it, you must start the green card application process all over again.

Unfortunately, the typical backlog at the USCIS means that, no matter which immigration strategy is selected, there is typically a long wait ahead of you. In some cases, it can be as short as six to eight months, but we are aware of applications taking up to 10 or more years! As a result, the USCIS has introduced the K and V visas (listed above) as a temporary solution. There are two ways of getting lawful permanent resident status (a green card) in the U.S.

1. FAMILY SPONSORSHIP

Family-based sponsorship is possible by U.S. citizens or green card holders. Landed permanent residence status is granted based on one of five "preferences" in the order listed below.

- Immediate relatives preference: for spouses (including same sex), parents, and unmarried children (under the age of 21) of U.S. citizens only. There is no limit to the number of green cards issued under this preference in any particular year, and they are granted in order of preference as outlined below.
- First preference: for unmarried children, age 21 and older, of U.S. citizens only.
- Second preference: for spouses and unmarried children under

age 21, or unmarried children age 21 and older, of green card holders.
- Third preference: for married children of U.S. citizens only.
- Fourth preference: siblings age 21 or older of U.S. citizens only.

2. BUSINESS OR PROFESSIONAL RELATIONSHIP

Lawful permanent resident status for business or professional reasons is also granted based on one of five "preferences" in the order outlined below.

First preference: for priority workers who have risen to the top of their profession. At least 40,000 first preference green cards are issued annually. This category is broken into three employment-based classes of immigrants:
- EB1-A extraordinary ability: for those with sustained national or international acclaim for ability in art, science, business, or athletics (Wayne Gretzky and Jim Carrey are examples).
- EB1-B advanced degrees: for researchers and professors with exceptional ability and international recognition coming to the U.S. to conduct full-time research for a company or university.
- EB1-C skilled workers: for executives and managers of multinational companies who have worked in a Canadian affiliate for one of the past three years, and now the U.S. affiliate is petitioning for permanent status.

Second preference: for priority workers whom the USCIS views as benefiting the "national interest" (i.e., helping the economic, cultural, educational, or general welfare of the U.S.) if employed in the U.S. This is sometimes called the "national interest" waiver (a company or institution doesn't have to obtain labor certification, as described under the third preference below). At least 40,000 second preference green cards are issued annually. They are broken into the following two categories:
- EB2-A advanced degrees: for professionals with advanced degrees (or equivalent experience) who display exceptional ability in science, business, or art. Proof of ability is not as

strenuous as in the first preference category, but you must prove you are the only one qualified (or the most qualified person) for the position.

- EB2-B exceptional ability: for those with more ability than ordinary folks in the areas of art, science, business, or athletics but who don't have the extraordinary ability of the first preference category. Defining ordinary versus exceptional versus extraordinary can be difficult.

Third preference: for skilled and unskilled workers who don't fit into the first or second preference areas. At least 40,000 third preference green cards are issued annually, but no more than 10,000 are issued to unskilled workers. Each of the third preference categories requires labor certification under which the U.S. employer must demonstrate to the satisfaction of the U.S. Department of Labor that there are no U.S. citizens or permanent residents able and willing to do the job. There are three categories:

- EB3-A workers with degrees: for professionals with a degree.
- EB3-B skilled workers: for those with at least two years of experience or higher training and education.
- EB3-C unskilled workers: for those with less than two years of experience or higher training and education.

Fourth preference: for special immigrants, including religious workers or those who have worked for the U.S. government abroad for 15 years. At least 10,000 fourth preference green cards are issued annually.

Fifth preference: since 1990, Congress has made available a fifth preference immigrant visa category known as an EB-5 investor green card or a "gold card." There are only 10,000 available per year, and the rules and regulations surrounding them are very specific (about 1,000 get approved annually, so don't do it yourself). An investor who establishes a business in the U.S. with an investment of $1 million ($500,000 if a USCIS "targeted employment area") can obtain a green card with conditions that last for two years. The USCIS wants the investment "locked in" for up to five years to ensure that it will benefit the U.S. economy and has directly or indirectly created at least 10 full-time jobs. Once filed, the investor's petition is normally approved by the USCIS within 60 to 90 days, so it is an unusually quick turnaround time. If approved, you move into the normal green card application process in which you get a physical and go through the interview process. Once the investment has been made, your "gold card" has been approved, and your entity has operated for two years, a petition can be filed to lift the restrictions from the "gold card," and you become eligible for an unencumbered green card. After holding the green card for an additional three years, you can apply to become a naturalized U.S. citizen. We have experience in getting the "gold card"(hard to find) and have experts available to assist you in implementing this complex but very convenient immigration strategy.

APPLYING FOR A GREEN CARD

To apply for a green card, the starting point is filing USCIS Form I-485 — Application to Register Permanent Status or Adjust Status, along with the U$985 filing fee for adults (U$635 for minors), plus a biometrics fee of U$85 (totals of U$1,070 and U$720 respectively), and two color photographs. There are other supplemental forms, such as the I-134: Affidavit of Support, which may be required, depending on your circumstances. Before undertaking this yourself, seek good counsel to save yourself a lot of time and to ensure you are filling out the right forms and submitting them in their entirety to the right location. One big "gotcha" we see quite often is when a U.S. citizen sponsors their Canadian citizen spouse for a green card and fails to meet the requirement to provide U.S. tax returns for the past three years. The reason you need to provide them is to show you can sufficiently support your spouse when you relocate to the U.S. (see our companion book *The American in Canada* for more details on the filing requirements of U.S. citizens and green card holders living in Canada). Needless to say, most American citizens and green card holders living in Canada are not in compliance with the IRS rules. If all of these requirements are not met, the USCIS may reject your application, delaying the process significantly.

U.S. CITIZENSHIP

For many Canadians, the prospect of becoming a U.S. citizen is terri-
fying, while for others it is the next most coveted nationality around.
Millions of people around the world would welcome the opportunity to
become a Canadian or U.S. citizen and be able to work and live anywhere
in Canada or the U.S. Once again, there are many rules and regulations
surrounding citizenship with which you must contend. U.S. citizenship
is obtained in one of the following three ways.

1. BIRTH IN THE U.S.

In general, if you were born in the U.S. (legally), you are a U.S. citizen
unless you effectively renounced your citizenship.

Loss of Citizenship

Before 1986, the U.S. Department of State involuntarily renounced your
citizenship if you performed an "expatriating act" (became a citizen of
another country, declared allegiance to it, enrolled in its military, or worked
for its government). Many U.S. citizens residing in Canada received a
Certificate of Loss of Nationality from the U.S. Department of State, but
in most cases citizenship can be reinstated. To regain it, you need to write
to the U.S. Department of State and ask it to revoke the Certificate of Loss
of Nationality. However, before you do so, realize that you become liable to
file U.S. tax returns and be subject to U.S. estate taxes, among other things.
Be sure you fully understand all the implications of reinstating your loss of
citizenship and the negative consequences that may be involved.

Reinstating Citizenship

Given the seemingly constant backlog at the USCIS, we recommend you
"short-circuit" the process of reinstating your citizenship by first applying
for a passport at the U.S. Department of State. You fill out Form DS-11
and submit it along with the U$140 application fee + U$25 execution fee,
plus two recent photographs of yourself (http://travel.state.gov/passport/
passport_1738.html). You will get an answer sooner this way and can determine the next course of action. Alternatively, you can file Form N-600 —
Application for Certification of Citizenship with the USCIS — along with

the U$600 fee and two photographs — to apply for U.S. citizenship. This approach will take longer and will require more time and effort.

Renouncing Citizenship

Formally renouncing your citizenship has now become a difficult (and, in some cases, costly) process because Congress is trying to stem the flow of people who are renouncing their citizenships and in turn no longer filing U.S. tax returns (remember, the U.S. taxes individuals based on citizenship and domicile, not physical presence). In particular, you will be subject to the expatriation rules if you have a worldwide net worth of U$2 million+ in 2015, or have paid an average of U$160,000+ (inflation adjusted) in annual income taxes for the preceding five years, or have failed to certify that you have complied with all U.S. tax filing require-ments for the five years prior to expatriation. Under these new rules, if you renounce your U.S. citizenship, or give up or are "deemed to have abandoned" your green card after having it for at least eight years, you may be subject to an "exit" tax. Effectively, such an individual (now referred to as a "covered expatriate") will be deemed to have sold all of their worldwide assets at fair market value on the date of expatriation. Upon the deemed sale, if there were any gains in excess of U$690,000 in 2015, they would be subject to capital gains tax at the maximum rate in effect at that time. Special rules apply to U.S. real estate and deferred compensation plans. However, if you have any U.S. retirement plans, including an IRA, these plans would be deemed sold and subject to ordi-nary income tax rates. However, the 10% penalty for distributions before age 59 will be waived. So if the exit tax does not get you on the way out, if you are a covered expatriate and you decide to gift assets to any U.S. citizen/resident family or friends beyond the annual gift tax exclusion (U$14,000 in 2015), the recipient of the gift will now pay tax at 45% on the gift received. See our companion book *The American in Canada* for more details on the new expatriation rules.

2. DERIVATIVE CITIZENSHIP

Many people living in Canada, though they have never physically lived in the U.S., may be U.S. citizens and not even know it! The derivative citizenship rules provide that you may be a U.S. citizen depending on where you are in your family tree. You may be able to claim U.S. citizenship if one or both of your parents were U.S. citizens and/or resided in the U.S. Determining whether you are a derivative citizen is a bit complex because the rules have changed over the years. The following decision tree (Figure 3.2) should assist you in determining whether you are a derivative citizen of the U.S., but you should consult with an experienced immigration attorney to confirm your derivative citizenship.

FIGURE 3.2
DERIVATIVE CITIZENSHIP DECISION TREE

Basically, if one or both of your parents were U.S. citizens and resided in the U.S. at some point, you may be a derivative citizen. However, in trying to establish derivative citizenship, it may be difficult to provide enough substantive evidence to the USCIS that your parents were U.S. citizens and/or resided in the U.S. for the required time periods. Birth certificates and proof of a U.S. address are typically required but often difficult to come by, particularly in small towns or counties. The rules surrounding derivative citizenship are complex, and you'll likely require the services of a good immigration attorney to build your case before exercising your right to derivative citizenship. However, before doing so, you should recognize that you become liable to file U.S. tax returns, could become subject to U.S. estate taxes on your worldwide assets, and so on, so ensure you fully understand all of the implications of exercising your right to derivative citizenship and what can be done beforehand to mitigate any negative consequences.

Applying for U.S. Citizenship

Again, given the current backlog at the USCIS, you can "short-circuit" the derivative citizenship process by applying for a passport at the U.S. Department of State. You fill out Form DS-11 — Application for a U.S. Passport and submit it along with the U$140 application fee + U$25 execution fee and two recent photographs of yourself. You will get an answer sooner this way and be able to determine your next course of action. Alternatively, you can file Form N-600 — Application for Certification of Citizenship with USCIS along with the U$600 fee and two photographs to determine your U.S. citizenship.

3. NATURALIZATION

The primary method used to obtain U.S. citizenship by Canadian citizens is becoming a naturalized citizen through an American spouse (after holding a green card for three years, like I did) or after holding a green card for five years. It is a relatively easy process that requires you to file Form N-400 — Application for Naturalization with the USCIS along with the U$675 fee (U$595 filing fee plus a biometrics fee of U$85), and two photographs. This form is onerous because you have to provide the details of every trip you have taken outside the U.S. since you received your green card, so start tracking them now! However, if you don't have this information and cannot rebuild the history, you can still obtain it under the Freedom of Information Act as outlined earlier.

Once the USCIS receives the form, you'll be fingerprinted, an FBI background check will be completed, and you will have a personal interview with a USCIS naturalization examiner. She will ensure you can both speak and write English and have a general understanding of U.S. history and government. Historically, there is a pool of 100 questions that the examiner will draw from for your interview, and she will typically pick 5 to 10 of these questions to test your speaking and writing abilities. These questions are intended to ensure applicants understand the meaning behind some of America's fundamental institutions rather than just memorizing names and facts. (See Appendix D for a list of the questions.)

REAL-LIFE EXAMPLE

Becoming a naturalized citizen of the U.S. can be a nerve-racking experience — you need to understand you are becoming a citizen of another country. My experience was particularly difficult because I had an older, experienced examiner who'd been lured out of retirement for the second time to handle the caseload. In the verbal interview, he asked, "If we went to war with Canada, would you fight for our side?" After getting a lump in my throat, I nervously replied, "A war with Canada would never happen!" He immediately replied, "The question still stands." That is when I realized the gravity of what I was doing. In the written portion of the interview, the examiner asked me to "demonstrate your writing skills by writing 'the color of my new flag is red, white, and blue.' Now underline 'blue.'" This was sobering to say the least, and I tried to keep my hand from shaking so the writing would be legible. Thankfully I passed and during my citizenship ceremony I exchanged my green card for a naturalization certificate (valuable document, so store in a safe-deposit box). My citizenship ceremony was a very interesting experience and we encourage you to participate in your own if you can (you don't have to). The most powerful part is generally the time people share their testimonies of how they got to the U.S. and how thankful they are to be U.S. citizens.

PROS AND CONS OF U.S. CITIZENSHIP

Table 3.2 presents some of the pros and cons you should consider before becoming a naturalized citizen of the U.S.

TABLE 3.2
PROS AND CONS OF U.S. CITIZENSHIP

Pros	Cons
• Able to work and live anywhere in North America, including Canada, where you can enjoy the safety of its socialized medical health-care system. • You do NOT relinquish your Canadian citizenship. • You get the same estate planning benefits that U.S. citizens do. • Unlimited gifting between spouses on an annual basis. • Able to use the higher quality/quicker U.S. health-care system for the balance of your life. • Able to vote in the U.S. and help shape the political landscape. • Able to carry both a U.S. and Canadian passport for traveling purposes. • You won't be called for jury duty. • You can run for municipal and state political office. • You will have unrestricted ownership of certain business entities in the U.S.	• Must file U.S. taxes for the balance of your life, no matter where you live in the world (including Canada). • To avoid filing U.S. taxes as noted above, you must renounce your citizenship, which is very difficult and costly to do. • You do not get the unlimited marital deduction at the first spouse's death. • Gifting between spouses is limited to $147,000 in 2015. • You may still be subject to Canadian income taxes on certain Canadian source income. • You can't run for President of the United States. • You may now be subject to certain U.S. legal proceedings. • You can be called for jury duty. • You may be subject to a military draft. • You may create diplomatic and consular difficulties when traveling outside Canada and the U.S.

Pros	Cons
• You can sponsor parents and siblings for U.S. permanent resident status. • You will be able to go through the U.S. citizen line when reentering the country, which is expected to be much faster now that permanent residents are subject to the U.S.-VISIT photo and finger scan requirements at entry. • You may qualify for in-state tuition. • You are protected from deportation.	

Obviously, becoming a U.S. citizen is a very personal decision and needs to be considered seriously in light of the pros and cons above.

FACTS AND MYTHS

There are many facts and myths surrounding U.S. citizenship. Here are the most common ones we have seen.

FACT: DUAL CANADIAN-U.S. CITIZENSHIP

I am living proof, and so are many of our clients! We have even worked with people who have moved from Australia to Canada to the U.S. and obtained citizenship in all three countries. Others have moved from the United Kingdom to Canada to the U.S., while still others have moved from Hong Kong to Canada to the U.S. and are citizens in all three countries. This is completely legal, and you do not have to give up citizenship in one country for that in another. You'll find some immigration officials who won't admit to knowing about it, and others have posters in the lobby announcing the joys of dual citizenship (USCIS office in Buffalo,

NY, for example). Dual citizenship comes about because the citizenship applications for both countries are separate. You do not apply for dual citizenship. You are simply a Canadian citizen applying for U.S. citizenship or a U.S. citizen applying for Canadian citizenship.

Since Pierre Trudeau declared his "once a Canadian, always a Canadian" policy in 1977, Canadians cannot lose their Canadian citizenship even if they take up citizenship in another country. This issue came up for debate in 2006 when tens of millions of dollars were spent to bring home from Lebanon non-resident Canadian citizens during the conflict there (they were not necessarily paying Canadian taxes). Some people incorrectly believe that U.S. citizenship requires that you renounce your Canadian citizenship because, in the citizenship oath ceremony, there is language to the effect of the individual "renouncing" all former citizenships or loyalties. However, the reality is that you can retain your citizenship with another country as long as that country recognizes you as a citizen, despite having taken up citizenship in another country. The U.S. government has neither the jurisdiction nor the power to dictate whom the Canadian government has as citizens (and vice versa). As a result, talking up U.S. citizenship will lead to dual citizenship, or even multiple citizenship, as long as each respective country continues to recognize it.

For Americans, becoming a Canadian citizen used to mean they automatically lost their U.S. citizenship. Before 1986, the U.S. Department of State involuntarily revoked your U.S. citizenship if you performed an "expatriating act," as previously outlined. Many U.S. citizens residing in Canada received a Certificate of Loss of Nationality from the U.S. Department of State in such circumstances. However, in most cases, your citizenship can be reinstated. Since 1986, the act of applying for Canadian citizenship does not automatically mean you intend to give up your U.S. citizenship. Refer to the section on "Loss of Citizenship" for information on how to get it back.

To me, dual citizenship is the ultimate in freedom since I can work and live anywhere in the two greatest nations in the world. In addition, what a heritage to pass on to your children! U.S. citizenship is not for everyone, though, so ensure you understand all that is involved before you make your decision.

If one or both parents are Canadian citizens and you have a child that is born or adopted after you moved to the U.S., you may be wondering if your child is a Canadian citizen. Under laws passed on April 17, 2009, which amended the Citizenship Act, if you are in the first generation born outside Canada after 1947, to at least one parent who is a Canadian citizen, then you are automatically a Canadian citizen without having to become a permanent resident in Canada. You don't need to apply for citizenship, but you may need to apply for a certificate to prove your citizenship. To apply for a certificate, you need to fill out Form CIT 0001 — Application for a Citizenship Certificate (and supplemental documents), and file it along with your C$100 application fee. For the adopted children of Canadian citizens living abroad, retaining Canadian citizenship wasn't an option until December 22, 2007, when Bill C-14 amended the Citizenship Act to make it permissible. With the amendment in 2009, children adopted abroad to a Canadian citizen automatically get Canadian citizenship as well, as long as they are a first-generation adoption. To get your adopted child Canadian citizenship, you are required to fill out Form CIT 0003 – Application for Canadian Citizenship — Minors (and supplemental forms), and submit it with a C$100 processing fee (see our companion book *The American in Canada* for more details).

MYTH: GREEN CARD LOTTERY

The green card lottery is really called the Diversity Immigrant Visa Lottery, and it does happen annually. Once and sometimes twice a year the U.S. will make 50,000 green cards available through an online lottery system. The intent behind this lottery is to equalize the immigrants entering the U.S. from around the world. Countries that do not get their "fair share," and where it is a political advantage for the U.S. to do so, will be put on the "list." Only those countries on the list will be eligible for the lottery. Unfortunately, Canada has its fair share of emigrants to the U.S., and since 1993 Canadians have been excluded from the lottery. In fact, any country that has more than 50,000 immigrants over the past five years is excluded. The list includes China, India, Pakistan, Mexico, and 14 other countries. However, if you have citizenship in another country that is still included in the lottery (Russia and Kosovo were recently added), you may be able to enter the lottery using that citizenship. Interestingly enough, there has been a shift in immigrants from European countries, to immigrants from Asian and Latin American countries.

BECOMING A U.S. RESIDENT

Once you have completed the transition to the U.S. and officially given up Canadian residency (but not citizenship!), there is a whole new set of items to consider.

FILE TAX RETURNS

As American residents, you are required to file U.S. tax returns — it's a primary responsibility now that you have taken up residency in the U.S. Don't forget your final Canadian tax-filing obligation by filing your exit return, and ensure that any Canadian source income has the appropriate withholding per the Canada-U.S. Tax Treaty. (See Chapter 5 for all the tax implications of your move.)

STAY OUT OF CANADA

To demonstrate that you have severed your ties with Canada and established U.S. residency, it is best if you postpone any lengthy stays in Canada for at least two years and preferably three. Do not return to Canada for extended periods of time (i.e., six months or more), and if you do go to Canada, be sure it is for short visits to family (it always helps to document your trips).

REVIEW YOUR ESTATE PLAN

As outlined in Chapter 7, now is the time to have your Canadian estate plan reviewed by a qualified U.S. estate planning attorney familiar with Canada-U.S. issues to determine its validity in the U.S. You need to ensure that your children are cared for and that all your financial affairs are managed according to your wishes in the event you become incapacitated. In addition, you need to ensure that your children have guardians and that your estate can be settled quickly (in both the U.S. and Canada) when you pass away. These are serious issues that need to be addressed immediately.

REGISTER, APPLY FOR, SUBSCRIBE

As outlined in the next chapter, you should register your vehicle in the state in which you are residing and get a valid driver's license (you typically have 30 days). You should also get the appropriate U.S. homeowner, auto, and liability insurance policies. See Chapter 2, "Cover Your Assets," for further details on these areas. A credit card is a must in the U.S., and you should apply for one upon your arrival. See Chapter 6, "Show Me the Money," for the difficulties and solutions in building a credit rating in the U.S.

CANCEL, CANCEL, CANCEL

This is the time to cancel your Canadian provincial health insurance, driver's license, vehicle registration, and credit cards to clearly establish your ties with the U.S. It is usually best to mail them back to the issuing authority along with a letter stating that you are now a U.S. resident. If you don't do this, you risk these items being used to show you never really intended to leave Canada.

RRSPS/RRIFS

Provided you have a well-thought-out plan by a transition planner knowledgeable in Canada-U.S. matters, now may be the best time to withdraw some, or all, of your RRSPs/RRIFs/LIRAs. Chapter 5 gives you further insights into severing your ties with Canada, as well as outlines the taxation of your registered plans. Chapter 10, "Money Doesn't Grow on Trees," addresses the issues in moving these accounts to the U.S.

ESTABLISH A U$ INVESTMENT PORTFOLIO

Depending on your tenure in the U.S., you should establish a U.S.-dollar-based investment portfolio at a discount brokerage firm. Provided it is structured correctly, your portfolio can reduce your tax bill by consuming foreign tax credits while funding your future U$-based liabilities during retirement, U.S. expenditures, and so on. See Chapter 10 for more details in this area.

MOVING 4
YOUR STUFF

*Take your flocks and herds,
as you have said, and go.*
— EXODUS 12:32

Despite the many tax, immigration, and estate planning issues you may encounter when making the transition to the U.S., moving your physical assets there is what garners most people's attention. In light of 9/11, Canada and the U.S. signed the Smart Border Declaration on December 12, 2001. The intent of this declaration was to outline an action plan to collaborate in identifying and addressing security risks without hampering the transfer of legitimate travelers and goods. The countries agreed to share information and intelligence to strengthen the coordination between both enforcement agencies in addressing common threats. However, there can still be much frustration in this process because, in my experience, when you contact U.S. Customs and Border Protection, the answer to your question is typically different every time you call. To that end, we suggest you document the time and date of each call along with the name of the agent and their badge/agent identification number. Call three times for any question; then take the best answer and be prepared to defend it with the documentation you have. You may still endure some inconvenience at the border, but you should get some marks with the customs agent for your efforts. Here are a few other things to consider when moving your physical assets to the U.S.

AUTOMOBILES

For some reason, many Canadians insist on taking their automobiles to the U.S. when they move. However, moving your automobile to the U.S. is a tricky proposition and should be avoided if at all possible, particularly for long-term or permanent moves. Because of the reasons listed below, you will typically get a higher price in Canada when you sell than you would in the U.S., and trust me . . . it is a lot easier to move cash! You will have to fill out U.S. Department of Transportation Form HS-7 — Declaration and Environmental Protection Agency Form 3520-1 — Import Declaration. In addition, there are several other issues that you should consider when trying to take your automobile to the U.S.

KILOMETERS VERSUS MILES

The primary denomination of both the speedometer and the odometer are in kilometers, so to have them converted to miles when your transition to the U.S. is complete will cost you some money. To convert your automobile from kilometers to miles in the U.S. costs approximately U$800, provided the requisite parts for your make and model can be found. If you choose not to spend the money, your vehicle will be worth less when you sell the auto in the U.S.

SAFETY STANDARDS

Your vehicle must pass the rigorous safety standards in the U.S., and it most likely will. These standards are enforced by the Department of Transportation, which has a say in whether or not your car meets the standards. If not, you could create some difficulties for yourself because you won't be able to register the vehicle until a safety certificate is issued.

EMISSIONS TEST

Your Canadian vehicle may fail the high (and ever-increasing) emission standards required in sunshine states such as California and Arizona. It will typically not meet the emission standards if it was not originally manufactured to comply with these tougher U.S. emission standards. As a result, you will be required to invest the money to bring it up to standards or destroy/deport the car. We are aware of individuals who have brought brand-new vehicles down to the U.S. assuming they would have no problem passing the emissions test, but in fact ended up failing it. The problem is that the emission devices placed on the vehicles in Canada may not be approved by the Environmental Protection Agency in the U.S. Once you get an emissions test failure, you are unable to register the vehicle, which means you can't drive it until you produce a passed emissions test certificate. This is becoming a greater issue in moving to the U.S. because of the high levels of smog in most U.S. cities. As a point of interest, the American Lung Association cites the following 15 cities as having the highest levels of smog in the U.S.: (1) Los Angeles, CA (plus five other cities in California), (7) Houston, TX, (8) Dallas-Forth Worth, TX, (9) Washington, DC/Baltimore, MD/Northern Virginia, (10) El Centro, CA, (11) San Diego/Carlsbad/San Marcos, CA (plus two more cities in California), (14) Cincinnati, OH/Middletown, KY/Wilmington, IN, (15) Birmingham/Hoover/Cullman, AL. In Canada, the 15 highest smog levels are: (1) Kitchener, ON, (2) Toronto, ON, (3) Windsor, ON (and three other cities in Ontario), (7) Montreal, QC, (8) St. Catharines, ON, (9) Kejimkujik, NS, (10) Oshawa, ON, (11) Halifax, NS, (12) Quebec, QC, (13) St. John, NB, (14) Vancouver, BC, (15) Calgary, AB.

DUTY

Depending on the year and make of your automobile, there may be duty to be paid at the border when you take your vehicle to the U.S., although most Canadian-manufactured vehicles enter duty free. The idea behind duty is to prevent what was happening with prescription drugs: buying a newly manufactured car in Canada at lower prices (due to currency exchange, different manufacturing costs) and then moving it to the U.S. You should contact U.S. Customs and Border Protection well in advance of your move to research your particular vehicle, and the applicability of any duties, so you don't get a nasty surprise at the border. These duties are required at the time of your crossing, or the vehicle will be impounded until you pay them. For returning U.S. residents, you are eligible for a U$800 duty exemption if duty applies to your particular vehicle.

INVESTIGATION

Be prepared for a lengthy stay at the border crossing. Officials don't allow automobiles into the U.S. easily because the government is trying to stem the flow of stolen vehicles from Canada being sold in the U.S. I watched as a customs agent checked every number inside and outside my car and compared it to the information contained in Customs' databases. There were countless questions on when the car was purchased, where, for how much, and so on. Be sure to have adequate documentation, bill of sale, title, etc. to prove evidence of ownership and ease this difficult process.

REGISTRATION

In most states, you must register your vehicle with your state of residence within 30 days of taking up residency, since your provincial plates will be considered expired, and you could face fines for driving an unregistered automobile. However, be prepared because the state auto registration fees can be punishing (U$400 or more) if they are based on the value of your vehicle (as in Arizona). The good thing is that a portion of your registration fees may be deductible on your U.S. tax return.

DRIVER'S LICENSE

Most states require you to obtain a local driver's license typically within 30 days of taking up residency in the U.S. Some states require extensive measures, such as writing the driver's exam and taking an eye test, a reaction test, and a road test. Others simply issue you a driver's license when you present a valid provincial driver's license (New York does this, for example). The rules vary by state, so you should check with your local state authorities on what is required from you and the appropriate timelines before you move.

Another alternative to getting a local state driver's license, particularly if your stay is going to be relatively short, is to obtain an international driving permit (IDP). An IDP is primarily aimed at tourists who wish to drive in another country without having to take additional tests or file applications. An IDP is proof that the holder has a valid driver's license issued by a competent authority in their country of residence. These function as an official translation of your Canadian driver's license and are accepted across America. An IDP is issued for one year and can be obtained through the Canadian Automobile Association before you depart for the U.S. The only problem with getting an IDP is that CRA could argue that this constitutes a tax tie, which would require the continued filing of Canadian tax returns (see Chapter 5). Further, getting an international driving permit requires just as much effort as getting a driver's license from your state, so we generally don't recommend it.

MISCELLANEOUS

Autos from Canada are not viewed as favorably as local cars in the southern states because of the toll the salt used in Canada during the winters takes on vehicles. There is typically a large decrease in value, particularly in the sunshine states where you can buy a car locally that hasn't experienced the effects of salt corrosion. Besides, you won't need the antirust undercoating and block heater in Florida.

If, after all this, you insist on bringing your vehicle with you to the U.S., the easiest way is to hire an auto importer to take care of all the details for you. If you need a referral, please contact us. If you don't want to incur the expense, here is how to import your vehicle to the U.S. To begin, you will need to contact the Canadian manufacturer of your vehicle and obtain a letter from them that very clearly states that your vehicle, VIN, make, and model meets U.S. Environmental Protection Agency (EPA) emission standards and U.S. Department of Transportation (DOT) National Highway Traffic Safety Administration safety standards. See Exhibit 4.1 for an actual letter with the necessary components. You also need to have a label on the driver's door certifying such compliance permanently affixed by the original manufacturer of the car. With this letter in hand and label on the door, you simply present it at the border when you drive across, along with U.S. DOT Form HS-7 — Importation of Motor Vehicles and Motor Vehicle Equipment Subject to Federal Motor Vehicle Safety, Bumper and Theft Prevention Standards, and U.S. Customs and Border Protection Form 7501 — Entry Summary. U.S. CBP will stamp Form 7501 that your vehicle meets the EPA and DOT standards outlined. When this happens, you can drive across the border having successfully imported your Canadian vehicle. You use your stamped CBP Form 7501 to register your vehicle in your state of residency.

EXHIBIT 4.1

ACCEPTABLE MANUFACTURER LETTER

Ford Motor Company of Canada, Limited
Ford du Canada Limitée

The Canadian Road
P.O. Box 2000
Oakville, Ontario
L6J 5E4

August 27, 2013

TO: Daniel

Calgary, AB

This is to advise the 2010 Explorer, VIN#   , equipped with Engine Calibration Number 9-U51-A50, as originally manufactured, met United States Environmental Protection Agency Exhaust Emission Standards in effect for the 2010 model year.

We also advise that, with the exception of minor labeling requirements and daytime running lights, the above noted vehicle, as originally manufactured, complies with the applicable United States Federal Motor Vehicle Safety Standards necessary to allow its importation into the United States from Canada.

Additionally, please be advised the above vehicle has no outstanding Ford of Canada safety or emission recalls.

Yours very truly,

Eric Trepanier
FORD MOTOR COMPANY OF CANADA, Limited
Loyalty & Retention Manager

If your letter states that your vehicle meets U.S. EPA standards, as well Canadian Motor Vehicle Safety Standards — and your door label says the same — but doesn't meet U.S. Safety Standards, you have a problem (see Exhibit 4.2).

EXHIBIT 4.2
UNACCEPTABLE MANUFACTURER LETTER

Kia Canada Inc.
180 Foster Crescent, Mississauga
Ontario L5R 4J5 Canada
T 905 755 6250

Mr. Brian Wruk

Gilbert AZ

Wednesday August 07, 2014

Reference: Vehicle Exportation/Importation Declaration

To whom it may concern:

Thank you for contacting KIA Canada Inc In reply to your request, KIA Canada Inc. would like to confirm that at the time of importation the following vehicle met or exceeded the Canadian Motor Vehicle Safety Standards (C.M.V.S.S). At the time of importation this vehicle also met Canadian *On-Road Vehicle and Engine Emission Regulations* under Environment Canada and the U.S. Environmental Protection Agency (E.P.A) regulations

We, further to consultation of our recall files, confirm that the following vehicle does not have any related or pending Canadian Motor Vehicle Safety Standards (C.M.V.S.S.) recalls.

Manufacturer:	KIA Canada Inc.
Model:	2008 RONDO 4 CYL EX 7 SEAT
VIN:	

Respectfully,

Gloria
Customer Experience Department
KIA Canada Inc.
1-877-542-2886

To import a vehicle into the U.S., it must be manufactured exactly to the specifications as if it were made in the U.S. Since Kia would not attest to this in my case, U.S. CBP wouldn't stamp Form 7501, which means I couldn't register that car in Arizona. Some think, "I will bypass this process and just go down to my local Department of Motor Vehicles to register the vehicle." The problem you will have is you need to provide your VIN. When they input that number, they will see the vehicle was manufactured in Canada and ask you for your stamped Form 7501. Without it, you cannot register the vehicle, so save yourself the time.

At this point, you will need to hire a government-registered importer to assist you (http://www.nhtsa.gov/cars/rules/import/ or call us for a referral). They will post a bond for the vehicle, replace the dash with miles as the primary measure of speed and distance on your odometer, and then take over 300 pictures of everything from the gauge of steel on your seat belt to the size of tires on the vehicle. All of this gets submitted to the DOT, who then approves the car as being brought up to U.S. manufacturing standards and issues the necessary permit. The importer takes this, along with your vehicle, to CBP who provides a stamped Form 7501. Your vehicle can now be registered in your state. The cost for all this? Around U$2,550, composed of U$1,850 for the importer, U$700 to replace the dash, plus the cost for registration and other assorted fees. I did this and my importer came and picked up the vehicle, got it all certified and approved, went down to the DMV and registered the vehicle, and then brought the vehicle back to my house ready to drive.

HOUSEHOLD GOODS

When moving to the U.S., you are permitted a one-time settling of your personal effects, tax and duty free. When you reach the border with your U-Haul, you will need to file U.S. Customs and Border Protection Form 6059B — Customs Declaration, which requires a complete inventory of all the goods you are importing. You can speed things up at the border by making a list of all the items (and their approximate values, if known) as you pack. Per U.S. Customs and Border Protection, you should break your items into the areas outlined below.

- Furniture: tables, chairs, sofas, bedroom furniture, home office and living room furniture, desks, lamps, mirrors, etc.
- Kitchenware: silverware, glassware, chinaware, pots, pans, utensils, electrical appliances, etc.

- Household goods: linens, towels, rugs, toiletries, cleaning products, decorative articles, art, framed pictures, toys, strollers, crafts, holiday decorations, fans, washers, dryers, DVD players, TVs, stereos, records, collectibles, etc.
- Sports equipment: bicycles, weights, stationary equipment, skis, skates, surfboards, etc. (Note: this category doesn't include firearms.)
- Clothes: for men, women, boys, girls, and infants.
- Books/printed materials: books, calendars, personal records, photo albums, etc.
- Home office equipment/tools of trade: computers (CPU, monitor, printer, software, etc.), filing cabinets, shredders, fax machines, telephone equipment, calculators, books, etc.
- Other personal effects: items not covered by the categories outlined above should be individually described.

Be sure to have available a full count of the boxes or pieces you have enclosed in the moving container/truck/trailer to ease the process as well. If you intend to leave some of your goods in Canada, you need to file Form 3299 — Declaration for Free Entry of Unaccompanied Articles when you go to pick them up later to "enter" them into the U.S. You should create this inventory at the same time you are packing the rest of your goods to make things easier on yourself. However, we caution you on storing your personal goods (particularly valuables) in Canada for an extended period of time since doing so can be considered a tie to Canada for income tax purposes (see Chapter 5).

PETS

There are certain requirements in moving your pets to the U.S. First, you will need a health certificate from your pet's veterinarian proving your pet has a clean bill of health. Second, each pet will also need a letter from its veterinarian confirming that it is coming from a rabies-free zone. In lieu of this letter, you can show proof that your pets have had valid rabies shots at least 30 days prior to entering the U.S. Depending on which border crossing you use when you enter the U.S., your pets may have to go through a pre-clearance process. Any unusual or exotic pets might be barred from entry to the U.S. As a result, you should call U.S. Customs in advance of your move to determine if there are any additional requirements.

ALCOHOL AND TOBACCO

Bringing your own wine cellar or cigars with you to the U.S. is permitted when you move, but for obvious reasons the process is much more involved than it is for your other belongings. If you are at least 21 years of age, you can import alcoholic beverages into the U.S. for your personal use. First off, law prohibits shipping alcohol by the U.S. postal service, but shipping it by courier is permitted (though you will have to pay duty and excise taxes). There is no limit on how much alcohol you can import to the U.S., but large quantities (like a wine collection) might raise the suspicion of the CBP Officer, who may require you to obtain an Alcohol and Tobacco Tax and Trade Bureau import license before releasing your collection to you. You should note this includes any homemade wine or beer. In addition to meeting federal regulations, you must also meet your state of residency's laws and regulations as well. Each state has its own alcoholic beverage control board with which you will need to consult.

FIREARMS

To keep its citizens safe, the U.S. has restrictions on bringing firearms into the country. Certainly "the right to bear arms" is part of the American Constitution, but that doesn't automatically give you the right to enter the U.S. with undeclared firearms. The Bureau of Alcohol, Tobacco, Firearms and Explosives (the ATF) is the agency that regulates the importation of firearms to the U.S. To begin, you will need to fill out ATF Form 6 — Application and Permit for Importation of Firearms, Ammunition and Implements of War that asks for detailed information about the firearms and ammunition you are importing. It generally takes four to six weeks to process your accurately prepared Form 6, so take this timeline into account in your moving plans. Once your Form 6 has been approved, you will need to complete and file Form 6A – Release and Receipt of Imported Firearms, Ammunition and Implements of War to complete the process of importing your firearms and ammunition.

MONETARY INSTRUMENTS

When moving to the U.S., do not take any significant amount of cash (greater than U$10,000), traveler's checks, personal checks, money orders, stock or bond certificates, or other negotiable instruments with you when you cross the border. For amounts in excess of $10,000, you must declare that amount at the Canadian border when you leave, and it stands to reason that you will be detained and asked to explain the source of it and why you are carrying it with you. You will need to fill out Canada Border Services Agency (CBSA) Form E677 — Cross-Border Currency or Monetary Instruments Report — Individual and file it with CBSA, which will forward it to the Financial Transactions and Reports Analysis Centre of Canada (FINTRAC) for assessment and analysis. If the amount is greater than U$10,000, you will need to fill out U.S. Department of the Treasury Financial Crimes Enforcement Network (FinCEN) Form 105 — Report of International Transportation of Currency or Monetary Instruments and file it with U.S. Customs and Border Protection (note: don't file the predecessor form to this one — Customs Form 4790). This is just part of Canadian and American attempts to stop money laundering and curb the flow of money to criminal and terrorist organizations.

To avoid these complications, you are well advised to transfer these items electronically through pre-established channels (wire from a bank) since they are traceable transactions, and the financial institutions will fill out and file the required forms for you. Note that the Canadian financial institution automatically reports any cash transactions (deposits or transfers) in excess of C$10,000 on Form E667 — Cross-Border Currency or Monetary Instruments Report — General and automatically sends it to the FINTRAC. Transactions in excess of U$10,000 are automatically reported by the U.S. financial institution on U.S. Department of the

Treasury Financial Crimes Enforcement Network Form 105 — Report of International Transportation of Currency or Monetary Instruments and filed with the Bureau of U.S. Customs and Border Protection. Remember that you need to declare any amounts above U$10,000 coming by mail or courier later on as well.

Now, we know what you are thinking . . . why not just move U$9,900 in a series of transactions to avoid all this reporting? Because it is considered a crime called "structuring," which is arranging to give or receive amounts of less than U$10,000 to avoid the reporting rules. You may recall Rush Limbaugh in the U.S. (a prominent Republican radio talk-show host), whose representative at U.S. Trust suggested he do that; U.S. Trust then paid a $10 million fine. See Chapter 10 for more details on how to legally move your cash, investment portfolio, and other financial instruments to the U.S.

HIRING A MOVER

When planning the move of your physical goods to the U.S., we don't recommend you flip through the Yellow Pages, close your eyes, and let fate decide which mover you are going to hire based on where you finger lands. We recommend you look for a certified mover through an organization such as the American Moving and Storage Association (moving. org). Its website is full of good information and gives you an opportunity for recourse in the event that a move goes awry, because companies approved to use the trademark agree to a code of conduct providing complete disclosure, written estimates, etc. If you need a referral, please contact us and we can provide one for you. For full disclosure purposes, we receive no compensation or referral fees of any kind from any moving companies for our recommendation. You can also contact the Better Business Bureau (BBB), but despite its great reputation, our experiences have shown it is an unreliable source for finding trustworthy vendors. Our firm has been solicited by the BBB to join, but we have refused because it is willing to admit almost any financial planner who submits a form and a check without undertaking the due diligence required to determine if the planner is held to a suitability standard or a fiduciary standard (see Chapter 13, "Mayday! Mayday!").

Hiring a professional mover is the easiest and most expensive way to get your stuff to the U.S. A family of four with 8,000 pounds of stuff moving 1,200 miles will cost approximately U$3,000 during the summer months, but you can usually save about 10% by moving during the off season (October to May). Be sure to deal with a reputable firm, or accompany the driver to the weigh station when the truck's weight is recorded when empty, and again when full, to ensure you are getting an accurate weigh-in of your goods. If you want to save some money, consider packing and unpacking all of your goods yourself, and buy your own packing boxes and tape from a discount retailer rather than from the moving company, since it will tend to mark them up 10 to 20%. If you want to save even more money, rent a truck through U-Haul, Ryder, or some other company. We had the good fortune of getting a new truck that U-Haul wanted to move from Calgary to Phoenix so it could be tested in the hot weather. As a result, we got a greatly discounted rate, and we got to drive a brand-new truck. Many new companies are now offering to do the driving for you. They drop off a crate or trailer at your home that you pack. When you are finished, they come and pick it up and drop it off for you at the address you specify. If you do some comparison shopping, you can see they are slightly cheaper than U-Haul and far cheaper than a full-service mover. Remember to keep track of all your expenses, and keep your receipts because they may be deductible on your U.S. tax return in the year you move.

VISITING CANADA

Once you have settled in the U.S. and begin making plans for your first trip back to "the homeland," consider the things listed below to make your trip easier.

PASSPORT
Be sure to take your American passport with you (if you have one) or your Canadian passport, because the Department of Homeland Security

requires a valid passport for Americans, Canadians, and Mexicans entering the U.S. under The Western Hemisphere Travel Initiative. You also want to take your American passport to ensure you have it on record when you left the country and when you returned. Some dual citizens believe it is better to show your Canadian passport when you enter Canada and your U.S. passport when you enter the U.S. again because, as a citizen of those respective countries, entry is automatic. In some ways, it is really irrelevant because your U.S. passport clearly states your country of origin as Canada, so border agents already know you are a dual Canadian-U.S. citizen. Further, as outlined earlier, the U.S. and Canada are now tracking your entry and exit from each country and sharing that data between them.

GIFTS

You are permitted to take back to Canada gifts of C$60 per recipient, tax and duty free. You are limited to 200 cigarettes, 50 cigars, 1.5 liters of wine, 1.14 liters of liquor, or 24 cans of beer/ale. You will have to fill out CBSA Form E311 — Declaration Card to declare all of the goods you are bringing into Canada. This is the tear-off form we are all familiar with when traveling to Canada as it is usually handed out on the plane before landing.

LUGGAGE

Be aware that virtually all airlines now charge a fee of $25–$50 or more if any of your bags exceeds 50 pounds. This is particularly true if you are planning on bringing back a lot of stuff from Canada. To protect yourself from this charge, do not buy the big suitcases on wheels that have expansion panels in them. Keep to the medium-sized suitcases, and pack a collapsible duffel bag in case you are over or want to bring back more goods than expected. Also be aware that most airlines will allow you one carry-on (which fits under the seat or in the overhead bin), one purse or similar item, and two pieces of checked luggage per person. If you exceed these amounts, you will face additional charges as well.

FOOD

A common question our firm fields is, "Are there any prohibitions on any foods taken to Canada?" It has been our experience that, as long as the food isn't grown in Canada, border agents will typically allow it in with little or no difficulty. I have taken citrus, nuts, Arizona sweet onions, and freshly caught shrimp and fish through the Canada Border Services Agency with little hassle. Just be sure to notify the customs agent you have food with you (or you risk a C$400 fine), and make sure you know the source of each item. You can check out which items are permissible at beaware.gc.ca or call 1-800-O-Canada.

BRINGING IT BACK

You are permitted to bring back to the U.S. U$400 per person duty free every 30 days. This amount applies to goods purchased or received as gifts and brought back with you when you travel (called "accompanied baggage"). You are also limited to 200 cigarettes, 100 cigars, and a liter of alcohol every 30 days. There may be restrictions at the state level as well, so you should check with the authorities in your state to ensure you don't violate their liquor transportation laws when you land. The value of alcohol and tobacco is included in your U$400 duty-free exemption; if you exceed this limit you will have to pay duty plus IRS taxes on the excess amount. All items must be for your own use and not for resale. Goods to follow via mail or courier are allowed duty free as long as they are valued at less than U$200.

TRAVEL TO CUBA

It is common for Canadians to travel to Cuba for business and vacation purposes. In fact, there are vacation package deals advertised regularly in Canada for leisure trips to Cuba. As you may be aware, Americans are generally prohibited from traveling to Cuba or engaging in commerce with Cuba (buying Cuban cigars) because of the Cuban Missile Crisis in the 1960s. For personal travel, it is only legal to travel to Cuba on "People-to-People" licensed trips involving cultural or educational exchanges with Cubans. The U.S. Treasury Office of Foreign Assets Control grants these licenses, and very few tour operators have been provided with one. Your itinerary must be full of cultural activities that exclude going to the beach, fishing, or sightseeing. To engage in business, you must be appropriately licensed by the Department of the Treasury or you'll face civil penalties and criminal prosecution when reentering the U.S. Furthermore, the U.S. government has set up enforcement of these rules at U.S. airports and pre-clearance facilities in third-party countries. Unfortunately, these rules apply to you, even though you are Canadian, because you are subject to U.S. jurisdiction when you relocate to the U.S. Therefore, beware of taking advantage of a good deal to Cuba! Instead, you may want to travel to Cuba before you make the transition to the U.S.

With Fidel Castro facing health problems and his powers passing to his brother Raoul, who appears to be more pro-American, President Obama opened negotiations with Cuba to eliminate the embargo that has been in place for 50 years and permit trading, commerce, etc. This is a welcome advance for some and a step back for others, but regardless, it appears many of these restrictions may be lifted soon so stay tuned.

DOUBLE TAXES, 5
DOUBLE TROUBLE

Is it right for us to pay taxes to Caesar or not?
— LUKE 20:22

Of all the areas to consider in your move, taxes are by far the most complex yet potentially beneficial area. This is particularly true if the planning is done before making the transition to the U.S. Some advisors make the generalization that you will always pay less tax in the U.S. than in Canada, and many people use that as their sole reason to move to the U.S. In our experience, retired Canadians in the U.S. generally pay less income tax than in Canada. However, if you look at income and payroll taxes combined (and health care), working Canadians may end up paying more income tax in the U.S. than they would in Canada (see the case studies in Appendices E and F). It depends a lot on your individual tax situation now, how it projects into the future, the state you are moving to, the makeup of your family, your sources and types of income, and what both governments end up doing with their respective tax systems in the years to come. Paying less income tax (along with the warmer weather) appeals to most people when considering a move to the U.S. Generally, the evidence is there to confirm that thinking, because in 2014 Tax Freedom Day fell on April 21st for Americans (according to the Tax Foundation) versus June 9th for Canadians (according to the Fraser Institute). It is interesting to note that for Albertans, Tax Freedom Day is the earliest, on May 23rd, while Newfoundland is latest, on June 22. In the U.S., tax freedom day is March 30th in Louisiana and May 9th in Connecticut and New Jersey. Income taxes are a large part of most everyone's budget, but with proper tax planning and then competent tax preparation to implement the planning there are some tremendous opportunities to take advantage of before exiting Canada. This chapter outlines some of the key things you need to know in the area of tax planning when making the transition from Canada to the U.S.

It is important to note the difference between tax planning and tax preparation. Tax preparation is purely a historical event. You simply take the tax slips recording the transactions from last year, input them into the tax software, and hit the calculate button. Based on the luck of the draw, you either get a refund or have an amount due. Tax planning, on the other hand, takes actions in the current tax year to use legal tax avoidance techniques to reduce your tax bill in advance of your tax preparation. It is also important to differentiate between tax avoidance and tax evasion. Tax avoidance employs techniques permitted by law to reduce your tax bill and ensure you pay the appropriate amount throughout the year. Tax evasion is the intentional defrauding of the tax authorities and what is legally due to them.

Interestingly enough, our firm receives the bulk of its calls from February to April of each year because that is when newly minted American residents realize they need to file a U.S. tax return for the first time. That also seems to be the time when people who have moved to the U.S. realize they should have done some pre-planning because they are confronted with the harsh realities of filing their tax returns. We get questions such as, "Do I need to file in Canada? What income do I declare? On which return?" To answer these complex questions, people typically turn to their reliable Canadian Chartered Accountant (CA), soon to be Certified Public Accountant (CPA) as all the designations in Canada are merging, to get their Canadian return filed — if they decide they need to file at all. Then, for the sake of convenience, the CPA geographically closest to them in their city prepares the U.S. return. Everything is filed on time, and they take comfort in the fact that they have made it successfully through their first U.S. tax season. Unfortunately, it's a false sense of security because in our experience very few accountants know how to properly prepare these returns unless they are practicing regularly and consistently in this area. Many tax preparers don't know how to coordinate the preparation of the Canadian and U.S. returns, they don't know how to properly apply the Canada-U.S. Tax Treaty, and they can't ensure that the necessary compliance issues related to foreign assets are fulfilled in both countries. Further, in our experience, if you have two different people preparing your Canadian and U.S. returns, the chance of your tax situation not being optimized, or your returns not being in compliance, goes up exponentially. It is only a matter of time before one of the taxing authorities catches a compliance issue and the "hate mail" starts to fill your mailbox, or your tax bill is higher than it should be and no one is the wiser. We have seen situations in which the compliance issue is caught and the client goes back to the original accountant to draft a response to the tax authorities or to explain the penalties and interest. Suddenly, that accountant is no longer an expert in Canadian or U.S. tax, phone calls are no longer returned, but your check has been cashed.

A recent example was someone who exited Canada, prepared his own Canadian tax return, and hired a local U.S. accountant to prepare the U.S. federal and state returns. Our firm reviewed the returns and noted numerous errors. An adjusted Canadian return was filed for an increased refund of C$17,000, and the U.S. return was amended to get him into compliance with the IRS and the appropriate state tax authorities (additional U$200 paid). The important thing to note is that this was not a high-income client! One more point before I tackle the complexities of Canada-U.S. taxes: if a lack of planning prior to your departure results in an unexpected large tax bill in Canada and/or the U.S., our firm will not condone or participate in any techniques we believe to violate current income tax laws to reduce your tax bill (yes, we have been asked).

TAX FILING REQUIREMENTS

CANADA

Many people move to the U.S. and just stop filing Canadian tax returns because they believe that, since they no longer live in Canada, they don't have to file tax returns there anymore. They are correct, Canada Revenue Agency taxes are based on Canadian residency, but what these folks aren't aware of is the departure tax when leaving Canada. When you leave Canada, you have to file a final T1 exit return, which is one of the criteria you use to sever your tax residency with Canada (but not your citizenship). This doesn't mean you are completely done filing taxes in Canada because, if you continue to have Canadian-source income in the future (e.g., dividends or rent or sell a Canadian property), you will continue to have a tax obligation in Canada through withholding per the Canada-U.S. Tax Treaty, filing to correct inaccurate withholding, or filing a non-resident tax return to declare that Canadian source income.

Exit Return

CRA agrees to stop taxing you on your worldwide income when you leave — but not before it takes its "pound of flesh." Certain property you own worldwide is "deemed" sold and repurchased again (whether you actually do so or not), and any gains are declared on your final tax return (affectionately known as the departure tax). Items such as stocks, bonds, mutual funds, partnerships, and income trusts in regular brokerage accounts, U.S. real estate, and certain businesses must be declared on your exit return. This can mean potentially huge capital gains on your final exit return and a large tax liability owing before you are sent on your merry way. Items not taxed at your exit include all items the government can "attach" itself to (called taxable Canadian property). These include the following:

- All registered plans (RRSPs, RRIFs, LIRAs, RCAs, Profit Sharing Plans, Pensions, Money Purchase Plans, Individual Pension Plans, etc.).
- All Canadian real estate.
- Property owned by a business but not the shares of that business.
- Employee stock options granted while in Canada.
- Life insurance policies or annuities.
- Trusts, depending on a variety of issues.

Note that you are not paying an extra tax — it is simply an early collection of tax because you are leaving Canada. This early collection of tax catches most people by surprise because it is not anticipated. On top of the departure tax, you must declare your worldwide income (any wages, interest, dividends, etc.) while resident in Canada. With the small tax brackets and high marginal rates, it doesn't take long to reach the top tax bracket of 45%+ when leaving Canada. One client we worked with paid in excess of C$55,000 in departure tax because she did not do the requisite planning before she left Canada! Her biggest frustration was that she didn't see it coming. Her employer never informed her of the things she needed to do before moving and she had to come up with a large amount of cash on short notice to pay the tax (posting security with the Canadian government is another option as outlined later). With proper planning before you leave Canada, you can use many techniques to mitigate your taxes significantly — while reducing your U.S. income and estate taxes at the same time. At a minimum, understanding your departure tax liability — and knowing you did everything you could to optimize it before you entered the U.S. — will make for a much better transition.

The exit return is filed on a T1 tax return, but you must fill in your departure date in the space provided. In addition, your basic personal amount is prorated based on the amount of time you spent in Canada up to the date of your departure. To ensure you are reporting the departure tax correctly, CRA requires Form T1161 — List of Properties by an Emigrant of Canada to be filed along with your T1 tax return when the value of all your property exceeds C$25,000. This form lists all of the items subject to the departure tax and establishes the fair market value of each item on the date you departed from Canada. You should note that there is a penalty of C$25 per day if the T1161 is not filed by April 30th, with a minimum penalty of C$100 and a maximum penalty of C$2,500. In addition, Form T1243 — Deemed Disposition of Property by an Emigrant of Canada provides a detailed record for CRA on how you are calculating your final departure gains (or losses). In certain situations, it may be worthwhile to file Form T1244 — Election under Subsection 220(4.5) of the Income Tax Act, to Defer the Payment of Tax on Income Relating to the Deemed Disposition of Property by posting security with CRA so you are not forced to come up with a large amount of cash up front. This strategy "freezes" your departure tax, but its applicability depends on your unique financial situation and the liquidity of your assets (e.g., shares of a small business).

For married couples who are leaving Canada at different times, CRA generally determines the exit date to be that of the spouse who leaves last because that is considered a significant tax tie back to Canada. Exit date planning is a critical component of your transition to the U.S. and, done correctly, can mitigate your taxes significantly. Your exit return is due by April 30th of the year after the last spouse leaves Canada. This tax return is filed with the International Tax Services office in Ottawa (not the Provincial Tax Centre you filed with previously), and your Notice of Assessment can take up to six months or a year to receive. It takes so long because CRA goes over these returns with a fine-toothed comb to ensure it is collecting every last bit of tax before granting you non-resident status. Remember, this is CRA's last chance to collect the resident income taxes owing; after that, the appropriate treaty/tax withholding rates and non-resident returns must be filed, which are typically lower than the ordinary income tax rates on a T1 tax return. That is why it is so important to get your address in the U.S. on all of these accounts as soon as you are a non-resident of Canada. See the case studies in Appendices E & F for strategies to reduce the departure tax.

Part XIII

Once you are in the U.S., Canada retains the right to tax any Canadian-source income (dividends, rents, etc.) according to the rates specified in the Canada Income Tax Act and adjusted per the Canada-U.S. Tax Treaty. If too much withholding is taken, you will be overtaxed, and if you are under-withheld you could begin receiving tax bills from CRA for the balance, along with any penalties and interest. You need to review all of your Canadian sources of income to ensure the correct withholding has been taken per the treaty or the Income Tax Act and, if necessary, prepare Form NR7-R — Application for Refund of Non-Resident Part XIII Tax Withheld to sort out your non-resident tax withholding refunds with CRA. This tax return needs to be filed by June 30th of the following year, costing you more in tax preparation fees. For the correct withholding rates on various types of income, see "Withholding Taxes in the Canada-U.S. Tax Treaty" later in this chapter. Failing to file this return with CRA could be considered a tax residency factor by CRA.

T1 Non-Resident Return

Just when you think you have escaped the clutches of CRA and your need to file a T1 tax return, you realize to your chagrin that there are different types of income for which no withholding applies. As a result, you cannot file a Form NR7-R, and you are back to filing a T1 non-resident tax return. Canadian sources of income such as wages, exercise of vested stock options, and the sale of real estate all must be filed on a T1 non-resident tax return. The problem is you don't get the personal amount or much of any deductions (see income-specific items below).

UNITED STATES

Unlike Canada (which taxes only its residents on worldwide income), the U.S. taxes its citizens and residents (including green card holders) on their worldwide income. This approach leads to difficulties because, if you are a U.S. citizen or a green card holder living anywhere in the world, you have a tax-filing obligation with the IRS. Specifically, when Canadians take up tax residency in the U.S., they must file a U.S. "start-up" tax return and report their worldwide income. Doing so can lead to double taxation because you have to file a Canadian exit return declaring your worldwide income, and then pay the appropriate withholding on any Canadian source of income after you exit Canada. Some folks decide to "straddle the border" and end up filing in both countries, which adds to the complexity and tax prep fees. There are different ways of filing your U.S. returns to minimize your tax liability, and depending on your situation several tax and compliance elections may need to be taken as well. These are complex tax returns to complete. Unfortunately, most U.S. CPAs have no idea how to handle Canadian issues on the U.S. return, and you usually end up being out of compliance with the IRS and your local state government from the very first tax return you file in the U.S. It is in your best interest to get the assistance of a professional who works regularly and consistently in the Canada-U.S. tax preparation arena to ensure you remain in compliance with the IRS and your local state, file the necessary exit return with CRA, and coordinate the preparation of both your U.S. and Canadian returns to optimize your tax liability in both countries with a good understanding of the Canada-U.S. tax treaty. Further, there is a lot to be said for doing your initial filing correctly so you can have peace of mind and avoid having the IRS, your local state, or CRA turn on the "hate mail" machines because something is not filed correctly.

Your "start-up" U.S. 1040 tax return (and your applicable state return) is due by April 15th of the year after you take up tax residency in the U.S. (due to your presence in the U.S. or the issuance of a green card). One unique aspect of the U.S. tax system that confuses some people is the ability to file an extension. Many Canadians believe that, by filing IRS Form 4868 — Application for Automatic Extension of Time to File U.S. Individual Income Tax Return before the deadline, they can postpone paying their taxes. Nothing is further from the truth. An extension, if approved by the IRS, means, "I am paying my tax now, and due to circumstances out of my control, my paperwork will follow later." If you choose not to pay your tax liability at that time, interest and penalties will accrue on that liability from April 15th until paid in full. Unfortunately, filing an extension still requires you to prepare a mock tax return using the information you have available to estimate whether you have a balance owing or not. You are allowed one extension after the April 15th deadline until October 15th (that's why most CPAs are so busy at that late time of year).

You will also have to file a separate state tax return depending on your state of residence (like Quebec, they all collect their own income taxes). You will file a "part-year" tax return for your particular state, and potentially a county and/or city tax return as well (as in New York). There are nine states with no income tax.

- Alaska
- Florida
- Nevada
- New Hampshire (interest and dividends only)
- South Dakota
- Tennessee (interest and dividends only)
- Texas
- Washington
- Wyoming

In contrast, all 10 provinces and 3 territories in Canada have an income tax in addition to the federal tax.

Foreign Account Tax Compliance Act

One reason to ensure your U.S. tax returns are prepared correctly (while properly disclosing all of your accounts remaining in Canada), is because of the Foreign Account Tax Compliance Act (FATCA). Commissioner Douglas Shulman was sworn in as the head of the IRS on March 24, 2008, after President George Bush appointed him and the U.S. Senate confirmed the appointment on March 14th. Commissioner Shulman's main focus after taking office was to develop strategies to increase international tax compliance, as tax avoidance is estimated to cost the IRS an estimated $100 billion per year . . . and he succeeded. In March 2010, Congress passed sweeping laws (known as FATCA) specifically to target noncompliant U.S. taxpayers committing tax evasion with foreign accounts. The intent of these laws is to target wealthy U.S. taxpayers living in the U.S. and committing U.S. tax evasion with assets offshore in a tax haven. However, these laws cast a huge net on far more taxpayers than intended, and as a result many innocent U.S. taxpayers are getting caught. This has created a lot of media attention and public outcry around the world, as well as in the U.S., from the innocent folks that are getting caught up in the large dragnet the IRS has created. Despite the outcry, there seems to be little sympathy from the IRS or concessions made on these ridiculously complex rules, and those who ignore FATCA will get into trouble . . . these laws have teeth!

In addition to the public outcry from individual U.S. taxpayers around the world, there was an international outcry from financial institutions. The reason is that, starting June 30, 2014 (delayed twice to give financial institutions time for implementation), FATCA requires foreign banks, investment firms, insurance companies, and other foreign financial instituitions (FFIs) to register with the IRS and, in doing so, agree to report to the IRS financial and account information for accounts with "substantial U.S. owners." Willing participants in the program may be required to withhold 30% on certain payments to their U.S. clients if those clients are not in compliance with FATCA, as outlined below. To encourage these financial institutions to "cooperate," firms choosing not to register will be subject to a 30% withholding tax on certain U.S. source payments made to them! The effects of these actions are far reaching.

For example, by disclosing this information to the IRS, financial institutions are likely in violation of local data protection, confidentiality, and bank secrecy laws in their home country. To get around this, the U.S. government entered bilateral agreements with over 100 foreign governments that allow the FFIs to report the details of U.S. account holders to their country's tax authority, which in turn will forward these details to the IRS. On February 5, 2014, Canada's Department of Finance announced it had signed an intergovernmental agreement with the U.S. under the existing Canada-U.S. Tax Treaty to share information on U.S. persons with accounts in Canada that total $50,000 or more effective July 1, 2014. (Happy Canada Day!) Incredibly, Canada negotiated with the U.S. that RRSPs, RRIFs, TFSAs, and RDSPs are exempt from reporting under FATCA and will not be disclosed. In addition, credit unions with less than $175 million in deposits are exempt from reporting. However, U.S. tax filers still need to declare these accounts on their tax return with the new foreign account disclosure forms the IRS has (as outlined later in this chapter).

Under the intergovernmental agreement with Canada, any client with aggregated accounts in excess of $50,000 will have the following information provided to CRA (and subsequently to the IRS) by their financial institution:

1. The name, address, and U.S. TIN [Tax Identification Number] of each Specified U.S. Person that is an Account Holder of such account;

2. the account number (or functional equivalent in the absence of an account number);

3. the name and identifying number of the Reporting Canadian Financial Institution;

4. the account balance or value (including, in the case of a Cash Value Insurance Contract or Annuity Contract, the Cash Value

or surrender value) as of the end of the relevant calendar year or other appropriate reporting period or, if the account was closed during such year, immediately before closure;

5. in the case of any Custodial Account:
    (a) the total gross amount of interest, the total gross amount of dividends, and the total gross amount of other income generated with respect to the assets held in the account, in each case paid or credited to the account (or with respect to the account) during the calendar year or other appropriate reporting period; and
    (b) the total gross proceeds from the sale or redemption of property paid or credited to the account during the calendar year or other appropriate reporting period with respect to which the Reporting Canadian Financial Institution acted as a custodian, broker, nominee, or otherwise as an agent for the Account Holder;

6. in the case of any Depository Account, the total gross amount of interest paid or credited to the account during the calendar year or other appropriate reporting period; and

7. in the case of any account not described in subparagraph 2(a)(5) or 2(a)(6) of this Article, the total gross amount paid or credited to the Account Holder with respect to the account during the calendar year or other appropriate reporting period.

In addition, according to the "Annex I: due diligence obligations," your financial institution is required to look for U.S. "indicia" by conducting electronic searches for:

1. Identification of the Account Holder as a U.S. citizen or resident;

2. Unambiguous indication of a U.S. place of birth;

3. Current U.S. mailing or residence address (including U.S. post office Box);

4. Current U.S. telephone number;

5. Standing instructions to transfer funds to an account maintained in the United States;

6. Currently effective power of attorney or signatory authority granted to a person with a U.S. address; or

7. An 'in-care-of' or 'hold mail' address that is the *sole* address the Reporting [FATCA Partner] Financial Institution has on file for the Account Holder.

If none of the U.S. indicia listed above is discovered in the electronic search, then no further action is required until there is a change in circumstances. One last point in addition to the above: any investment manager that has "actual knowledge" that their client is a "specified U.S. person" has an obligation to include that account information so it can be reported to CRA as well. As you can see, this IRS initiative is very pervasive but has proven to be effective. At the time of writing, a lawsuit was filed against the Canadian government by two American citizens living in Ontario to block their information from being passed to the IRS. Their attorney is arguing that any of their personal information given to the IRS violates their rights as Canadians under the Charter of Rights and Freedoms. This will have to be worked out in the courts, so stay tuned.

Likewise, the IRS is now exchanging the same information so that these foreign governments can root out their own tax evaders at the same time. Another imposition of these rules is that FFIs are now required to ask their existing and prospective clients if they have ties to the U.S. It is yet to be seen if a U.S. person who does not disclose this information to the foreign financial institution, or lies, could be caught by cross-referencing information from the IRS. Many financial institutions are simply refusing to do business with U.S. persons anymore and are involuntarily forcing them to move their accounts. Foreign hedge funds, mutual funds, and private equity funds are liquidating U.S.-based assets to avoid any issues with the IRS. The bottom line is that the U.S. is using its economic muscle to coerce cooperation from financial institutions around the world to successfully root out U.S. tax evaders. It started in Switzerland, with some of the toughest bank secrecy laws in the world, when UBS was permitted by the Swiss government to hand over thousands of names and account details of U.S. owners to the IRS.

From the 2011 tax year forward, FATCA requires virtually all U.S. tax filers to file Form 8938 — Statement of Specified Foreign Financial Assets with their tax returns if the total value of "specified foreign financial assets" is above U$50,000 at year end (U$100,000 for married couples) or exceeds U$75,000 at any time during the tax year (U$150,000 for married couples). If you are living abroad, the threshold for filing Form 8938 is U$200,000 at year end (U$400,000 for married couples) and U$300,000 during the tax year (U$600,000 for married couples). Specified foreign financial assets include foreign accounts at foreign financial institutions (but not the foreign branch of a U.S. institution), foreign partnership interests, foreign securities (mutual funds, stocks, bonds), foreign trusts in which you are the grantor, foreign-issued life insurance and annuities, foreign hedge funds, and private equity funds. However, these items are not included in the definition of specified foreign financial assets: foreign real estate held directly for personal use, foreign currency held directly, personal property held directly (art, antiques, precious metals, jewelry, cars, collectibles), or foreign pensions. Failure to report foreign financial assets on Form 8938 may result in an IRS penalty of U$10,000 (up to U$50,000 for continued failure after IRS notification). Are we having fun yet?

In addition to filing Form 8938, there is a host of other onerous tax filing requirements that you need to be aware of. First, you are required to file U.S. Department of the Treasury Financial Crimes Enforcement Network (FinCEN) Form 114 (formerly TD F 90-22.12 — Report of Foreign Bank and Financial Account, or FBARs) requiring you to disclose your interest in financial accounts outside the U.S., including RRSPs, RRIFs, bank accounts, LIRAs, etc. in Canada. These must be electronically filed through FinCEN's website. "Non-willful" violations because of reasonable cause will not be penalized, but all others are subject to a U$10,000 penalty per violation. "Willfully" failing to file can lead to penalties as high as the greater of U$100,000 or 50% of the balance of the foreign account. Second, if you own Canadian mutual funds, income trusts, and registered plans, or own or have an interest in a foreign trust, you will be required to file Form 8621 – Information Return by a Shareholder of a Passive Foreign Investment Company or Qualified Electing Fund and possibly Form 3520 — Annual Return to Report Transactions with Foreign Trusts and Receipt of Certain Foreign Gifts as well (or if you still have a Tax-Free Savings Account (TFSA) in Canada. In this case, the failure-to-file penalty is the greater of U$10,000 or 35% of any distributions from your Canadian investments, trusts, and registered plans! In addition, you may be required to file Form 3520A — Annual Information Return of Foreign Trust with a U.S. Owner. Failure to do so may subject you to penalties of the greater of U$10,000 or 5% of the gross value of the trust assets. If you have an RRSP/RRIF in Canada, fortunately, you no longer need to file Form 8891 — U.S. Information Return for Beneficiaries of Certain Canadian Registered Retirement Savings Plans. On October 7, 2014, the IRS simplified the tax treatment of these plans by automatically recognizing the tax deferral of these plans per the Canada-U.S. Tax Treaty. Third, if you have an interest in a Canadian company, you need to file Form 5471 — Information Return of U.S. Persons with Respect to Foreign Corporations, or another myriad of IRS filing requirements and penalties can be imposed (see Chapter 11, "The Business of Business"). In most cases, applying the foreign-earned income exclusion and foreign tax credits should result in no additional tax, which begs the question: why are U.S. taxpayers subject to these ridiculous rules to begin with?

So what if you are one of the thousands of Canadians with accounts in Canada that have not been declared on your U.S. 1040 and state tax returns? Or suspect that your returns have not been filed correctly? Thankfully, the IRS has instituted "streamlined offshore procedures" for innocent folks like you that you can take advantage of. First, here's a brief history.

Offshore Voluntary Disclosure Program

When the IRS announced FATCA and was in the process of receiving thousands of names from the government of Switzerland, it announced the first Offshore Voluntary Disclosure Program (OVDP) in 2009. This program resulted in 15,000 disclosures and $3.4 billion in back taxes. With this success, the IRS launched another Offshore Voluntary Disclosure Initiative (OVDI) in 2011 that resulted in another 15,000 disclosures and $1.6 billion in back taxes. Starting in January 2012, the IRS began an open-ended Offshore Voluntary Disclosure Program (OVDP) that allowed folks with foreign accounts to come forward and disclose them, pay any taxes, interest and penalties owing, and get right with the world rather than risk detection by the IRS through FATCA, under which criminal prosecution is possible. Through OVDP, the IRS has reduced (though still substantive) standardized penalties that give noncompliant taxpayers the opportunity to calculate, with some certainty, the total cost of getting into compliance with the IRS. So far, 45,000 taxpayers have taken advantage of the program with $6.5 billion in taxes, penalties, and interest collected. However, for those with accounts in Canada, there has been much controversy surrounding voluntary disclosure because the intent is not to evade taxes as Canada is not considered a tax haven. Moreover, if taxes have been/will be paid to Canada, there would be a foreign tax credit against most, or all, of any additional U.S. taxes owing, but this does not erase the hefty penalties owing through OVDP (as outlined previously).

On June 18, 2014, IRS Commissioner John Koskinen announced new "streamlined offshore procedures" for U.S. tax filers living both outside and inside the U.S. who have not been properly reporting their foreign accounts and the income from them. We believe these are very positive changes that will give many "U.S. persons" a better way to come into compliance because of the substantial reduction in penalties. This comes after many "U.S. persons" with accounts in Canada have illustrated to the IRS that they weren't trying to evade taxes and they shouldn't be penalized so harshly for failing to simply report these accounts. Here is how to get into compliance with the IRS and begin sleeping at night.

Nonfilers Living Inside the U.S.

For those Canadians living in the U.S. with accounts in Canada, you have likely been filing U.S. returns but you are out of compliance because you have not filed any FBARs, treaty elections, or other disclosure forms as outlined above. If your nonfiling was due to "non-willful conduct," no "failure-to-file," "failure-to-pay," "accuracy-related," "information return," or "FBAR" penalties will apply! However, states the IRS on its website, "the Title 26 miscellaneous offshore penalty is applied in your situation and is equal to 5% of the highest aggregate balance/value of the taxpayer's foreign financial assets that are subject to the miscellaneous offshore penalty during the years in the covered tax return period and the covered FBAR period." This is indeed good news, but it is important to define an important term:

Non-Willful Conduct — "conduct that is due to negligence, inadvertence, or mistake or conduct that is the result of a good faith misunderstanding of the requirements of the law."

If you meet the definition of "non-willful" as stated, you are eligible to file under the new streamlined OVDP procedures, which require:

1. **File Amended Returns** — For each of the three most recent tax years that have passed (with extensions), file amended Form 1040X tax returns along with all required disclosures (Forms 3520, 3520A, 5471, 8938). At the top of each return you file (paper filing only, no e-filing) write in red ink "Streamlined Foreign Offshore" to ensure they are processed through the new procedures. In addition, you must remit all taxes due, all applicable statutory interest, and all Title 26 miscellaneous offshore penalty amounts for each return at the time you file your returns!

2. **File FBARs** — You will need to file the most recent six years' delinquent FBARs (FinCEN Form 114 — previously Form TD F 90-22.1) electronically at FinCEN (fincen.gov/forms/bsa_forms/) and follow the instructions there. If you have trouble, you can call the FinCEN helpline at 1-703-905-3975.

3. **Certification** — Complete and sign Form 14654 - Certification by U.S. Person Residing in the United States for Streamlined

Domestic Offshore Procedures, which is a new form the IRS is providing (see Figure 5.1 below). This document is the taxpayer (1) certifying they are eligible for the streamlined procedures; (2) all FBARs have been filed; (3) attesting to "non-willful" conduct.

4. **Failure to Make a Timely Treaty Election** — For example, if you have made a charitable contribution to a Canadian charity and declared it on your U.S. return without taking a treaty election, you are required to: (1) submit a statement requesting an extension of time to make the election along with the applicable treaty provision; (2) sign a statement under penalties of perjury describing what led to the failure to make the election, how you discovered the failure, if you relied on a professional advisor, and the engagement with the advisor and his/her responsibilities; (3) complete Form 8833 — Treaty-Based Return Position Disclosure Under Section 6114 or 7701(b) for each return where applicable in the past three years.

Mail everything to:
Internal Revenue Service
3651 South I-H 35, Stop 6063 AUSC
Attn: Streamlined Foreign Offshore, Austin, TX, 78741

FIGURE 5.1

CERTIFICATION OF U.S. PERSON RESIDING IN THE U.S.

Form **14654** (January 2015)	Department of the Treasury - Internal Revenue Service **Certification by U.S. Person Residing in the United States for** **Streamlined Domestic Offshore Procedures**	OMB Number 1545-2241

Name(s) of taxpayer(s)	TIN(s) of taxpayer(s)

Note: Spouses should submit a joint certification if they are submitting joint income tax returns under the Streamlined Foreign Offshore Procedures. If this certification is a joint certification, the statements will be considered made on behalf of both spouses, even though the pronoun "I" is used. If spouses submitting a joint certification have different reasons for their failure to report all income, pay all tax, and submit all required information returns, including FBARs, they must state their individual reasons separately in the required statement of facts.

Certification

I am providing amended income tax returns, including all required information returns, for each of the most recent 3 years for which the U.S. tax return due date (or properly applied for extended due date) has passed. I previously filed original tax returns for these years. The tax and interest I owe for each year are as follows

Year (list years in order)	Amount of Tax I Owe (Form 1040X, line 19)	Interest	Total
			$0.00
			$0.00
			$0.00
Total	$0.00	$0.00	$0.00

I failed to report income from one or more foreign financial assets during the above period.

I meet all the eligibility requirements for the Streamlined Domestic Offshore procedures.

If I failed to timely file correct and complete FBARs for any of the last 6 years, I have now filed those FBARs.

During each year in either my 3-year covered tax return period or my 6-year covered FBAR period, my foreign financial assets subject to the 5% miscellaneous offshore penalty were as follows

Year

Name, City, and Country of Financial Institution/Description of Asset	Account Number	Year Account Was Opened or Asset Was Acquired	Year-End Balance/ Asset Value (state in US Dollars)
Total			$0.00

If you held no assets subject to the 5% miscellaneous offshore penalty during this year enter "N/A" next to "Total" in the above table. Attach a continuation sheet if necessary. If you attach a continuation sheet, it must be signed with taxpayer name(s) and TIN(s) printed.

Year

Name, City, and Country of Financial Institution/Description of Asset	Account Number	Year Account Was Opened or Asset Was Acquired	Year-End Balance/ Asset Value (state in US Dollars)
Total			$0.00

If you held no assets subject to the 5% miscellaneous offshore penalty during this year enter "N/A" next to "Total" in the above table. Attach a continuation sheet if necessary. If you attach a continuation sheet, it must be signed with taxpayer name(s) and TIN(s) printed.

Catalog Number 67044W	www.irs.gov	Form **14654** (Rev. 1-2015)

CERTIFICATION OF U.S. PERSON RESIDING IN THE U.S.

Year

Name, City, and Country of Financial Institution/Description of Asset	Account Number	Year Account Was Opened or Asset Was Acquired	Year-End Balance/ Asset Value *(state in US Dollars)*
Total			$0.00

If you held no assets subject to the 5% miscellaneous offshore penalty during this year enter "N/A" next to "Total" in the above table. Attach a continuation sheet if necessary. If you attach a continuation sheet, it must be signed with taxpayer name(s) and TIN(s) printed.

Year

Name, City, and Country of Financial Institution/Description of Asset	Account Number	Year Account Was Opened or Asset Was Acquired	Year-End Balance/ Asset Value *(state in US Dollars)*
Total			$0.00

If you held no assets subject to the 5% miscellaneous offshore penalty during this year enter "N/A" next to "Total" in the above table. Attach a continuation sheet if necessary. If you attach a continuation sheet, it must be signed with taxpayer name(s) and TIN(s) printed.

Year

Name, City, and Country of Financial Institution/Description of Asset	Account Number	Year Account Was Opened or Asset Was Acquired	Year-End Balance/ Asset Value *(state in US Dollars)*
Total			$0.00

If you held no assets subject to the 5% miscellaneous offshore penalty during this year enter "N/A" next to "Total" in the above table. Attach a continuation sheet if necessary. If you attach a continuation sheet, it must be signed with taxpayer name(s) and TIN(s) printed.

Year

Name, City, and Country of Financial Institution/Description of Asset	Account Number	Year Account Was Opened or Asset Was Acquired	Year-End Balance/ Asset Value *(state in US Dollars)*
Total			$0.00

If you held no assets subject to the 5% miscellaneous offshore penalty during this year enter "N/A" next to "Total" in the above table. Attach a continuation sheet if necessary. If you attach a continuation sheet, it must be signed with taxpayer name(s) and TIN(s) printed.

FIGURE 5.1

CERTIFICATION OF U.S. PERSON RESIDING IN THE U.S.

Year

Note: Use this seventh year only if your 3-year covered tax return period does not completely overlap with your 6-year covered FBAR period (for example, if your 3-year covered tax return period is 2011 through 2013 because the due date for your 2013 tax return is passed, but your covered FBAR period is 2007 through 2012 because the due date for the 2013 FBAR has not passed).

Name, City, and Country of Financial Institution/Description of Asset	Account Number	Year Account Was Opened or Asset Was Acquired	Year-End Balance/ Asset Value (state in US Dollars)
Total			$0.00

If you held no assets subject to the 5% miscellaneous offshore penalty during this year enter "N/A" next to "Total" in the above table. Attach a continuation sheet if necessary. If you attach a continuation sheet, it must be signed with taxpayer name(s) and TIN(s) printed.

The assets listed in this certification are my only foreign financial assets subject to the 5% miscellaneous offshore penalty.

My penalty computation is as follows

Highest Account Balance/Asset Value *(enter the highest total balance/ asset value among the years listed above)*	
Miscellaneous Offshore Penalty *(Highest Account Balance/Asset Value from above multiplied by 5%)*	

My payment information is as follows

Total Tax and Interest Due	
Miscellaneous Offshore Penalty	
Total Payment	

Note: Your payment should equal the total tax and interest due for all three years, plus the miscellaneous offshore penalty. You may receive a balance due notice or a refund if the tax, interest, or penalty is not calculated correctly.

In consideration of the Internal Revenue Service's agreement not to assert other penalties with respect to my failure to report foreign financial assets as required on FBARs or Forms 8938 or my failure to report income from foreign financial assets, I consent to the immediate assessment and collection of a Title 26 miscellaneous offshore penalty for the most recent of the three tax years for which I am providing amended income tax returns. I waive all defenses against and restrictions on the assessment and collection of the miscellaneous offshore penalty, including any defense based on the expiration of the period of limitations on assessment or collection. I waive the right to seek a refund or abatement of the miscellaneous offshore penalty.

I agree to retain all records (including, but not limited to, account statements) related to my assets subject to the 5% miscellaneous offshore penalty until six years from the date of this certification. I also agree to retain all records related to my income and assets during the period covered by my amended income tax returns until three years from the date of this certification. Upon request, I agree to provide all such records to the Internal Revenue Service.

My failure to report all income, pay all tax, and submit all required information returns, including FBARs, was due to non-willful conduct. I understand that non-willful conduct is conduct that is due to negligence, inadvertence, or mistake or conduct that is the result of a good faith misunderstanding of the requirements of the law.

I recognize that if the Internal Revenue Service receives or discovers evidence of willfulness, fraud, or criminal conduct, it may open an examination or investigation that could lead to civil fraud penalties, FBAR penalties, information return penalties, or even referral to Criminal Investigation.

Note: You must provide specific facts on this form or on a signed attachment explaining your failure to report all income, pay all tax, and submit all required information returns, including FBARs. Any submission that does not contain a narrative statement of facts will be considered incomplete and will not qualify for the streamlined penalty relief.

Catalog Number 67044W   www.irs.gov   Form **14654** (Rev. 1-2015)

CERTIFICATION OF U.S. PERSON RESIDING IN THE U.S.

Provide specific reasons for your failure to report all income, pay all tax, and submit all required information returns, including FBARs. If you relied on a professional advisor, provide the name, address, and telephone number of the advisor and a summary of the advice. If married taxpayers submitting a joint certification have different reasons, provide the individual reasons for each spouse separately in the statement of facts. The field below will automatically expand to accommodate your statement of facts.

Under penalties of perjury, I declare that I have examined this certification and all accompanying schedules and statements, and to the best of my knowledge and belief, they are true, correct, and complete.

Signature of Taxpayer	Name of Taxpayer	Date
Signature of Taxpayer *(if joint certification)*	Name of Taxpayer *(if joint certification)*	Date

For Estates Only

Signature of Fiduciary		Date
Title of Fiduciary *(e.g., executor or administrator)*	Name of Fiduciary	

Privacy Act and Paperwork Reduction Notice

We ask for the information on this certification by U.S. person residing in the United States for streamlined domestic offshore procedures to carry out the Internal Revenue laws of the United States. Our authority to ask for information is sections 6001, 6109, 7801, 7803 and the regulations thereunder. This information will be used to determine and collect the correct amount of tax under the terms of the streamlined filing compliance program. You are not required to apply for participation in the streamlined filing compliance program. If you choose to apply, however, you are required to provide all the information requested on the streamlined certification. You are not required to provide the information requested on a document that is subject to the Paperwork Reduction Act unless the document displays a valid OMB control number. Books or records relating to a document or its instructions must be retained as long as their contents may become material in the administration of any Internal Revenue law. Generally, tax returns and return information are confidential, as required by section 6103. Section 6103, however, allows or requires the Internal Revenue Service to disclose or give this information to others as described in the Internal Revenue Code. For example, we may disclose this information to the Department of Justice to enforce the tax laws, both civil and criminal, and to cities, states, the District of Columbia, and U.S. commonwealths or possessions to carry out their tax laws. We may also disclose this information to other countries under a tax treaty, to federal and state agencies to enforce federal nontax criminal laws, or to federal law enforcement and intelligence agencies to combat terrorism. Failure to provide this information may delay or prevent processing your application. Providing false information may subject you to penalties. The time needed to complete and submit the streamlined certification will vary depending on individual circumstances. The estimated average time is: 2 hour

SEVERING TAX TIES WITH CANADA

When making the transition to the U.S., you must ensure you properly sever your tax ties with Canada so you are not subject to the higher Canadian rates and deemed a resident of Canada for tax purposes. If done improperly, you can create untold complexities, paperwork, and double taxation. The Canadian courts have held "residence" to be "a matter of the degree to which a person in mind and fact settles into or maintains or centralizes his ordinary mode of living with its accessories in social relations, interests, and conveniences at or in the place in question." Interestingly, CRA has rules surrounding *if* you are a non-resident, but nothing about *when* you become a non-resident (hint, hint — this is a great planning opportunity!). Therefore, the key to severing your ties with Canada is to ensure you move your community of interest, vital interests, family and social relations, cultural and other activities, place of business, and place of property administration clearly from Canada to the U.S. The CRA does not look at any one item in particular but at an accumulation of things together to determine your residency, as outlined in Form NR73 — Determination of Residency Status. There is no obligation to file this form, and we don't recommend you file it unless specifically requested to do so. CRA uses this form to determine if you are still a resident of Canada for tax purposes. It is intentionally tricky, so get competent assistance when filling it in to avoid any additional complications. To ensure you sever your ties properly with Canada, you should review the checklist below for those items that pertain to you.

- Move your spouse and children at the same time you move, where possible.
- Sell your principal residence and your vehicles if possible.
- Take all your personal possessions with you, especially expensive and cherished items.
- Terminate all memberships (or convert to non-resident status) to churches, civic leagues, clubs, and cultural and other religious organizations.
- Terminate memberships (or convert to non-resident status) to all professional associations.

- Close all checking and savings accounts except those for convenience only, and ensure they are converted to a non-resident account with your U.S. address on it.
- Convert all brokerage accounts to non-resident status and ensure your U.S. address is on the account. Move all brokerage accounts to the U.S.
- Sell or "wind up" any business interests (except as needed for your immigration strategy).
- File a Canadian exit return.
- Terminate all family allowance or child tax benefit payments.
- Terminate all Canadian credit card accounts.
- Mail in your provincial driver's license (may be difficult to do).
- Terminate your Canadian auto insurance and provincial auto registration.
- Mail in your provincial health-care card (may be difficult to do).
- Notify the post office of your address change in the U.S.
- Close all post office boxes and terminate any other addresses in Canada. Do not have any mail addressed to you delivered to a Canadian address, including those of family!
- Close all safe-deposit boxes.
- Terminate all subscriptions to magazines and newsletters or inform them of your address change (there may be a surcharge).
- Notify all financial institutions of your U.S. address.
- Terminate all utility services (electric, water, sewage, trash collection, cell phone, telephone, internet access, Canadian email addresses, cable, etc.).
- Do not make frequent or regular visits to Canada or remain there for an extended period of time. Try to remain outside Canada for as long as possible after you initially leave.
- Don't vote in Canada (stayed tuned, this was recently appealed as outlined in chapter 14).
- Establish ties in the U.S. by ensuring you do the reverse of all the items above, such as getting a state driver's license, registering your automobile, opening up bank accounts,

starting up memberships, establishing cell phone service from a U.S. provider, establishing a U.S.-based email address, and generally moving your community of interest to the U.S.

BECOMING A TAX RESIDENT OF THE U.S.

Nothing can be more confusing than knowing when you have left Canada as a tax resident and when you have become a tax resident of the U.S. Knowing this requires a thorough understanding of the U.S. residency rules and how the Canada-U.S. Tax Treaty overrides them in certain circumstances. Again, properly planning your Canadian exit date with your U.S. entry date can provide many benefits and simplify your tax-filing situation. Whatever you do, try to avoid "straddling" the border unless your unique tax situation warrants it and the appropriate advice is sought. In our experience, people trying to maintain tax ties in both countries generally haven't done much planning before leaving Canada, and are playing a dangerous game of Russian roulette that could have many unintended negative consequences. The risk you run is, if the Canada-U.S. Tax Treaty "tiebreaker" rules need to be used to determine your residency and you end up having closer connections to the U.S., you could be deemed a U.S. tax resident by the Canadian authorities and automatically subject to the departure tax when planning is restricted or no longer can be done. We encourage you to do your planning before you go — and don't try to straddle the border.

SUBSTANTIAL PRESENCE TEST

Overall, the rules for determining when you become a tax resident of the U.S. are generally a black-and-white proposition due to the substantial presence test the IRS uses. Generally, if you reside in the U.S. for more than four months per year for three consecutive years, you will be considered a tax resident for U.S. purposes (unless Form 8840 is filed and accepted, as referenced below). What is interesting about this is you don't need any form of working immigration status to become a tax resident for U.S. purposes! This creates an interesting conundrum: a B-1 or B-2 visitor's visa allows you to remain in the U.S. for up to six months, but neither allows you to earn wages in the U.S. However, you are substantially present in the U.S. (and considered a tax resident for U.S. purposes) if you have been in the U.S. for 183 days or more in the current year (no closer connections exemption here but the treaty "tiebreaker" rules may come in to play), or over the past three years, based on the following formula in Table 5.1.

TABLE 5.1
SUBSTANTIAL PRESENCE TEST

Days present in the U.S.	Multiplier	Total
Current year (t)	1	# days x 1
Previous year (t-1)	1/3	# days x 1/3
Year before that (t-2)	1/6	# days x 1/6
Grand total		???*

*If less than 183 days, you are not a U.S. tax resident

*If 183 days or more, you are a U.S. tax resident (or must file Form 8840).

Some further clarification of definitions is needed. You must count a day in the U.S. when you are physically present in the U.S. (even if you visit just to fill up with gas, shop, and return to Canada). It is important to note that the days don't have to be consecutive — any day you are in the U.S. counts toward the substantial presence test. Finally, a year is considered a calendar tax year, January 1st through December 31st inclusive. As with any government rules, there are always exceptions. If you are in the U.S. for less than 31 days in the current year, the substantial presence test does not apply in that year no matter how many days you were in the U.S. previously. There is a commuting exception as well. Exempt individuals (e.g., students, professional athletes, and foreign government representatives) can reside in the U.S. and not have any of those days count. Likewise, if you are in the U.S. for less than 24 hours when in transit between two places outside the U.S., it does not count. Finally, if you develop a medical condition in the U.S. that prohibits you from leaving, those days will not count toward the substantial presence test either. For those "snowbirds" who end up exceeding 183 days over the three years, they must file IRS Form 8840 — Closer Connection Exception Statement for Aliens to demonstrate that they have closer tax ties to Canada than to the U.S. to avoid being deemed a U.S. resident and having to file a U.S. tax return (see Chapter 11 for more details). Failing to file can lead to a long list of IRS penalties. If you exceed 183 days in any one calendar tax year, you have bigger problems as you are now a tax resident of the U.S. and need to file a tax return. If you do not, you need to file with Competent Authority to have them determine your tax residency. Yes, but Brian, how will I get caught? Because beginning June 30, 2014, Canada and the U.S. implemented the final Entry/Exit Initiative related to the Perimeter Security and Economic Competitiveness Action Plan where they will compare entry and exit information to determine nonfilers, those in violation of immigration rules and tax compliance issues. Each country will now be able to tell how many days you spent in each country so it is only a matter of time before you get caught.

GREEN CARD TEST

Currently, there are thousands of people with U.S. green cards who have since moved back to Canada to live for an extended period of time. The bad news is the IRS considers you a resident for tax purposes if you are a "lawful permanent resident" (green card holder) at any time during the calendar year under the "green card test." This means that, if you are given the privilege of residing permanently in the U.S. as an immigrant, you are considered a resident for tax purposes and must file the requisite U.S. tax returns annually. However, the good news is the Canada-U.S. Tax Treaty can override this IRS rule (being a treaty resident of Canada), and you won't have to file U.S. tax returns except to declare U.S. source income. One note of caution: if you choose to use the treaty and not file U.S. federal and state tax returns as a green card holder, the USCIS will likely impose the "intent to abandon" rules (see Chapter 3, "A Pledge of Allegiance"), which means your green card will be confiscated the next time you cross the border.

DUAL STATUS

Generally, you are a dual-status tax filer if you are both a resident alien and a non-resident alien of the U.S. in the same tax year (typically in the year you move into or out of the U.S.). Different U.S. rules apply to that part of the year you resided in Canada versus the time you resided in the U.S. Generally, you will have to file a 1040NR and declare any U.S.

source income for the period of time you resided in Canada. For the time you were considered a tax resident of the U.S., you have to file a 1040 tax return and declare your worldwide income for that portion of the year.

To simplify things and reduce your tax liability, you may want to take the full-year residency election per IRC §6013(g), which allows you to be declared a U.S. tax resident for the entire calendar year. This election can simplify your U.S. "start-up" return filing and offer some tax advantages but it means you have to do any pre-entry planning by December 31st of the previous year. Determining whether to use this election to file your tax returns depends on your individual circumstances and on the reduction of your overall tax liability. If you take the full-year residency election, one interesting provision in the Internal Revenue Code permits you to exclude up to U$100,800 in wages earned in 2015 while residing outside the U.S. Another election you can take is IRC §6013(h), which allows you to file a married filing joint return with a non-resident alien spouse remaining in Canada. This election allows you to avoid filing "married filing separately" and can lower your tax liability, particularly if you have a low-income-earning spouse. The catch is you have to declare your spouse's worldwide income on your U.S. tax return along with your own, so you should analyze this election to see if it is in your best interest.

THE CANADA-U.S. INCOME TAX TREATY

To resolve some of the complications citizens create in moving back and forth, Canada and the U.S. have negotiated the Income Tax Convention between the United States of America and Canada. Put simply as the "Canada-U.S. Tax Treaty" (or the "treaty"), it was first negotiated and signed on September 26, 1980. Since then, the treaty has been revised only five times: June 14, 1983; March 28, 1984; March 17, 1995; July 29, 1997; and December 15, 2008 (known as the Fifth Protocol). Compared with the U.S. Internal Revenue Code or the Canadian Income Tax Act, it is evident that treaty changes occur infrequently. The purpose of the treaty is to prevent the double taxation of Canadian and U.S. residents on the same income, to provide mutual assistance between the authorities in the collection of taxes, and to authorize the sharing of information to improve compliance.

The Canada-U.S. Tax Treaty "overrides" certain areas of the Canadian Income Tax Act and the U.S. Internal Revenue Code to afford protection from, among other things, double taxation in both countries. An example may help to understand this treaty. If you are residing in the U.S. and you generate C$100 in dividends from a Canadian brokerage account, Canada retains the right to tax this income as "Canadian-source" income. However, as a U.S. resident or U.S. citizen, you are required to declare your worldwide income on your U.S. return, including the C$100 from Canada. Without the Canada-U.S. Tax Treaty, Canada Revenue Agency takes a 25% default withholding tax on the dividend (C$25), while the U.S. taxes the dividend at the qualified income tax rate of 15% (C$15). In total, you have now paid C$40 on C$100 of income (see the detailed example later in the "Foreign Tax Credit Planning" section of this chapter). With the treaty, CRA withholds the treaty rate of only 15%, and the IRS permits a foreign tax credit of that amount against your U.S. taxes. As a result, C$15 tax paid = U$15 tax credit = zero additional tax out of your pocket. As you can see, tax preparation of this nature requires a thorough understanding of the treaty coupled with the experience in knowing how to apply it optimally to your unique situation. The key provisions are outlined below.

DETERMINING TAX RESIDENCY

Once you or the government authorities have determined you meet each of their respective residency laws and are deemed a tax resident of both the U.S. and Canada, the treaty "tiebreaker" rules are used to sort out in which country you are resident. The tiebreaker rules are generally applied in the order they are listed in the treaty:

1. the location of your permanent home (principal residence);

2. your center of vital interests — where your personal and economic relations exist;

3. where you "habitually" reside;

4. where you are a citizen; and

5. if none of the above can determine your residence, the Canadian and U.S. competent tax authorities will agree between themselves who gets to tax you.

SHARING INFORMATION

To catch those who might evade taxation on income from one country while residing in the other, both countries have agreed to share tax information on you. In fact, the treaty allows either tax authority to ask for your complete tax file (electronic, paper, or otherwise) from the other country's tax authority. This means that, if you have a Canadian source of income that is not taxed in Canada (e.g., OAS or CPP), or an NR4 designated as U.S., and you don't report it on your U.S. return, the chances of the tax authorities catching it has increased significantly (particularly with the implementation of FATCA as outlined earlier). Furthermore, the two countries have agreed to collect each other's taxes in certain circumstances. This means that CRA can use the IRS's "long arm of the law" to collect Canadian taxes from Canadians in America, although we have yet to see this be done. Interestingly enough, CRA will not enforce IRS tax claims if you are a Canadian citizen and resident. However, don't ever plan on taking your grandkids to Disneyland or visiting that hospitalized relative in the U.S. As noted earlier, your chances of getting caught evading income tax or tripping up on a compliance issue are more pronounced than ever before. To stem the tax evasion occurring in foreign accounts, CRA has modified the T1 tax return to require disclosure of accounts outside Canada on Form T1135 — Foreign Income Verification Statement, and is signing tax treaties with countries around the world to allow them to exchange tax information to ferret out those not declaring income.

FOREIGN TAX CREDITS

The IRS allows taxes paid to Canada as a foreign tax credit against that income on the U.S. return to avoid double taxation. Using the example above, you would take the C$25 you paid to Canada, convert it at the prevailing exchange rate, and use it as a foreign tax credit on your U.S. return. The treaty allows you to take the taxes paid to Canada and use them against any tax liability that income generates on the U.S. return. See the "Foreign Tax Credit Planning" section of this chapter for more details.

EXEMPTING CERTAIN INCOME

The treaty sorts out what income is taxed in which country, as well as exempts certain income altogether. For example, it provides direction on who taxes capital gains first and exempts up to $10,000 in employment income earned in one country from being taxed in both countries. It also contains specific provisions to eliminate double taxation between the two countries should it occur. For example, the most recent protocol of the treaty provides a treaty election to "step-up" the cost basis for tax purposes on all assets in the U.S. subject to Canada's departure tax. This means all assets are "reset" to fair market value on the day of your departure from Canada for U.S. purposes as well.

WITHHOLDING TAXES

The treaty specifies the withholding tax rates for different types of income sourced out of that country. In the previous example, the withholding tax on dividend income is reduced to 15% rather than the default 25% withholding for nontreaty countries as outlined in the Canadian Income Tax Act. For Canadian sources of income accruing to those in the U.S., the current treaty withholding rates are as follows:

- interest — 0%
- dividends — 15%
- Canada Pension Plan — 0%
- Old Age Security — 0%
- company pension — 15%
- periodic RRIF/LIF payments — 15%
- rental income — 25%

TAXATION OF RRSPS AND OTHER REGISTERED PLANS

The most frequent question our firm fields from Canadians in America, U.S. CPAs, Canadian CAs, and financial planners is, "How are RRSPs (or any other registered plans in Canada) taxed in the U.S.?" These registered plans are so misunderstood in the U.S. — and the complexities so diverse — that a competent Canada-U.S. transition planner should be sought before doing anything with them (ideally, you did the requisite planning before you took up tax residency in the U.S.). We often get a number of inquiries each month from U.S. financial planners and investment advisors who have stumbled across a Canadian living in the U.S. who has a Canadian registered account. Many of them want to move the money to the U.S. so they can manage it but are completely unaware of the adverse Canadian and U.S. income tax consequences of transferring these assets to the U.S. For a review of the issues in moving these accounts to the U.S., see Chapter 10.

Listed below are the key myths and facts about the taxation of Canadian registered plans in the U.S. To simplify things, we refer to RRSPs, but generally we are referring to all types of registered plans in Canada, including the following:

- RRIFs — registered retirement income funds
- LIRAs — locked-in retirement accounts
- LIFs — life income funds
- LRIFs — locked-in retirement income funds
- TFSAs — tax-free savings accounts
- RCAs — retirement compensation arrangements
- DPSPs — deferred profit sharing plans
- RPPs — registered pension plans (e.g., a money purchase RPP)

FACT: RRSPS/RRIFS/LIRAS ARE TAXABLE IN THE U.S.

Few people (including most CAs and CPAs!) realize that the IRS does not recognize the tax-deferred status of RRSPs like CRA does. In fact, the IRS considers them similar to a regular brokerage account with all interest, dividends, and capital gains being taxable on your U.S. return. However, this is where the Canada-U.S. Tax Treaty saves you. Article XVIII(7) gives you the ability to defer the tax on any income inside your RRSP/RRIF until you make a withdrawal. Until recently, the IRS required Form 8891 — U.S. Information Return for Beneficiaries of Certain Canadian Registered Retirement Plans to be filed with your tax return every year to take this treaty election. In a surprise announcement in late 2014, the IRS now automatically acknowledges the treaty election to defer the income inside your RRSP starting with the 2014 tax year, so no formal election or RRSP form needs to be filed anymore.

However, you aren't on easy street yet. First, RRSPs can be considered foreign trusts. As a result, in any year you make contributions to or withdrawals from your registered plan, you may be required to file IRS Form 3520 — Annual Return to Report Transactions with Foreign Trusts and Receipt of Certain Foreign Gifts, as well as Form 3520-A — Annual Information Return of Foreign Trust with a U.S. Owner, instead of Form 8891. Second, there are other tax filing requirements as well, including reporting these foreign accounts on FinCEN Form 114 as mentioned earlier, in addition to Form 8938, and to properly account for and use any foreign tax credits generated at withdrawal, you will need to file IRS Form 1116 — Foreign Tax Credit. Finally, the day will come when you voluntarily, or involuntarily through an RRIF payment, make a withdrawal from your registered plan. This is when you will need to understand the adjusted cost basis in your registered plan for IRS tax purposes and confusion sets in . . . this is when our firm gets a call. Ideally, it is best to establish the cost basis in your RRSPs for IRS purposes by selling everything in your RRSPs before you take up tax residency in the U.S. Despite popular opinion, you do not get an automatic "step-up in basis" when you take up tax residency in the U.S.

Determining the taxable amount of your RRSPs, etc. in the U.S. is a complex undertaking, and most Canada-U.S. tax experts we correspond with have varying opinions. Exactly how the IRS taxes RRSPs is open to debate. Many believe your original contributions are returned to you tax free so a portion of your RRSP/RRIF withdrawal is tax free on your U.S. return. Others believe the entire amount is taxable like a pension. Still others believe you declare the individual income inside the RRSP/RRIF in its individual baskets of interest, dividends, and capital gains. It is best to consult with an experienced Canada-U.S. tax expert to understand the risks, and take a position and be prepared to defend it in the unlikely scenario the IRS challenges it. To further complicate things, you must take into account the appropriate exchange rates in establishing the "cost basis" of your RRSP/RRIFs for IRS purposes because there may be currency gains or losses that need to be accounted for as well. If you have moved to the U.S. and did no pre-entry planning with your registered plans, you should start now by locating the statement closest to your entry date into the U.S., and tracking what has happened in your RRSP since you entered the U.S. You may have to contact your RRSP custodian to begin looking it up on microfiche!

The next issue to contend with is taxation of the RRSP/RRIF at the individual state level. The IRS has one set of rules and forms to deal with registered plans, but the states don't necessarily follow along. Some states don't have an income tax, while others do. Some states don't recognize the automatic IRS treaty election to defer the income inside the RRSP/RRIF, so the income needs to be reported each year and state income taxes paid even though the IRS allows the deferral! Some states will allow a foreign tax credit against the income, and some will not. As you can see, each situation needs to be dealt with on a case-by-case basis.

When faced with all of this, many Canadians throw up their hands and just want to withdraw their RRSPs/RRIFs from Canada. Determining the best course of action for your registered plan depends on your individual circumstances and what you are trying to achieve (see Chapter 10 for details on the management and movement of these accounts to the U.S.). You may be focused on getting your registered plans out of Canada, but what are you going to do with the funds once withdrawn? Good RRSP planning considers how your funds are invested, the best means of collapsing it (lump sum or staged), and the best use of the funds once collapsed. Some nonworking spouses may be able to get their RRSPs out of Canada tax free depending on their circumstances. As you can see, the complexities surrounding these decisions require a thorough understanding of your unique financial situation accompanied by much thought and analysis.

FACT AND MYTH: WITHDRAW YOUR RRSP TAX FREE!

We have seen advertisements and other pronouncements that declare "Withdraw your RRSP tax-free or close to zero tax from Canada!" This has misled some people into thinking this is a regular occurrence. These tax "schemes" are generally based on a legal opinion letter (with you signing a nondisclosure agreement and little disclosure of the details to you) and involve setting up complex offshore structures that essentially "lock" you in to the provider where you can't leave their services, no matter how bad their customer service gets. At first, it seems like you can save some taxes but the complexity it adds, and the fact that you are locked in to ongoing high fees, has many telling us it wasn't worth it. That being said, it is possible to withdraw an entire RRSP or RRIF tax free from a Canadian perspective in certain unique financial situations, and our firm has succeeded in doing so when the requisite planning, tax preparation, and investment management are all coordinated. However, this shouldn't be considered the norm. With proper planning and tax preparation, it's possible to pay a rate lower than CRA's 25% lump-sum withholding rate. A lot depends on your individual financial circumstances and what you will do with the money once your RRSP has been collapsed and the funds moved to the U.S. The other important component is ensuring the appropriate tax preparation is done. The most effective tax planning in the world won't amount to much if it is not properly implemented on your tax return. This is where comprehensive planning and a competent Canada-U.S. transition team come into play.

MYTH: ROLL YOUR RRSP INTO A U.S. IRA

Many people believe they can simply maintain the tax-deferred status of their RRSPs by rolling them tax free into an individual retirement account (IRA) in the U.S. This cannot be done. The only way you can make a contribution to a regular IRA is with cash. This means you have to collapse your RRSP, pay the requisite taxes in both Canada and the U.S., and then move the cash into an IRA if eligible. Sometimes there is confusion surrounding transfers into a "rollover" IRA that can come from a U.S. qualified plan, such as a 401(k), 403(b), not a Canadian registered plan (see Chapter 8, "Financial Freedom," for more details on these qualified plans).

MYTH: LUMP-SUM RRSP/RRIF WITHDRAWALS HAVE A 10% WITHHOLDING

People have told us we were wrong about the withholding of lump-sum RRSP withdrawals because the financial institution told them 10% needs to be withheld per withdrawal instead of the treaty mandated 25%. In fact, the confusion lies with the financial institution that processed the withdrawal because for residents of Canada the following rates apply (see Table 5.2).

TABLE 5.2

RRSP/RRIF WITHDRAWAL RATES

RRSP Withdrawals	Rest of Canada	Quebec
C$0 – 5,000	10%	21%
C$5,001 – 15,000	20%	30%
$15,000 +	30%	35%
RRIF withdrawals in excess of annual minimum	30%	16%

The usual reason the institution withholds 10% per withdrawal is because there is still a Canadian address on the account — your financial institution hasn't been told you moved to the U.S. and are no longer a resident of Canada for tax purposes. According to the Canadian Income Tax Act, the correct withholding on each lump-sum withdrawal is 25%, and you are required to submit the remaining 15% through a Part XIII tax filing with CRA or they will be looking for a T-1 return. Likewise, our firm has filed Form NR7-R for clients who have a 5% refund coming because their financial institution took the default 30% on lump-sum withholding in excess of C$15,000.

MYTH: WITHHOLDING TAX CAN BE PAID FROM OUTSIDE THE RRSP

Often an RRSP may contain nothing but investments that you may not want to sell (deferred sales charges, etc.). As a result, you may want to keep all the investments intact and pay the withholding tax by separate check so that nothing has to be sold. Unfortunately, the withholding (hence the term) must come from within the RRSP account. This means you will be forced to sell enough investments (and incur any deferred sales charges, etc.) to pay the required withholding before you can collapse the RRSP.

TAXATION OF TAX-FREE SAVINGS ACCOUNTS

Similar to Roth IRAs and Roth 401(k) plans in the U.S., TFSAs are the Canadian equivalent of a tax-free savings vehicle (see Chapter 8 for more details). These accounts allow annual contributions (C$5,500 in 2015 and soon maybe C$10,000 with the pre-election budget) that are not deductible on either your Canadian or your U.S. tax return. The earnings grow tax free from a Canadian perspective, but unfortunately there is no treaty protection like Roth IRAs in Canada yet. TFSAs were in the early stages of formulation by the Canadian government when the Fifth Protocol of the Canada-U.S. Tax Treaty was being negotiated and, as a result, did not make it into the treaty. Since Roth IRAs were well established in the U.S., the tax-free status of these accounts made it into the treaty. As a result, TFSAs are taxed like regular brokerage accounts (or like trusts by some practitioners) on your U.S. return, so you may want to "run the numbers" before starting one if you are going to move to the U.S. In fact, you may want to consider collapsing them completely while a non-resident of the U.S., rebuild your TFSA contribution "room" with CRA, and move those funds to the U.S.

MEDICARE SURTAX ON NET INVESTMENT INCOME

With the passing of Obamacare came additional taxes on high-income earners to pay for it all. In addition to the 0.9% Medicare payroll tax on those exceeding the thresholds below (see payroll taxes later in this chapter), a 3.8% Net Investment Income Tax (NIIT) is added on top of the regular income tax of those in the following modified adjusted gross income thresholds.

TABLE 5.3

INDIVIDUALS SUBJECT TO NET INVESTMENT INCOME TAX

Filing Status	Threshold (U$)
Married, Filing Jointly	250,000
Married, Filing Separately	125,000
Single, Head of Household	200,000

The 3.8% surtax is due on the lesser of your net investment income for the year or the amount your modified adjusted gross income (MAGI) exceeds these income thresholds. As we begin the discussion on various types of investment income, you have to remember the 3.8% net investment income tax (NIIT) is added for higher-income U.S. tax filers. To

further complicate things, the IRS has issued new regulations (Treas. Reg. § 1.1411-1[e]) stating that a foreign tax credit is *not* available against the NIIT. This means high-income taxpayers will likely owe some tax to the IRS on top of what they owe to CRA. However, this additional tax should be used as a foreign tax credit on your Canadian return. Throughout this chapter we have provided simplified examples of a taxpayer in Alberta (which has the lowest tax rates in Canada, but the top marginal rate is reached at approximately C$135,000 in taxable income) versus Texas (no state tax, but the top marginal rate is reached at U$457,600 in taxable income filing jointly and U$406,750 filing singly) for the highest income earners in each jurisdiction for comparison.

TAXATION OF INTEREST AND DIVIDENDS

INTEREST

Both Canada and the U.S. tax interest as ordinary income subject to your marginal tax rate. In the U.S., you will receive a 1099-INT slip that will outline your taxable, partially taxable (federal interest), and nontaxable interest (municipal bonds). For U.S. residents, interest from a Canadian bank account, for example, is subject to a 0% withholding tax at source, and your financial institution should issue you an NR4 slip at tax time showing you how much interest was paid. In addition, the Canadian government amended the Canadian Income Tax Act to completely eliminate the withholding on Canadian-source interest to any non-resident, regardless of what country they live in and whether that country has a tax treaty with Canada or not. As a result, there is no withholding on any Canadian source interest paid to you.

TABLE 5.4

TAXATION OF INTEREST EXAMPLE

Texas		Alberta	
Federal	39.6%	Federal	29%
State	0%	Provincial	10%
NIIT	3.8%		
Total	43.4%	Total	39%

As this example shows, you can actually pay more on interest income in the U.S. than Canada, but this does not take into account the use of muni bonds or federal obligations that would be applicable here, nor the large taxable income (U$400k+ vs. C$135k+) you need to get to for these rates to apply.

DIVIDENDS

The taxation of dividends in both countries is a bit tricky because the income distributed by corporations has already been taxed at the corporate level. When the dividend ends up in your hands, it is taxed at the personal level as well, so the federal governments in both countries have put accommodations in place to alleviate the double taxation. In Canada, eligible dividends are grossed up by 138% (to reflect what the company earned pretax), and then your marginal tax rate is applied at 39% for an Alberta taxpayer. You then have to subtract the dividend tax credit of 19.29% in Alberta (but it varies by province) to reflect the tax the company has already paid on that dividend.

In the U.S., qualified dividends are taxed differently than non-qualified dividends. Qualified dividends are dividends from U.S. corporations and corporations that reside in a country that has a treaty with the U.S. (like Canada). Non-qualified dividends include those from real estate investment trusts, commodity mutual funds, money market or bond funds, and corporations in countries where the U.S. does not have a tax treaty.

TABLE 5.5

DIVIDEND TAXATION IN THE U.S.

Marginal Tax Bracket (%)	Ordinary Dividend	Qualified Dividend
10	10	0
15	15	0
25	25	15
28	28	15
33	33	15
35	35	15
39.6	39.6	20

Dividends from American and/or Canadian sources are included on Schedule B of your Form 1040 and taxed in accordance with Table 5.5 above. In the U.S., you will receive a 1099-DIV slip outlining your qualified and non-qualified dividends. Residents of the U.S. receiving Canadian dividends are subject to a 15% treaty withholding tax at source by your Canadian financial institution, which should issue you an NR4 slip at tax time. Sometimes, we have seen a 0% withholding because there is still a Canadian address on the account. Just because no withholding was taken does not mean there is no tax owing to CRA. You have the obligation to file a Canadian Part XIII tax return and remit the 15% as stipulated in the Canada-U.S. Tax Treaty, otherwise CRA will send you a notice to file a tax return because they have a resident tax slip with no accompanying tax return. Like interest, this dividend income must be reported on your U.S. return as part of your "worldwide income," resulting in the potential for double taxation. With proper planning and tax preparation you can recapture some, or potentially all, of this 15% tax on your U.S. return.

TABLE 5.6

TAXATION OF QUALIFIED AND ELIGIBLE DIVIDENDS EXAMPLE

Texas		Alberta	$100 Dividend
Federal	20%	Gross Up	$138
State	0%	Federal	29%
NIIT	3.8%	Provincial	10%
Total	23.8%	Tax	$53.82
		Fed Div Tax Credit	-$20.73
		AB Div Tax Credit	-$13.80
		Total	19.29%

TAXATION OF CAPITAL GAINS AND LOSSES

In comparing the taxation of capital gains between Canada and the U.S., Canada includes 50% of the total gain in taxable income and then taxes it at your progressive marginal rates. This means that, if your marginal rate is 39% in Alberta, your net capital gains rate is 19.5%. The U.S. capital gains rate depends on how long you have held the investment and what marginal tax bracket you are in. For investments held one year or less, the capital gains are taxed at ordinary income tax rates, just like interest, at your marginal rates. For investments held greater than one year, the following rates apply.

TABLE 5.7

CAPITAL GAINS TAXATION IN THE U.S.

Marginal Tax Bracket (%)	Short-Term Capital Gain (%)	Long-Term Capital Gain (%)
10	10	0
15	15	0
25	25	15
28	28	15
33	33	15
35	35	15
39.6	39.6	20

Realized capital gains and losses are reported on Schedule D of your Form 1040. Canadian capital gains are reported on CRA Form T5008 while in the U.S., they are reported on Form 1099B — Proceeds From Broker and Barter Exchange Transactions. You should note that all financial institutions in the U.S. are required to track the cost basis on all taxable accounts and report all taxable transactions to the IRS annually. As a result, the capital gains and losses on your tax return must match the tax information the IRS has from the financial institution. If not, the financial institution's reporting overrides your return!

TABLE 5.8

LONG-TERM CAPITAL GAINS TAXATION EXAMPLE

Texas		Alberta	
Federal	20%	Federal	29%
State	0%	Provincial	10%
NIIT	3.8%	50% is taxable	-19.5%
Total	23.8%	Total	19.5%

The treatment of capital losses is fairly different in Canada than in the U.S. In Canada, capital losses can be applied against taxable capital gains in that year, with any excess losses carried back three years (through an adjusted return) or carried forward indefinitely. In the U.S., capital losses can be applied against capital gains in the current year, plus an additional U$3,000 (U$1,500 if married filing separately) can be applied against other income. Any unused losses can be carried forward indefinitely and netted against future gains or deducted up to the U$3,000 annual limit on any other type of income until fully used up. Unlike in Canada, capital losses can't be carried back in the U.S. against gains in prior years.

For those making the transition to the U.S., capital gains are typically reported only in the country of residence, but it depends on what type of investment you are selling. For example, CRA reserves the right to tax Canadian real estate, business interests, and trusts, and the IRS will tax those transactions as well, leading to potential double taxation. This is a primary reason you should use caution when a Canadian investment firm manages your investment portfolio, as they generally do not understand the U.S. tax implications of managing your portfolio, and could subject you to a lot of short-term gains or Passive Foreign Investment Corporation income (PFICs — addressed later in this chapter). They need to have a thorough knowledge of the U.S. tax rules and be registered in your state of residence in the U.S. to provide investment advice; otherwise, you could receive an unnecessarily large tax bill, and your advisor's compliance department will have a fit!

PASSIVE FOREIGN INCOME CORPORATIONS (PFIC)

As a U.S. Form 1040 tax filer, you need to be aware of some ridiculously complex rules if the source of the interest, dividends, or capital gain distributions we just wrote about are coming from any Canadian investment vehicles, as this may change the taxation of these income items significantly. These regulations came about as part of the 1986 Tax Reform Act. The purpose of the regulation was to eliminate the beneficial tax treatment for certain foreign investments. Under prior law, U.S. taxpayers could accumulate tax-deferred income from foreign investments and then, upon sale of the investment, recognize the gain at the long-term capital gains tax rate. The prior law put U.S. mutual funds at a disadvantage as they are required to pass through all income to the shareholder in the year earned. The new PFIC regulations were designed to create a more level playing field for U.S. funds but add an incredible level of complexity to even the simplest of situations.

Then in 2010, after a policy review, the IRS determined that all foreign (non-U.S.) mutual funds and Exchange Traded Funds (ETFs) are to be classified as corporations (rather than trusts) for U.S. tax purposes, and they are now subject to the extremely complex and onerous tax consequences of the PFIC tax regime. Consequently, anyone required to file a U.S. 1040 tax return still holding Canadian mutual funds, ETFs, etc. in a brokerage account in Canada are subject to the ridiculously complex set of PFIC rules if they had more than U$25,000 filing singly (U$50,000 filing jointly) as well as the foreign trust rules required on Form 3520.

WHAT IS A PFIC?

Before going any further, it may be helpful to understand the precise definition of a PFIC. A PFIC is essentially a non-U.S. corporation that generates most of their income from passive investment sources such as dividends, interest, rents, royalties, and capital gains. Specifically, if 75% or more of the foreign company's income is passive income, or 50% or more of the foreign company's holdings are held to generate passive income, then the company is considered a PFIC. As a result of this definition, all Canadian (foreign) mutual funds, ETFs, labor-sponsored funds, money market funds, real estate funds, and pension funds fall squarely into this definition.

PFIC SHAREHOLDER FILING REQUIREMENTS

Beginning in 2011, the IRS required any U.S. 1040 tax filer who owned shares of PFICs to disclose certain information to the IRS on Form 8621 annually. In previous years, there was a reporting obligation with respect to PFICs only if there was a transaction related to that investment. Now, reporting must be made even if there is no activity, but the IRS provided some relief by forgoing the requirement to file in 2011 and 2012 but making Form 8621 mandatory for tax years 2013 forward. Disclosure of a PFIC is required in a "nonregistered" account (regular taxable brokerage account); however, there was much debate about PFICs held in a "registered" account (e.g., RRSP, RRIF, or LIRA) until the IRS issued guidance saying PFICs inside these accounts do not have to be disclosed. Further, the Canada-U.S. Tax Treaty provides protection from the taxation of PFICs in a registered account as RRSPS, etc. are now automatically tax-deferred. However, to further complicate things, the IRS revised Form 8621 in December 2014 and included Part I — Summary of Annual Information that may apply to all PFICs no matter where they are held, including RRSPs. It is best to have a conversation with your tax preparer to decide the best way to go to ensure everything is disclosed appropriately

In the meantime, if you are subject to the PFIC requirements, you must file IRS Form 8621 for *each* PFIC you own with your tax return, and you have the option of taking one of two tax treatment elections for each one. The first election is to treat the PFIC as a qualified electing fund (QEF), probably the most advantageous of the three methods. The second method is the mark-to-market method, which requires the shareholder to report annual increase in market value of the PFIC as ordinary income. If neither of these options is selected, the "default" method is employed, and the investment is treated like a Section 1291 Fund (excess distributions).

TAX TREATMENT OF A PFIC

The QEF Election

If the QEF election is taken, a U.S. taxpayer's investment in a PFIC is generally subject to the same tax rules and rates as a domestic investment, except dividends are not considered qualified dividends and are subject to ordinary income. The taxpayer includes a pro rata share of the PFIC's ordinary earnings and net capital gains on their U.S. tax return each year. Let's look at an example.

An investor owns five shares of ABC mutual fund, a Canadian mutual fund that qualifies as a PFIC. At the end of the year, the mutual fund as a whole earns $50,000 in investment income and $75,000 in capital appreciation. To figure out the tax due according to the QEF method, the investor needs to know their proportionate ownership of the mutual fund so they can calculate the income and gains attributed to them. If there are 500 shares outstanding, we can calculate the investor of five shares owns 1% of the fund. Therefore, the investor is taxed on $500 of investment income and $750 of capital gains on their U.S. return.

This method seems quite straightforward. However, there is one huge obstacle. In order to take the QEF election, the mutual fund (PFIC) must comply with substantial IRS reporting requirements. The PFIC must provide an annual information statement to the shareholder that must include the shareholder's pro rata share of the PFIC's ordinary earnings and net capital gains for that tax year. Because most Canadian mutual fund managers are unaware of these requirements, or may not be willing to comply because of the costs involved (that is changing quickly as people pull their money from these mutual funds), the QEF election is not frequently available to U.S. 1040 tax filers invested in Canadian mutual funds.

The Mark-to-Market Election

The shareholder can elect to treat the PFIC using the "mark-to-market" method if the PFIC is considered a "marketable" stock or fund. To be considered a "marketable" stock or fund, the PFIC must be regularly traded on either a national securities exchange that is registered with the SEC, the national market system established by the Securities Exchange Act of 1934, or a foreign exchange regulated by a governmental authority of the country in which the market is located (e.g., Toronto Stock Exchange). If the mark-to-market election is taken, the PFIC holder recognizes the gain or loss on the shares of the fund as if they had sold all shares at fair market value at the end of the taxable year. The gain or loss is treated as ordinary income on the U.S. return, an unfavorable tax treatment for most individuals. Unrealized losses are only reportable to the extent that they offset previously reported gains. Upon the sale of the PFIC shares, all gains are reported as ordinary income, whereas losses are reported as capital losses on Schedule D. Let's look at some examples to illustrate the potential adverse tax consequences of the mark-to-market method.

First, let's look at the issue of taxation on unrealized capital gains from mutual funds. Let's assume you purchase $50,000 of XYZ fund, a Canadian mutual fund that qualifies as a PFIC, but does not provide the necessary information to select the QEF option. Therefore, you elect the mark-to-market tax treatment. At the end of the year, your position in the fund is worth $60,000, a 20% gain. Let's also assume that the fund is managed in a tax-efficient manner, so no capital gain distributions occurred during the year. On your Canadian tax return, no tax is due from this investment since no distributions were made from the fund. However, for U.S. tax purposes, you would be taxed on the $10,000 gain in value according to the mark-to-market tax method. Furthermore, this gain would be characterized as ordinary income for U.S. tax purposes ... an unfavorable tax outcome. The same tax disadvantages hold true for Canadian-listed Exchange Traded Funds and all other funds that qualify as PFICs.

Let's turn to an example involving the sale or disposition of an asset using the mark-to-market method. To start the illustration, let's assume you buy $50,000 of QRS fund that is *not* a PFIC. The investment does very well, and you sell it later the same year for $75,000. In Canada, half of the gain is taxable. Let's use the highest tax rate for this illustration. If the investor is a resident of Nova Scotia, the top tax rate is 50%. Therefore, the tax rate on the capital gain would be 25%. For U.S. purposes, the gain would be taxed at 20%, the top long-term capital gains tax rate (we assume the 3.8% NIIT does not apply). Since the Canadian tax exceeds the U.S. tax, no tax is due in the U.S. because of the foreign tax credits permitted by the Canada-U.S. Tax Treaty.

Let's look at the scenario again, but this time the investment qualifies as a PFIC. For U.S. tax purposes, you pay the top ordinary income tax rate on the gain, which is currently 39.6% (once again we assume the NIIT of 3.8% does not apply). The tax rate in Nova Scotia remains at 25%. Since the U.S. tax exceeds the Canadian tax, you could owe the IRS 14.6% of the $25,000 gain, an additional $3,650 in tax if no other foreign tax credits were available.

Excess Distributions (Section 1291)

If neither election is made, the PFIC will be considered a Section 1291, and the shareholder will be subject to even more complex and generally less favorable treatment. The general penalty for investing in a PFIC is that "excess distributions," including gains from the sale of the PFIC, are thrown back over the shareholder's holding period and subject to tax at the shareholder's highest ordinary income tax rate in each throwback year. The definition of an "excess distribution" is twofold:

1. The part of the distribution received from a section 1291 fund in the current tax year that is greater than 125% of the average distributions received in respect to such stock by the shareholder during the three preceding tax years (or, if shorter, the portion of the shareholder's holding period before the current tax year).

2. Any capital gains that result from the sale of PFIC shares.

Let's look at an illustration of the "excess distribution" rules at work. A Canadian resident buys 100 shares of REM fund (a PFIC) on January 1, 2016, valued at $1,000 per share for a total investment of $100,000. The fund distributes $80 per share in dividends every year. On December 31, 2015, the shares were sold for $250,000. Since the dividends each year never exceeded the prior year's amount, there are no excess distributions relating to dividends. However, since the sale resulted in a capital gain of $150,000, the gain is an excess distribution and will be allocated over the life of the investment. In particular, the excess distribution would be allocated $50,000 for 2016, $50,000 for 2017, and $50,000 for 2018. The taxable amounts in 2016 and 2017 are taxed at the highest marginal tax rate for those tax years (35%). Further, the resulting additional tax for 2016 and 2017 draws an interest charge as if it were an underpayment of taxes for the year in question. Fortunately, amended returns don't need to be filed; the underpayment of taxes is simply included on line 16c of Form 8621. The allocation of the final $50,000 of gains is added to ordinary income on line 21 on the 2018 1040 and subject to the taxpayer's marginal tax bracket for that year.

Moreover, the taxable amounts allocated to the prior year PFIC period are not included in the investor's income. Rather, the tax and interest are added to the investor's tax liability without regard to other tax characteristics. This means that tax and interest is payable even if the investor otherwise had a current loss or net operating carryovers.

As you can see, the complexity and punitive nature of the PFIC rules render most individual U.S. 1040 tax filers incapable of filing their own returns without qualified, professional assistance. The American Institute of CPAs (AICPA) wrote a letter to the IRS in May 2013 asking the IRS to provide an exemption for certain shareholders in PFICs, including shareholders with ownership of less than 2% in a PFIC, shareholders that don't know they own a PFIC, or PFICs that did not notify their shareholders of their status as a PFIC. This would eliminate many innocent taxpayers from having to comply with these complex, draconian tax rules. Hopefully, the IRS will heed some of what the AICPA is saying . . . soon!

TAXATION OF PENSIONS

COMPANY PENSION PLAN

In Canada, your employer's pension is fully taxable but is offset with a C$2,000 nonrefundable tax credit. However, when you move to the U.S., your Canadian company pension plan is subject to a 15% treaty withholding tax at source, and must be reported on your U.S. tax return as part of your "worldwide income," resulting in the potential for double taxation. Proper planning and tax preparation can recapture some, or all, of this 15% on your U.S. return.

There is some difference of opinion amongst tax professionals about whether any of your contributions into the pension plan come out "tax free" from a U.S. perspective. The majority of these plans are employer only contributions and are therefore fully taxable in the U.S. You may want to contact the pension administrator if you have employee contributions into the plan to see if those can be quantified; in so doing, you can have a discussion regarding the tax implications to you.

One strategy that may save you some Canadian withholding tax on your pension is using Section 217 of the Canadian Income Tax Act, which will tax you more favorably and as if you were still a tax resident in Canada. The rules for this are complex, but if your annual pension income (including RRSPs or RRIFs) is around C$10,000 to $20,000, and you have virtually no other income from outside Canada, this tax filing will allow you to claim the personal amount, age amount, and pension amount (along with some other potential nonrefundable credits) against pension type income. You will still have the 15% withholding at source but you get some or all of it refunded when you file your tax return by June 30th of the following year. If you think you are going to qualify for a Section 217 filing in the next tax year, you can file Form NR5 — Application by a Non-Resident of Canada for a Reduction in the Amount of Non-Resident Tax Required to be Withheld with CRA by October 1. Once approved by CRA, your financial institution will be authorized to reduce the withholding tax at source.

Your best bet with these plans is to take the commuted value of the pension and roll it into a LIRA before moving to the U.S. There are several reasons this may be your best option. First, most company pensions are not adjusted for inflation. This means your purchasing power declines over your lifetime, slowly leading to a decline in your lifestyle. Second, if you are living life in the U.S., your living expenses will be in U.S. dollars but your pension will be paid in Canadian loonies. This subjects you to currency exchange risk and as the exchange rate normalizes around C$1 = U$0.80, you could find it more difficult to manage your expenses. Third, in the LIRA, you can invest the funds in line with your own risk tolerance (more aggressively than a big pension plan might), in addition to getting everything into U.S. dollars to eliminate the exchange rate risk. Finally, there are opportunities to move some of the LIRA to an RRSP to unlock it and move it to the U.S. very tax efficiently (see Chapter 10 for more details).

U.S. SOCIAL SECURITY

In the U.S., Social Security benefits are partially taxed on the U.S. return. The first 15% of your benefits are tax free no matter how much money you make. If your income is between U$32,000 and $44,000 (U$25,000 and $34,000 if filing single), 50% of your benefit is taxable. Income in excess of U$44,000 ($34,000 if filing single) means the maximum 85% of your benefit is taxable in the U.S. (see Chapter 8 on how to qualify for U.S. Social Security). Interestingly enough, the Canadian tax return allows this 15% deductible benefit for those living in Canada collecting U.S. Social Security (see our companion book *The American in Canada* for further details).

OLD AGE SECURITY

In the U.S., OAS is taxed similarly to U.S. Social Security in that the first 15% of your benefits are tax free, and the remaining 85% may be taxable (at the lower U.S. rates) depending on your income. One of the most compelling reasons for moving to the U.S. is that the OAS recovery tax (the "clawback") no longer applies to U.S. residents. This means that Canadian residents with an income of more than C$71,592 in 2015 no longer lose any of their OAS due to the clawback (15% of the difference between the threshold and your income is clawed back). If your net income exceeds C$116,103 (adjusted quarterly), all of your OAS is clawed back, essentially resulting in a 100% tax on your OAS benefits. Not only can you begin collecting up to an additional C$6,764.88 annually (adjusted quarterly for the CPI) per person in 2015 if you move to the U.S., but because of the elimination of the clawback there is also no withholding on your OAS by CRA.

CANADA PENSION PLAN/QUEBEC PENSION PLAN

CPP/QPP is not subject to any Canadian withholding, but is fully reportable on your U.S. tax return as part of your worldwide income. Like OAS, your CPP/QPP is taxed like U.S. Social Security benefits at the lower U.S. rates, with the first 15% of your benefits being tax free and the remaining 85% taxable depending on your income. Also, be aware that your CPP can affect your Social Security benefits through the Windfall Elimination Provision (WEP), discussed further in Chapter 8.

TAXATION OF RENTAL PROPERTIES

For some valid reasons, many Canadians insist on keeping their home in Canada to rent it out. We have seen this done numerous times, but what people aren't prepared for is the potential tax, estate planning, and paperwork nightmare that comes with keeping a rental property in Canada. This complexity needs to be considered in your overall decision to rent out your current home in Canada along with consideration of this tax tie to Canada.

CANADA

Even if you live in the U.S., CRA retains the right to tax all Canadian-source rental income or capital gains on real property, and you are required to appoint an agent in Canada to ensure taxes owing are paid. If you don't pay the tax, your agent residing in Canada must do so. This way, CRA has assets and people it can attach itself to for any claim of taxes owing. To appoint an agent, you need to file Form NR6 — Undertaking to File an Income Tax Return by a Non-Resident Receiving Rent from Real Property or Receiving a Timber Royalty each year with CRA. Once approved, this option allows you to remit 25% withholding tax on the net income each month (if any) when the rent is collected. If you don't file an NR6 in a timely fashion, you are subject to a 25% withholding tax on the gross rental income, which could lead to a significant cash outflow problem, particularly if you have a mortgage on the property. You must also file a Section 216 tax return each year to properly account for your expenses against any rental income, which may result in a refund or a balance owing.

When you sell your rental property, you are subject to even more complexity. As a non-resident of Canada selling Canadian real estate property, you are subject to a flat 25% withholding tax on the gross sale price. This means if you sell a property in Canada for C$200,000, $50,000 will be withheld and remitted to CRA by your attorney. However, if you file Form T2062 — Request by a Non-Resident of Canada for a Certificate of Compliance Related to the Disposition of Taxable Canadian Property, you can reduce the amount withheld to 25% of the net gains only. This means if you get an approved T2062 from CRA before, or within a month or two of the closing, you only have to remit C$200,000 (current sale price of the property) less C$100,000 (original cost of the property) = C$100,000 gain, multiplied by 25%, which = C$25,000. It is therefore important to get a formal appraisal of your property to establish its fair market value when you leave Canada or convert it to a rental property.

Finally, if capital cost allowance is taken on the Canadian return, there could be a nasty "recapture" upon the sale of the property that you should plan for. Recapture is the taxation of the cumulative capital cost allowance taken on the property over the years — all in the year of sale.

All of this is captured on a T1 non-resident tax return where the final tax liability is determined.

UNITED STATES

Since you are required to report your worldwide income on your U.S. return, the rental income you derive from Canada must be reported on your U.S. return after converting everything to U.S. dollars. This income gives rise to the potential for double taxation because of the 25% withholding paid to CRA. Proper tax planning and preparation can recoup some of the tax paid to Canada as a foreign tax credit on your U.S. return. Interestingly enough, you must depreciate the rental property on your U.S. return even though claiming capital cost allowance is optional in Canada. Again, when it comes time to sell the property, there is the "recapture" of the depreciation on your U.S. tax return in the year of sale, and it can lead to a nasty tax surprise as it is taxed at a flat 25%. Proper tax planning can make this a much easier transaction.

TAXATION OF PRINCIPAL RESIDENCE

If you move to the U.S. and retain your principal residence in Canada, it converts to a "second home," and added complications can result. Since both the Canadian and U.S. tax authorities recognize only one principal residence, your principal residence in Canada now becomes a vacation home, and your new home in the U.S. becomes your principal residence. For Canadian purposes, gains accrued while you lived in the home are exempt from taxation. For U.S. purposes, gains accrued while you lived in the home are subject to U$500,000 capital gains exemption per married couple, U$250,000 per single person. However, to claim this capital gains exemption when you sell, you must have lived in the home for two out of the five years leading up to the date of sale or your exemption is prorated and a portion of it is taxable. For planning purposes, you may want to rent out your property for a maximum of three years in order to get the full capital gains exemption; if you don't, all of the appreciation in the home will be taxable from the time you originally purchased it.

SOCIAL SECURITY NUMBER (SSN)

Similar to the Social Insurance Number (SIN) issued in Canada, the U.S. issues a Social Security number, but note that they are two completely different numbers for two different countries! Your SIN is of no use in the U.S. except to get a credit rating, as noted in Chapter 6. Do not attempt to give your SIN to a U.S. bank or use it on a U.S. tax return; you will cause yourself no end of grief because the IRS will not recognize your SIN and kick out your tax return. Further, any tax payments made with your return will not be accepted because there isn't a valid SSN to deposit those funds in your account. As a result, you may be subject to penalties or interest. Besides, it can be considered fraud if you try to pass off your SIN as an SSN!

Once you have taken up residency in the U.S. and are permitted to work via a valid immigration visa or green card, you are required to apply for a Social Security number using Form SS-5 — Application for a Social Security Card. Once you complete it, file it with the Social Security Administration, not the IRS! You need an SSN because income paid to you from an employer, interest from a bank account, or dividends from a mutual fund at a brokerage firm need to be tracked to an SSN for income tax purposes. Likewise, any wages and payroll taxes need to be tracked to your SSN to ensure you establish the necessary coverage to qualify for U.S. Social Security and Medicare.

The SSN is divided into three parts to help make it a unique configuration as outlined below:

XXX	XX	XXXX
Area	Group	Serial Number

Your area number indicates your state of residence. For example, Arizona is 526-527, 600-601, California is 545-573, 602-626, Florida is 261-267, 589-595, while Texas is 449-467. The group number has no particular significance — it is just there to "break the numbers into blocks of convenient size for SSA's processing operations." The serial numbers are simply issued from 0001 to 9999 within each group, except every fifth

SSN is assigned 2001-2999 and 7001-7999. Serial number 0000 is never used. The SSN is an important number, and by simply inputting it into a system, government officials can tell whether it is valid or not.

INDIVIDUAL TAXPAYER IDENTIFICATION NUMBER (ITIN)

Dependent family members of valid visa holders residing in the U.S. (but who are ineligible to work) may still be eligible to be claimed as dependents on your taxes to get the ensuing tax benefits. To do so, each family member must have an ITIN (starts with a "9"), or the IRS will deny any tax benefits for your dependents. To obtain an ITIN, you must fill out and submit Form W-7 — Application for Individual Taxpayer Identification Number and provide the required documentation to the IRS (not the Social Security Administration), which will issue an ITIN in approximately 8 to 12 weeks. Unfortunately, the IRS is becoming more stringent in issuing ITINs, as there has been much fraud in this area; a demonstrated "U.S. tax purpose" is therefore now required to get an ITIN. Starting in 2016, an ITIN that has not been used in at least one tax return in the past five years will automatically be canceled. As a result, you need to fill out the form appropriately and submit all of the required documentation (which usually includes original documents like a passport or a certified copy from the issuing agency!). Please note that an ITIN does not qualify you for any Social Security benefits, nor does it change your immigration status, including your ability to work. Once you or your family member receives authorization to work in the U.S., an SSN will be needed to replace the ITIN. To do this, just fill out Form SS-5 outlined above and submit it to the Social Security Administration (SSA). There is a spot on the form to provide your ITIN, and the SSA will ensure it is replaced in the IRS system with your new SSN.

Please note that sometimes a spouse ineligible to work will be issued an SSN, but stamped across it will be, "Not eligible for employment." In this case, do not file an ITIN, since you will have two tax numbers to identify yourself, causing untold confusion among the U.S. government authorities.

FOREIGN TAX CREDIT PLANNING

By far the most complex, least understood, yet potentially beneficial area in your move is that of foreign tax credit planning. Foreign tax credits are a dollar-for-dollar credit allowed by the IRS and the treaty to eliminate the double taxation of the same income by both the U.S. and Canada. The aim is to alleviate the U.S. taxpayer of taxes owed in the U.S. when taxes are required on the same income in Canada (or any other country). Despite its good intentions, the IRS makes it difficult to completely avoid being double taxed on the same income, for the following reasons.

- The IRS limits the amount of foreign tax credits you can use in any one year by a ratio of your U.S. income to your total world income.
- Foreign tax credits are thrown into two different "baskets" depending on the type of income they are derived from: passive (dividends, interest, etc.) or general limitation (wages and pretty much anything else not fitting in passive).
- Foreign tax credits are given a "life" of the current year when generated, one year back, and ten years to carry forward. If they are not used up in the specified time frame, they expire.

The key to good foreign tax credit planning is having a well-designed withdrawal strategy for your assets in Canada, a properly structured and ample investment portfolio in the U.S. to generate foreign income, and competent tax planning and preparation. Any income generated by the portfolio goes on your U.S. tax return, but the tax liability associated with that income is paid by the taxes withheld in Canada (which is much better than having to pay them out of pocket). This is where an experienced Canada-U.S. investment manager should be brought onto your transition team. The degree to which you are able to reduce your effective Canadian withholding rate is dependent on many factors, such as the timing of your RRSP or RRIF distributions, the size of your investment portfolio, and the amount of other foreign income you have. Foreign income can be generated within your investment portfolio, but the amount is dependent primarily on your risk tolerance and the performance of financial markets. That's why you need to be cautious of claims to "remove your RRSP from Canada at no or very low tax." In either case, the key is not to let the "tax tail wag the investment dog."

A SIMPLIFIED EXAMPLE

Assumptions

- You have C$10,000 in a Canadian junior oil stock in a taxable brokerage account.
- The Canadian stock pays a 5% dividend (C$500).
- The prevailing Canada-U.S. exchange rate is C$1 = U85¢.
- You have exited Canada and are a U.S. resident and taxpayer.

Canadian tax

- According to the Canada-U.S. Tax Treaty, the withholding on dividends is 15%.
- Therefore, C$500 x 0.15 = C$75 is remitted to CRA.

U.S. tax

- C$75 x 85¢ = U$63.75 in passive foreign tax credits on your U.S. tax return. Declare C$500 x 85¢ = U$425 as ordinary dividend income on Schedule B of your U.S. return.
- Assuming the dividend is non-qualified in the U.S. and you are in the 25% tax bracket, U$425 x 0.25 = U$106.25 tax liability.
- Use U$63.75 in foreign tax credits to offset U$106.25 in tax.
- Net out of pocket U$106.25 – U$63.75 = U$42.50 U.S. tax out of pocket.
- If not for the foreign tax credits, you would pay 25% + 15% = 40% tax on your dividend (U$170) versus 25% alone in the U.S. (U$106.25).

As you can see by this simple example, without proper understanding and accounting of the foreign tax credits, double taxation is inevitable. Many people have gone to their local CPA (unfamiliar with foreign tax credits) and ended up paying far more taxes than they were legally obligated to pay.

KEY TAX DIFFERENCES

Following are some of the key differences in the tax systems between Canada and the U.S. (see also Tables 5.9 and 5.10).

- For married couples in the U.S., you can choose married filing jointly or married filing separately when filing your tax return.
- In Canada, each person files his or her own tax return, while in the U.S. you have several filing statuses, including single, head of household, or qualifying widow.
- In Canada, common-law and same-sex marriages are accepted as a filing status, but for the U.S. federal return you must be legally married. Individuals living common law must file single at the federal level or jointly in the states where common-law marriages are recognized, as listed below.
  - Alabama
  - Colorado
  - District of Columbia
  - Georgia (if created before January 1, 1997)
  - Idaho (if created before January 1, 1996)
  - Iowa
  - Kansas
  - Montana
  - New Hampshire (for inheritance purposes only)
  - New Mexico
  - Ohio (if created before October 10, 1991)
  - Oklahoma (maybe)
  - Pennsylvania
  - Rhode Island
  - South Carolina
  - Texas (no state income tax)
  - Utah
- In Canada, your deductions are calculated as a credit against your tax liability.
- In the U.S., you deduct the higher of the basic standard

deduction the government gives to you or your "itemized" deductions (add up your mortgage interest, state income or sales taxes, property taxes, auto registration, charitable giving, etc.) from your income before arriving at your taxable income.

- In the U.S., separate tax returns are filed with the IRS and the applicable state, while in Canada you file these tax returns together and send them to the federal government (except in Quebec).

TABLE 5.9

2015 FEDERAL TAX BRACKETS

Canadian Taxable Income ($)	Per Return	U.S. Taxable Income ($)	Filing Single
0–44,701	15%	0–9,225	10%
44,702–89,401	22%	9,226–37,450	15%
89,402–138,586	26%	37,451–90,750	25%
138,587+	29%	90,751–189,300	28%
		189,301–411,500	33%
		411,501–413,200	35%
		413,201+	39.6%

TABLE 5.10

2015 DEDUCTIONS

2015 Deductions	Canada ($)	U.S. ($)
Personal amount/spousal amount	11,138/11,138	
Standard deduction/personal exemption		6,300/4,000
Mortgage interest	x	✓
Property taxes	x	✓
Auto registration	x	✓
Provincial/state or sales taxes	x	✓
Medical expenses	3% threshold	10% threshold
Charitable contributions	75% of income	50% of income
Contributions to political parties	✓	x
Safe-deposit box	✓	✓
Tuition and education	✓	✓

TABLE 5.11

2015 CREDITS

2015 Credits	Canada ($)	U.S. ($)
Child tax credit	x	1,000 per child
Foreign tax credit	✓	✓

U.S. PHASE-OUTS

With Congress finally settling on some new tax laws, it also brought back the phase-out of itemized deductions and personal exemptions for high-income taxpayers. For married couples with adjusted gross income (AGI) in excess of U$309,900 (U$258,250 for single), they will lose 2% of their personal exemption(s) for every U$2,500 of AGI above the threshold. This means married couples will lose all of their personal exemptions when their income reaches U$432,400 and filing single at U$380,750.

Itemized deductions (mortgage interest, state taxes, property taxes, charitable contributions) are reduced by 3% of the amount exceeding the same thresholds. Thankfully, there is a limit on the phase-out, and you will still be able to deduct at least 20% of your itemized deductions. These policies are part of the mindset in Congress to have the wealthiest taxpayers pay more — I thought we already had a progressive tax system for that (higher tax brackets for higher incomes?).

Now let's compare one of the most expensive tax states in the union (California) with the cheapest tax province in Canada (Alberta), using the latest data available.

TABLE 5.12

2015 PROVINCE/STATE TAX INFORMATION

Alberta Taxable Income ($)	Per Return	California Taxable Income ($)	Filing Single
0 +	10%	0–7,749 (est.)	1%
		7,750–18,371	2%
		18,372–28,995	4%
		28,996–40,250	6%

40,251–50,869	8%
50,870–259,844	9.3%
259,845–311,812	10.3%
311,813–519,687	11.3%
519,688+	12.3%

2015 Deductions	Alberta	California
Standard deduction/personal exemption	17,787	3,992/108
Mortgage interest	x	✓
Property taxes	x	✓
Auto registration	x	✓
Provincial/state taxes	x	✓
Medical expenses	3% threshold	7.5% threshold
Charitable contributions	75% of income	50% of income
Contributions to political parties	✓	x
Safe-deposit box	✓	✓

When you move to the U.S., you should familiarize yourself with the tax slips and forms in Table 5.13 so you are better prepared when it comes time to file your first tax return.

TABLE 5.13
TAX SLIPS AND FORMS

Tax Slip	Canada	U.S.
Wages/bonuses/commissions	T-4	W-2
Self-employment	T4(A)	1099-MISC
Interest	T3, T5	1099-INT
Dividends	T3, T5	1099-DIV
U.S. Social Security	T4A(P)	SSA-1099
Canada Pension Plan	T4A(P)	NR4
Old Age Security	T4A(OAS)	NR4(OAS)
Company pension	T4A	1099-R
RRIF	T4RIF	NR4
RRSP	T4RSP	NR4

Tax Form	Canada	U.S.
Personal tax return	T1	1040
Changed personal return	T1-ADJ	1040X
Capital gains/losses	Schedule 3	Schedule D
Dividends/interest	Schedule 4	Schedule B
Charitable donations	Schedule 9	Schedule A
Corporate tax return	T-2	1120
Partnership tax return	T5013	1065 or K-1
Trust tax return	T-3	1041

To see how these tax systems work compared with each other, see the comprehensive case studies in Appendices E and F of this book.

ALTERNATIVE MINIMUM TAX

Both Canada and the U.S. have an alternative minimum tax (AMT) system. In the U.S., the AMT system was brought into the tax code in 1969 to prevent high-income taxpayers, with lots of deductions, from paying no tax (hence the minimum tax). The tax policy behind the AMT is to force these people to pay some tax into the system, and the intention is similar in Canada.

For higher-income taxpayers moving to the U.S., there is a looming tax nemesis to be aware of as tax planning brings your ordinary income down. In the U.S., when your taxes are prepared, your tax situation is run through the normal 1040 tax return, and your "regular" income tax liability is calculated based on your itemized deductions, personal exemptions, and so on. This amount is compared with the amount you had withheld during the year, and a refund or balance owing is calculated. What most folks don't realize is that their tax situation is also run through IRS Form 6251 — Alternative Minimum Tax — Individuals at the same time, and they pay the higher of their regular income tax or the affectionately known "stealth tax." The problems with the AMT system are listed below.

- You don't get all of the deductions under the regular income tax system (namely, state income taxes and property taxes only).

- With higher-income taxpayers, the basic AMT exemption for 2015 of U$83,400 (for married couples)/$53,600 (for singles) is phased out.
- Up until recently, the exemption amount has not been increased with inflation or in conjunction with the exemptions given in the "regular" tax system. As a result, more and more U.S. taxpayers are getting caught in the net of the AMT. AMT rates are 26% on the first U$185,400 of AMT income for married couples and for singles, and 28% thereafter (essentially a flat tax) but the phase-out of the AMT exemption starts at U$158,900 for married and U$119,200 for single filers).

If you are a high-income taxpayer, with lots of deductions, moving to the U.S., you should be aware of the impact the AMT may have on you.

PAYROLL TAXES

Often the savings in income taxes becomes the focal point in justifying a move to the U.S. For retirees, this move has many advantages, as outlined in Chapter 8. However, if you are moving to the U.S. to resume work, you must be aware that payroll taxes in the U.S. are much higher than in Canada, potentially challenging your premise for moving to the U.S. In Canada, payroll taxes consist of Canada Pension Plan and Employment Insurance. For 2015, the Canada Pension Plan contribution is 4.95% on a maximum amount of C$53,600 in "pensionable earnings" less the basic yearly exemption of C$3,500. As a result, the maximum Canada Pension Plan contribution is C$2,479.95. In 2015, the Employment Insurance contribution rate is 1.88%, with maximum insurable earnings of C$49,500, leading to a maximum contribution of C$930.60. Combined, there is a maximum payroll tax of C$3,410.55 for 2015.

In the U.S., the first U$118,500 of your wages in 2015 is subject to the Social Security (known as FICA) contribution of 6.2%. That equals a payroll tax of $7,347 annually. You are also subject to the Medicare contribution of 1.45% with no income limitations. With the introduction of new taxes to pay for Obamacare, there is an additional 0.9% Medicare tax (for a total of 2.35%) on all wages exceeding U$250,000 for married couples (U$125,000 married filing separately) and U$200,000 filing single (or head of household). If you earn U$118,500 in U.S. income in 2015, you will pay a total of U$7,347 + U$1,718.25 = U$9,065.25 in payroll taxes compared with a maximum of C$3,410.55 in Canada. However, the benefits differ between the systems, as outlined in Chapter 8. In summary, Canadians are eligible for a maximum CPP benefit of C$12,780 annually in 2015 plus a maximum OAS benefit of C$6,764.88 annually, for a total maximum benefit of C$19,544.88 per person. Adding the OAS for a nonworking spouse, the maximum CPP and OAS benefits could be as high as C$26,309.76 for a married couple.

In the U.S., the maximum Social Security benefit you can receive is U$31,956 in 2015, and your spouse automatically qualifies for half of your amount even though they paid nothing into the system. This means the maximum Social Security benefit for a married couple in the U.S. could be as high as U$47,934. As you can see, you pay more — but you may get more!

In the U.S., it is more common to control the amount of income tax you want withheld from your paychecks. Through Form W-4 — Employee's Withholding Allowance Certificate, you are able to increase or reduce the amount of income tax withheld. The idea is to allow you to pay in the amount you are required without being forced to overpay, essentially giving the IRS an interest-free loan. Alternatively, having too little withheld (violating the IRS "safe harbor" rules) could result in underpayment penalties being assessed. The IRS wants its money when you make it; otherwise, everyone would reduce his or her withholding to zero and pay it all on April 15th (if they have it). There is no way the government could function under such a system. If you reside in a state that also has an income tax, it will have a form similar to the W-4 to enable you to adjust your state withholding as well. In Canada, Form TD1 — Personal Tax Credits Return is used to accomplish the same thing as a U.S. W-4, Form, but its use is generally reserved for when you change employers, get divorced, or face some other unique tax circumstances.

As explained earlier, the level of Social Security taxes (FICA and Medicare) payable in the U.S. is significantly higher than the Social Security taxes (CPP and EI) payable in Canada on the same level of income. For individuals moving to and working in the U.S. on a short-term assignment (not greater than five years), there can be the opportunity to opt out of paying U.S. Social Security taxes on their U.S.-source employment income. By filing CRA Form CPT56 — Certificate of Coverage under the Canada Pension Plan Pursuant to Article V of the Agreement on Social Security between Canada and the United States, an individual sent to the U.S. by his or her Canadian employer can continue to be covered by Canada Pension Plan and Employment Insurance as opposed to the U.S. Federal Insurance Contributions Act (FICA) and Medicare during their assignment in the U.S. To claim this exemption, the Canadian employer files Form CPT56 and requests a Certificate of Coverage from the Ottawa Tax Services Office, CPP/EI Rulings Division, Social Security Unit. The U.S. employer's payroll department then maintains the approved certificate. The Canadian employer files a T4 each year indicating CPP contributions with a footnote on the T4 that should read, "Filed for purposes of the Canada-U.S. Totalization Agreement." It is also recommended that if you are eligible for this exemption you attach a copy of the approved Form CPT56 with your U.S. Form 1040 on an annual basis. Please note that this exemption is available only for U.S. assignments through a Canadian employer for no longer than five years. If you are moving to the U.S. with a new or unrelated Canadian employer, this exemption is not available to you. You will lose the opportunity to qualify for U.S. Social Security and Medicare benefits, but you will be contributing to a bigger benefit in Canada, where you plan to remain. If there is a chance you may return to the U.S. at some point in the future, you may want to pay into the Social Security system in the U.S. to qualify for Medicare and Social Security benefits.

SALES TAXES

Another factor to consider in your move is state sales taxes. In Canada, there is the Goods and Services Tax (GST) of 5% which is a federal sales tax. There may also be a provincial sales tax (PST, except for Alberta), which can easily add another 8%. This is a total of 13% in additional sales taxes on most items purchased. In Ontario, New Brunswick, Newfoundland and Labrador, Nova Scotia, and PEI, there is the Harmonized Sales Tax

(HST), which essentially combines the GST and PST. The problem with the HST (and why it was repealed in BC) is that it adds a provincial sales tax to items that are subject to GST but were not under PST. Examples include gasoline/diesel and services (haircuts, advisory services . . . yikes!). Believe it or not, most folks residing in Canada and the U.S. end up paying more taxes to their local governments than they do to their federal governments. When you take into account property taxes (generally lower in the U.S.), sales taxes (gas, alcohol, tobacco), license fees (motor vehicle, hunting/fishing), and income/estate taxes, you typically end up paying over half of your tax bill to your local state and province. In the U.S., there is no federal sales tax like the GST, but most states have a sales tax that ranges from 4% to 6%, similar to most provinces. In addition, most municipal governments have a sales tax that typically ranges from 0% to 7%. The amounts of these taxes depend on what state and county you reside in when you move to the U.S.

SHOW ME 6
THE MONEY

For the love of money is a root of all kinds of evil.
— 1 TIMOTHY 6:10

This chapter aims to clear up some of the misconceptions about exchanging money and to provide some insights into overcoming a seemingly difficult issue for some folks. When making the transition to the U.S., you will have to convert your Canadian loonies to American dollars at some point. The technical term, cash management, deals specifically with matters related to your net worth (assets less your debts), currency exchange, and cash inflows/outflows. In our experience, assets on both sides of the border lead to a lot of complexity and inconvenience, so we generally recommend that you try to consolidate all of your assets on the U.S. side of the border where prudent. There can be some other hidden landmines in keeping assets in Canada, particularly if they remain in Canadian loonies. Here are some items to consider in the area of cash management when making the transition to the U.S.

CURRENCY EXCHANGE FACTS AND MYTHS

Ask most Canadians, and they can tell you within a penny or two what the current Canadian-American exchange rate is. In our opinion, some of Canada's national pride rises and falls in relation to the exchange rate of the Canadian loonie versus the U.S. dollar. Nowhere have we dealt with more confusion or deliberation of decisions than the area of currency exchange. This section aims to clear up some misconceptions and confusion so you can begin to move forward with confidence in this area. With the meteoric rise of the Canadian loonie against the U.S. dollar over the past few years and, recently, the rapid decline, there are calls to peg the Canadian loonie to the U.S. dollar or to create a common currency in North America similar to the euro. As of this writing, it appears the record-high closing rate for the Canadian dollar occurred on November 7, 2007, at $1.0905, with the record low closing set on January 18, 2002, at $0.6199 (a 76% increase in six years).

MYTH: YOU LOSE MONEY WHEN YOU CONVERT

One of the biggest misconceptions is that you lose money when you exchange Canadian loonies for U.S. dollars. Nothing could be further from the truth. The thinking goes, if you lose money during currency exchange, there must be ways of making money too! On one day, the following exchange rates were observed.

> $1 Canadian
> = € 0.7124 Euro
> = $ 0.862 U.S. dollar
> = $ 6.683 Hong Kong dollar
> = $ 98.52 Jamaican dollar

The first thing to notice is that most of these countries use the "dollar" as the name for their currency, and therein lies the problem. Because the currency has the same name, people assume it should have the same value. It does not. This is because they are different currencies, from different countries, with a different value associated with each one. A British pound sterling is different from a U.S. dollar, which is different from the European euro, which is different from a Canadian loonie. Different currencies from different countries (even if they have the same name) have different values ascribed to them by the supply and demand of a particular country's currency in the world. If you stop thinking about Canadian dollars and start calling them Canadian loonies, then you'll be better able to deal with the currency exchange issue.

To further illustrate the point, suppose you exchange one Canadian loonie for one U.S. dollar. According to the example above, you will receive U$0.862 for your Canadian loonie. People believe that, since they are getting 13.8¢ less, they have "lost" money. If that argument holds true, if you take your Canadian dollar and exchange it into Jamaican dollars, you'll "make" $98.52! If you exchange just over 10,150 Canadian loonies, you could become a millionaire in Jamaica! But we all know a Jamaican millionaire is a lot different from a Canadian millionaire, who is different from an American millionaire. Consider as well, if you were to convert your U$0.862 right back into Canadian loonies the next day, how much would you receive? You're right, pretty much one Canadian loonie (less any transaction fee), so where did you lose money in the currency exchange? And where did you gain money?

The real issue is the difference in living expenses that you will incur in the U.S. versus Canada. If the expenses (food, shelter, taxes, gas, autos, health care, etc.) are lower in the U.S. and your currency conversion leaves you with fewer dollars in your pocket, then the currency exchange may be inconsequential because you have lower living expenses in the U.S. for the same lifestyle. We all know it is cheaper to live in Jamaica, but you have to look at the other aspects of the lifestyle to get some insight into whether becoming a millionaire in Jamaica is worthwhile.

The other factor that comes into play is the fluctuation in exchange rates over time. For example, if you have a fixed Canadian pension, you could face a loss of purchasing power in the U.S. if the Canadian-U.S. exchange rate declines. This is particularly true if your Canadian pension is your primary source of income.

MYTH: SOMEONE KNOWS WHERE THE EXCHANGE RATE IS GOING

We don't know how many times people have asked for our opinion on where the Canadian-U.S. exchange rate is going. The resounding answer is that we have no idea, but in our view, "a bird in the hand is better than 1.01 birds in the bush." First, as seen in Figure 6.1, waiting for a better exchange rate has been the wrong thing to do as of late. There are some people who are still waiting for the loonie to reach parity again and are now sitting on $0.81 dollars. Second, who knew this would be the case? Research has shown that even the most prudent currency traders, economists, and investment managers can't make successful predictions over any extended period of time. If they could, they wouldn't tell you, and they would no longer need to make predictions — they would have more money than they had ever dreamed of getting.

FIGURE 6.1

CANADA-U.S. EXCHANGE RATES, 1973–2014

Canada-U.S. Exchange Rates 1973 to 2014

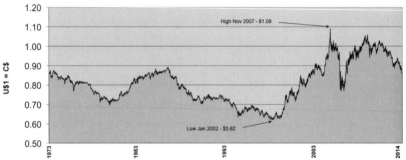

A number of factors influence the Canada-U.S. exchange rates and make it impossible to predict with any consistency where the rate is going over the long term. The causes of currency exchange fluctuations are what economists love to talk about at parties. We have limited knowledge in this area and offer you the following key factors that the experts agree influence the Canadian-U.S. exchange rate:

- the difference in inflation rates between Canada and the U.S.;
- the difference in productivity performance;
- the tax system and the tax burden imposed on the citizens of each country;
- the difference in interest rates;
- the difference in nonenergy commodity prices;
- the difference in trade and current account balances;
- the difference in fiscal balances;
- the economic growth prospects of each country;
- the political issues and political stability in each country; and
- the need to borrow money by each government.

Despite all of this economist jargon, the bottom line is, whichever currency is more desired by the world, that currency will enjoy a higher exchange rate. It is simple supply and demand, and the world wants U.S. dollars more than it wants Canadian loonies at this time. Canadian economists have often theorized about how to fix the problem, including abandoning the floating currency and adopting the U.S. currency whole-sale, "pegging" the Canadian dollar to the U.S. dollar, or forming a North American "dollar" with the U.S. and Mexico. We will leave all of this to the economists, but the question to ask is, "What do we do now?"

If you will need U.S. dollars in the future, be sure you have U.S. dollars available, and put the "currency speculating" aside. Likewise, if you need Canadian dollars in the future, be sure you keep some Canadian dollars to meet that need. We have seen folks compromise their U.S. retirement plans because they decided to currency speculate and leave their money in Canadian loonies when they had an ongoing permanent need for U.S. dollars. They watched their retirement nest eggs decline significantly and kept hoping for the Canadian loonie to bounce back. This unintended overconsumption of their Canadian-loonie retirement assets could have long-term effects on their financial security.

Even though we don't know where the currency rate is going, we do know the Canada-U.S. exchange rate fluctuates about 100 basis points every day. If you need to exchange currency at some point in the future, be aware that there are some currency exchange tools available that you may want to consider using to take advantage of the normal fluctuations in the exchange rate. For example, if you have a purchase you need to make in the short term but want to buy at the lower end of the daily fluctuation, you may want to make a "currency bid" with your currency broker. A currency bid is an agreement to purchase a certain amount of foreign currency at a fixed price sometime in the future. This scheme will allow you to avoid the current spot rate and make a bid to purchase the currency at the lower end of the daily fluctuation. The problem is if the currency exchange is in an upward pattern, your bid may never get filled. A currency bid can be put out for a maximum of 30 days and canceled or amended at any time with no penalty. Another tool available is a forward contract, an agreement to purchase a certain amount of foreign currency at some point in the future at a rate set today. This is for those that know they are going to need foreign currency in the future to fund a purchase and want to lock in the exchange rate now. The saying "a bird in the hand is better than two in the bush" is reflected by a forward contract because it can be set for up to a year in advance. The drawback is there is an expense in the currency rate you receive the further out you want the contract to go.

Nobody can predict the future, and it is really our emotions that are driving our decisions . . . and this spells trouble. For example, when we ask, "What rate does the exchange have to achieve for you to convert?" we typically get an off-the-cuff answer. Sure enough, when that exchange rate arrives, the decision to wait for an even better rate is made, and the tendency is to ride the exchange rate back down again. Soon your life revolves around the currency exchange section of the newspaper, and your mood for the day is dictated by what happened in currency exchange markets overnight. Is this any way to live? What a way to spend your golden years . . . glued to the newspaper watching the exchange rates (or the stock market, for that matter).

MYTH: WAIT TO CONVERT

Often people struggle with deciding when to convert their Canadian loonies into U.S. dollars, and "waiting for a better exchange rate" is the game they decide to play. The typical thinking is you can do better if you wait. What many don't realize is they have just made a prediction — the exchange rate will improve by the time you need to exchange loonies into dollars. You have now entered the realm of currency speculation, and frankly there are better ways of speculating on the currency exchange direction, such as buying currency futures contracts. Besides, there are currency traders with millions of dollars and all kinds of equipment monitoring global currency markets in the hope of conducting currency transactions to pay their bills. If there is money to be made in currency speculation, many others will make it ahead of you. So how do you determine when to convert?

The decision to convert should be determined by what you are trying to achieve (your personal goals and objectives). If you are moving to the U.S. permanently to retire, never to return to Canada, you will have an ongoing need for U.S. dollars, and it may make sense to convert your loonies now because you know with certainty what the exchange rate is today and how much you'll end up with. If the current exchange rate is sufficient now and the long-term projections of your financial situation in the U.S. show a high probability of your assets lasting your lifetime, why not exchange now, avoid any currency speculation, and get on with your life? Why not just do it now and avoid the other issues that come with leaving assets in Canada — such as the potential for double probate, double estate and income taxes, etc. — as outlined in the other chapters of this book? At a minimum, understand the sensitivity of your financial situation to currency exchange fluctuations and make an informed decision. A prudent, deliberate, ongoing strategy of currency exchanges over a period of time may make the most sense in your situation. Your financial plan provides the guidepost for your decision making because, without it, important decisions such as exchanging your loonies are driven by emotions, not sound financial reasons. The time to exchange your assets is when you can achieve your desired lifestyle per your financial plan. This approach allows you to remove the currency fluctuations from your retirement projections.

Exchanging your Canadian loonies to U.S. dollars can be an emotional experience, but your Canada-U.S. transition planner can help you make the decision that is right for you. You want to avoid currency exchange whenever possible because you have to pay the currency exchange broker or bank (see below). Therefore, it may make sense to leave some funds in a Canadian bank account if you plan on making regular trips to Canada for the summer, to visit friends and family, and so on (see our companion book *The American in Canada*). As long as you leave a nominal amount for convenience purposes only, it shouldn't be considered a "tax tie" by CRA.

FACT: HOW TO CALCULATE EXCHANGE RATES

Another misconception we often encounter involves the calculation of exchange rates. Typically, when C$1 = U85¢, folks think that C$1.15 = U$1, which is simply not the case. Here is how currency exchange calculations work:

- If C$1 = U85¢, you have to take 1 divided by 0.85 to find the reverse currency. Specifically, 1/0.85 = $1.176, which means when C$1 = U85¢, U$1 = C$1.176.

To make it easier on yourself, take the price of an item and divide it by the appropriate exchange rate to determine how much it will cost in your desired currency. For example:

- A sombrero at the premium outlet mall in Chandler, Arizona, costs U$11: 11/0.85 = C$12.94;
- A toque at West Edmonton Mall, Alberta, costs C$11: 11/1.176 = U$9.35.

FACT: THERE IS AN EXPENSE TO CONVERTING

Although, as we previously discussed, you don't lose money when you convert Canadian loonies into U.S. dollars, there is a transaction expense that you need to be aware of. Financial institutions "shade" the "spot" rate of the Canada-U.S. exchange rate and use it as another source of profit for shareholders. You can tell by comparing the exchange rate online or in the newspaper (the spot rates in the market) with those posted at your local bank or at the "currency exchange carts" at the airport. The difference can be significant. Understand that this service is unregulated and a huge source of profits for the banks. In some cases, using your Canadian credit card in the U.S. for purchases in U.S. dollars may be better or worse. By shading the exchange rate on your purchases in the U.S. or applying additional fees, the credit card companies make a small fortune, and you may have no idea. The next time you get your credit card statement, look for any additional fees or the rate the company exchanged your purchase at, and then locate the historical rate — you may grimace. We encourage you to be informed beforehand.

Here are some things you can do to reduce the expense of converting your Canadian loonies into U.S. dollars.

- Ask your currency exchange provider to give you a rate as close to the current spot rate as possible (don't prevent the provider from making a living, but make sure you aren't getting gouged). The spot rate is what the market is paying at that moment, when the currency exchange is not shaded at all.
- Accumulate your loonies together and convert them in one lump sum rather than making several smaller transactions,

because bigger transactions generally get a better exchange rate.

- Determine the expenses associated with using your Canadian-dollar credit card for U.S.-dollar purchases, and if prohibitive avoid using your Canadian-dollar credit card at all; find a credit card company that issues U.S.-dollar cards instead so you can control the exchange rate better rather than taking the prevailing rate the credit card company decides for that day.
- Avoid using your bank unless you have a good relationship with it; then ask your banker to give you the spot rate or something as close to it as possible.
- Avoid the currency exchange carts in airports or be sure to compare their rates to a discount currency broker or the spot rate in the newspaper or online whenever possible.
- Avoid converting cash since doing so is more expensive. Consider traveler's checks, bank drafts, money orders, or personal checks instead (but watch when you cross the border with such instruments in excess of $10,000 — see Chapter 4, "Moving Your Stuff").
- Make sure you do comparative shopping, particularly if you are exchanging large sums.
- If you have an account at a Canadian brokerage firm, it may offer you competitive exchange rates as part of its customer service to you, particularly if you already have a U.S.-dollar account.
- U.S. casinos typically provide excellent exchange rates in the hope you will leave some of your money in their machines or at their tables.
- Unless you go to the casinos, don't typically wait until you get to the U.S. to exchange your currency. Most U.S. banks will not convert your Canadian loonies to U.S. dollars. However, banks in the U.S. owned by a Canadian bank are more inclined to offer this service to their clients.
- Leave sufficient U.S. dollars in the U.S. to meet your currency needs each year or, as mentioned previously, enough Canadian dollars in Canada to meet your needs there.

MORTGAGES

There are huge differences in mortgages between Canada and the U.S., and they clearly favor the U.S. Since buying a home is typically the single largest purchase you will make in your lifetime, getting the right mortgage should be of primary consideration as well. Make sure you get the right mortgage with the right terms from the right (read honest) mortgage broker versus a captive agent at a bank.

AMORTIZATION

In Canada, the typical mortgage is amortized over 25 years, while it is 15 or 30 years in the U.S. A 30-year mortgage will obviously lower your monthly payments from a 15-year mortgage, but which mortgage you select in the U.S. depends on your individual circumstances. There are a number of other loan options (e.g., adjustable rate) to consider besides these conventional loans that may better suit your goals and objectives.

FIXED INTEREST RATE

In Canada, the typical mortgage fixes your interest rate for up to five years (at an increasingly higher interest rate), and then it is adjusted to the prevailing rate when it matures. You are required to bear the risk of any interest rate changes. This is where a U.S. mortgage has a big advantage over those in Canada, because you can fix your interest rate for the full 15- or 30-year amortization — the bank bears the interest rate risk. This can make a huge difference in stabilizing one of your largest debts over the long term. The other nice thing with mortgages in the U.S. is if rates decline significantly at any point, you can refinance your mortgage and lock it in for another 15 or 30 years at an even lower rate, lowering your monthly payments even further. In addition, mortgages in the U.S. use simple interest calculations, while in Canada interest is compounded semiannually. This means you will pay more interest in the U.S. if you make the minimum payment for the entire term of the mortgage, but you will pay less if you ever get in arrears, because there is no interest on the interest, as there is in Canada. Likewise, U.S. lenders will typically charge a late fee for payments made in arrears, while these fees are typically prohibited in Canada.

One thing we have noticed many times with Canadians moving to the U.S. is they justify a much larger mortgage than they otherwise would consider because it is deductible. Indeed, mortgage interest in the U.S. is deductible if your individual tax situation permits it (your itemized deductions aren't phased out), but be sure you understand exactly how it works. If you have a 7% mortgage and you are in the 25% marginal tax bracket, it means that for every $1 you give to the bank in interest the IRS gives you 25¢ back. Notice that you are still out of pocket 75¢. We have an even better deal: you give us $1, and we'll give you 99¢ back. We'll do that all day long, but who will end up with all of your money? Your mortgage is still an out-of-pocket expense to you.

We also see the strategy of investing the mortgage amount, rather than paying off the mortgage, to get a better return. Your after-tax mortgage rate can be calculated as $7 \times (1 - 0.25) = 5.25\%$. The argument goes, "I should be able to do better than 5.25% in the markets, so I'll get a bigger mortgage, make the minimum payments, and maximize my investments." The flaw in this argument is you can do better than 5.25% in the markets. If your money goes into a tax-deferred vehicle, the benchmark is 5.25%. But what if your money is in a taxable brokerage account and you get a return of 7%? You will have to pay taxes on the interest earned, so guess what — you are no further ahead. If you invest the money for capital gains, which can be taxed more favorably (flat 15%), you have to remember that markets don't go straight up. If you take a bigger mortgage so you can watch your portfolio go up, your business case falls apart if the markets go down (we saw this with the popping of the tech bubble in 2000 and more recently the real estate bubble).

PREPAYMENTS

Here is another area that makes U.S. mortgages far superior to Canadian mortgages. Most U.S. mortgages have no prepayment penalties, while Canadian financial institutions typically impose penalties for prepayments, restrict them to the loan anniversary, or simply do not allow any prepayments at all. In the U.S., you can send in as much additional money above your monthly mortgage payment as you wish, and it all gets applied to the principal. This means you can pay off your mortgage whenever you have the funds to do so (if you get a conventional mortgage). Many Canadians often set up biweekly payment schedules on their U.S. mortgages because it is an effective strategy in Canada to pay off your mortgage sooner. In the U.S., you have to be careful: U.S. financial institutions are often happy to oblige with a similar plan because there are many hidden costs and fees. This approach typically doesn't make sense; you can accomplish the same thing by making an extra payment on your mortgage per year.

DOWN PAYMENTS

To purchase a home in Canada, you are required to put 25% or more down to avoid paying for mortgage insurance from the Canada Mortgage and Housing Corporation (CMHC). In the U.S., the requirement is only 20% to avoid paying for mortgage insurance from the Federal Housing Authority (FHA) or a private insurer such as Fannie Mae. Depending on your situation, there are ways of structuring your mortgage to avoid the mortgage insurance while putting less than 20% down.

CLOSING COSTS

It has been our experience that closing costs in Canada are typically higher than those in the U.S. In particular, lender fees in the U.S. are around U$400 versus C$1,000 in Canada. In addition, legal fees and land title fees are seen in the closing costs in Canada but not in the U.S. However, you typically don't need a termite inspection fee in Canada! The other difference when closing on a house in Canada is that you typically use an attorney to handle the transaction. In the U.S., you use a title company almost exclusively to complete the transaction, and title insurance is a good thing. Note that realtor commissions are generally higher in the U.S. In Canada, the typical commission is 6% on the first C$100,000 and then 3% on the balance. In the U.S. it is typically a flat 6%. This is why there are many firms popping up that will help you sell for a flat fee or a reduced rate.

POINTS

You will see points only in the U.S., and they can offer substantial benefits if planned correctly. There are three types of points: discount points, loan origination points, and seller paid points. Discount points allow you to "buy down" the interest rate on your mortgage. A point is typically 1% of the loan amount and can reduce your interest rate by one-eighth or so. This gives you more flexibility in creating a mortgage that works for you. Origination points, on the other hand, are fees charged by the lender for the evaluation, preparation, and submission of your mortgage loan application (typically "junk" fees). There are also seller paid points to provide an incentive to buyers by offering a discount of a certain percent on the sale of a home. The important thing to note is that points may be deductible on your U.S. tax return, so careful planning here can provide an added benefit to you in getting the house you want with terms beneficial to you.

IMPOUND (ESCROW) ACCOUNTS

Impound accounts are another item seen only in the U.S. There, the mortgage lender will automatically roll your homeowner insurance and property taxes into your monthly payment so they can be "pre-collected." The insurance company or local government sends the bill directly to the mortgage company, which pays the money out of your escrow/impound account. The rationale behind these accounts is that, since the mortgage company owns 80% or more of your home, it can legally ensure the property taxes are paid and the home is protected in the event of fire or some other catastrophe. The company collects the money for these items in advance as part of your monthly mortgage payment and earns interest on it until the money is due. However, the bank is usually willing to reduce your interest rate if you use the impound accounts — a convenience that is hard to beat.

APPLYING FOR A MORTGAGE

In qualifying for a mortgage, things can get a little tricky (see "Establishing a Credit Rating" below). First, be sure to provide copies of your RRSP statements and other investment accounts you have in Canada (or the U.S.) to your mortgage broker or bank, who should take this into account in the underwriting process. It helps to have a letter of introduction from your banker in Canada that outlines your mortgage and line of credit history with the bank and your history of repaying borrowed amounts. You should also have a letter typed up by your mortgage broker outlining your Social Insurance Number in Canada and your Social Security number in the U.S. so they can match up the two records. In the letter, request the broker contact the Canadian credit agencies to get a full credit report from Canada. Your Canadian credit rating should satisfy the U.S. mortgage underwriter and result in a favorable interest rate and mortgage terms for you. Thankfully, some Canadian banks have acquired banks in the U.S. that can better handle your needs for a mortgage (see Canadian-friendly companies later in this chapter).

ESTABLISHING A CREDIT RATING

Many Canadians with an excellent credit rating in Canada move to the U.S. and are shocked when utility companies want payment in advance before starting service, they can't get a U.S. credit card, or they can't qualify for a mortgage. Don't take it personally; this is common because you don't have any kind of credit rating tied to your Social Security number with the U.S. credit agencies. To resolve this problem, there are some things you can do in anticipation of your move.

FICO SCORE

FICO stands for Fair Isaac & Co., the Minnesota-based firm that created this scoring system in the early 1950s and updated to the FICO®8 Score in 2009. These scores range from 300 to 850 and gauge the level of your credit risk (the higher the score, the less risky you are to extend credit to, and the lower the interest rate offered). A score under 620 is considered high risk or "subprime," and it's likely you won't be extended any credit. The score is created by giving different weights to the various criteria in your financial situation and is comprised of the following:

- 35% — your payment history (paying your bills on time);
- 30% — amounts owed (your total debt outstanding);
- 15% — length of credit history (yours will be short);

- 10% — new credit (recently applied for or issued debt);
- 10% — the type of credit used (mortgage versus auto loan versus credit card).

In the 1990s, mortgage lenders started using the score to rate prospective customers, and then in 1999 California passed a law requiring the lenders and the three national credit bureaus (Experian, TransUnion, and Equifax) to disclose your credit score to you. Today your credit score is used by most Canadian and American lenders to make instant decisions on extending credit to you, but this has led to increased credit-reporting errors that have negatively impacted innocent people's credit scores. As a result, the federal government recently mandated that all three credit-reporting agencies have to provide a free credit report annually upon request, and we recommend you take advantage of it to review and monitor your credit rating. You can get a host of information on your credit at the U.S. Government consumer website at usa.gov/topics/money/credit/credit-reports/bureaus-scoring.shtml.

BEFORE YOU APPLY

Before you start the process of establishing a credit rating in the U.S., you need to have a Social Security number, which you will need for every credit application you complete (see Chapter 5 on how to obtain one). Note that an Individual Taxpayer Identification Number (ITIN) will not do since it is viewed as a temporary number not typically eligible for credit purposes. In desperation, some folks start applying for credit cards at every bank, department store, or gas station, anywhere to get some form of credit. They don't realize that they may actually be damaging their credit rating. Each credit application you make is reported to the credit-reporting agencies in the U.S. and reduces your credit rating (new-credit component). They think you are getting desperate for money and are applying wherever you can to keep yourself afloat. If your applications are subsequently rejected, your credit rating will sink even lower. This means that, when you are approved for a mortgage, for example, you will have to pay a higher interest rate because you are perceived as being a higher credit risk (i.e., your FICO score is low). Table 6.1 shows how your FICO score can affect your monthly payments for a $216,000 fixed rate mortgage for a 30-year term.

TABLE 6.1

FICO Score	Interest Rate	Monthly Payment
760–850	6.14%	$1,315
700–759	6.36%	$1,346
680–699	6.54%	$1,371
660–679	6.76%	$1,402
640–659	7.19%	$1,464
620–639	7.73%	$1,545
	1.59% difference	$2,760 difference annually

TRANSFER YOUR CREDIT RATING

We have seen some success in transferring a credit rating to the U.S. by using your current Canadian credit card to apply for and secure a new credit card with the U.S. subsidiary of the same company. I did this with American Express in 1996 when I moved to the U.S. from Canada. However, prepare yourself because this tactic will typically take many phone calls to both the Canadian and the U.S. sides of your credit card company before you are successful in moving your credit rating and membership rewards points (exchanged at the prevailing exchange rate) to the U.S. The beauty of this strategy is it allows you to get an instant credit rating with your desired credit card in the U.S. based on your credit rating established in Canada, and you don't lose any of your membership points.

APPLYING FOR A CREDIT CARD

When you apply for a credit card, it's best to do so in person with an officer at the bank of your choice. The bank may tell you it isn't necessary since this is a routine process, but tell the bank you are new in the country and have an established credit rating in Canada it will need to obtain. You'll be surprised at how familiar most U.S. banks, owned by a Canadian bank, are with this process, so it should go smoothly. To prepare for this meeting, gather the following.

- Letter of reference: get a letter of reference signed by your bank manager in Canada that lists all of your credit transactions with that bank (mortgages, credit lines, etc.) and your history in paying on time, never defaulting, etc. This letter carries a lot of weight in the process, especially since the U.S. institution can call the bank manager in Canada and verify everything.
- SSN/SIN: have original Social Security and Social Insurance cards available. Instruct the loan officer to use your Social Insurance Number to contact the Canadian credit-reporting agencies to obtain a Canadian credit report. Equifax and TransUnion (see below) are credit-reporting agencies located in both Canada and the U.S., but their systems are separate, and it has been our experience that they rarely, if ever, talk to each other.
- Identification: be sure to provide an original passport or birth certificate to verify who you are.
- Credit card: take your current Canadian credit card with you so the institution can make copies and verify your existing credit history.
- Pay stubs: if applicable, take both your Canadian pay stubs and your current U.S. pay stub if you have one. You should also take your employment offer letter, stating your starting salary in the U.S.
- Deposit: it helps a lot if you have a U.S. bank draft for some amount that you are ready to deposit into your bank account when opened. You will typically get a higher level of service because the loan application officer is more motivated if you have money deposited with the institution. You'll most likely be able to secure a bank credit card at the time of your deposit as well.
- Company credit union: if you move to the U.S. to work with a large employer, it may have its own credit union set up (e.g., the Motorola Employees' Credit Union). This may be a good starting place to establish credit since credit unions tend to view you as a better credit risk since you are an employee of a large, established employer.

You will need to fill out the standard credit card application with the bank to start the process. Be sure a copy of all the information above is attached to the application along with a letter signed by the loan application officer requesting a Canadian credit bureau check be done as well. This letter should clearly outline your Social Security Number and Social Insurance Number so that the appropriate match is made when your credit reports come in. Also ensure your previous Canadian address(es) are on the application form and in the letter. All of this information should allow the bank to issue a credit card to you with a healthy limit and low interest rates. As you begin using it, be sure to pay off your balances in a timely fashion to start establishing a credit rating in the U.S. You should obtain a copy of your U.S. credit report at least annually from the three primary credit-reporting agencies for the first few years to confirm that your credit rating is getting established in the U.S.

CANADIAN-FRIENDLY COMPANIES

It has been our experience that there is more success with American Express (call New Accounts — Special Handling at 1-800-453-2639) than with Visa and MasterCard when transferring your credit card to the U.S. subsidiary. We have also confirmed that First National Bank of Omaha (Customer Service 1-800-688-7070) has figured out there is a market for Canadians moving to the U.S. First National appears to know how to obtain a Canadian credit report and is willing to issue a U.S. credit card even while you are still in Canada. When moving to the U.S., just inform First National of your new address; your account and credit rating already exists with them in the U.S. Many of the Canadian banks, such as Toronto Dominion (owns TD Bank in the U.S., formerly TD Bank North), Bank of Montreal (owns Harris Bank), and Royal Bank of Canada (owns RBC Centura), are good starting places for Canadians to obtain a credit card or secure a mortgage. Because these companies have locations on both sides of the border, they tend to have a better idea of how to obtain a Canadian credit report and give it its due weight in the underwriting process. There are two Canadian credit-reporting agencies they will need to contact: Equifax Canada (1-800-465-7166 or consumer.equifax.ca) and TransUnion (1-800-663-9980 or tuc.ca). If you have a Canadian-friendly company you have dealt with, please let us know (book@transitionfinancial.com), and we will be sure to include it in the next edition of this book or on our website at transitionfinancial.com.

7 TILL DEATH DO US PART

*Man is destined to die once
and then the judgment.*
— HEBREWS 9:27

By far the most neglected area we see with folks making the transition to the U.S. is will and estate planning. Unfortunately, the judgment of your estate plan won't come to light until after you can no longer do anything about it. Many Canadians mistakenly believe they should get their Canadian wills updated before their move to the U.S., but your simple Canadian will just won't cut it in the U.S. When moving to the U.S., wills and estates become much more complex, particularly when property spans both countries and non-U.S. citizenship issues are added. The use of more sophisticated estate planning techniques, such as trusts, is more common in the U.S. because of the complex estate and gift tax rules and the fact that trusts are a "flow-through" entity for tax purposes. We received a call from a desperate estate planning attorney in California. A man of substantial wealth living in the U.S. had suddenly passed away, and his widow, living in Canada, had no access to any funds to pay the family's bills. The man had a simple Canadian will, but most of the accounts had been frozen in both Canada and the U.S. because they were in his name only. Needless to say, it was a difficult situation at an already stressful time. In our opinion, estate planning is the most important area of planning you can do for yourself and your family. Consider the following questions.

- Is your Canadian will valid in the U.S.?
- What would happen to your spouse and dependents if you died suddenly in the U.S.?
- Will your spouse be able to get access to any funds to meet family obligations?
- What taxes would you pay in the U.S. and/or Canada in the event of your death?
- What would happen to your assets in Canada? Those in the U.S.?
- Can your heirs in Canada receive any of your assets?
- Who would care for your children if you and your spouse died simultaneously?
- Who would file your taxes, pay your bills, or care for your children in the event of your incapacity?
- In the event that you end up in a coma, will you want the "plug pulled"? How will that decision be communicated?
- Will you want your body buried or cremated? In Canada or the U.S.?
- If you inherit assets from Canada, are they taxed? Where?

Estate planning is all about how much control you want in a variety of circumstances, including death and incapacity. A secondary consideration is saving every court cost, attorney fee, and tax possible. Sometimes we hear "If I'm dead, I'm dead. What do I care?" If you don't want to determine the course of events in the situations listed above (don't want to spend the money to get an estate plan), your state of residence (or province where the asset is located) has default laws called intestate laws (intestate literally means to "die without a will") that will decide for you, and your estate will incur the attendant costs and delays that come with having no control. However, most people, when presented with the options, aren't content to let anybody but them decide what to do with what has taken a lifetime to accumulate, their health-care decisions, or their bodies. A U.S. estate plan is needed. You just need to consider the cost of a U.S. estate plan as part of the overall expense of moving to the U.S.

Estate planning for Canadians relocating to the U.S. can be extremely complex. It deserves much more attention than this book can provide because some areas have been tested in U.S. and Canadian courts, there are some gray areas, and some scenarios have yet to be played out. We recommend you use a qualified Canada-U.S. estate planning attorney to get the appropriate counseling to determine what estate planning documents you need to achieve the level of control you want. How much counseling will you get with a downloaded do-it-yourself will or trust kit? In our experience, the majority of U.S. estate planning attorneys have no idea of the complexity involved when planning for the Canadian in America. The estate planning attorney drafts the documents; once they are completed and executed, most folks sit back, let out a sigh, and take comfort that their estate plans are done. Unfortunately, it's a false sense of security because there is much to do in implementing your estate plan. Assets need to be re-titled, documents need to be filed where they can be retrieved easily, and those having a role in your estate plan need to be briefed on your intentions. In our biased opinion, a team approach with an experienced Canada-U.S. transition planner as the quarterback is generally your best option.

TAXES AT DEATH

CANADA

Many people wrongfully assume there is no estate or death tax in Canada. They simply aren't aware of the "deemed disposition tax" in Canada that occurs at one's death. Similar to the departure tax when you leave Canada, this tax kicks in when you die and applies to your worldwide assets. At the first spouse's death, things such as RRSPs/RRIFs can be rolled over to the surviving spouse to continue their tax deferral (provided the surviving spouse is named as the beneficiary on the RRSP/RRIF account). However, at the second spouse's passing, you must report on your Canadian T1 tax return the full value of your RRSPs, the capital gains in all investment real estate (including those properties in the U.S.), stocks or bonds, shares of your small business, plus any other income realized in the year of death. Needless to say, with Canadian income tax rates in some provinces reaching 48% or more, this can be a significant tax burden on your estate, particularly if you have illiquid assets. In addition to the federal tax burden, the provinces get their share of the proceeds plus a variety of additional probate fees that they levy individually (although they are fairly nominal and are coming under some legal scrutiny as of late). Probate fees alone aren't that expensive, but when an attorney is brought in to sort out the complexities, the expense can go up significantly, particularly since the probate process can last a year or more in certain provinces.

Once you are in the U.S. and a non-resident of Canada, the Canadian death tax situation changes a bit. Unfortunately, you are still subject to the deemed disposition at death, but it is at Canada Income Tax Act or Canada-U.S. Tax Treaty rates and is only on your Canadian assets, not your worldwide estate. For example, RRSPs/RRIFs are subject to a flat 25% withholding tax per the Income Tax Act because they are distributed at the second spouse's death. Canadian investment property is deemed disposed of as well, and a T1 tax return must be filed to declare any capital gains and ensuing income taxes paid to CRA.

UNITED STATES

For anyone moving to the U.S., the myriad of taxes at your passing needs to be considered carefully. There can be up to five different taxes at your death, including estate taxes, gift taxes, generation-skipping transfer taxes, state death taxes, and federal/state income taxes. Most of these are cumulative taxes and, without the proper forethought and estate plan in place, could result in the loss of the bulk of your estate. As you can see in Table 7.1, with no or improper estate planning, these taxes can be more punitive than the deemed disposition tax at death in Canada.

TABLE 7.1

ESTATE DEPLETION OF THE RICH AND FAMOUS

	Gross Estate	Settlement Costs	Shrinkage
Walt Disney	$23,004,851	$6,811,943	30%
Alwin C. Ernst, CPA	$12,642,431	$7,124,112	56%
J.P. Morgan	$17,121,482	$11,893,691	69%
Elvis Presley	$10,165,434	$7,374,635	73%
John D. Rockefeller, Jr.	$160,598,584	$24,965,954	16%

Settlement costs include the estate taxes, court fees, legal and accounting fees, probate fees, and so on that go into settling these estates after death. Your first line of defense in taking control of your financial affairs no matter what happens to you (death or incapacity) and reducing the settlement costs is a full "trust-centered" estate plan, which is discussed below. Even though Rockefeller's estate was the largest, he was able to keep more of his estate through proper estate planning and by including charitable gifting as part of his plan. A brief discussion of each of these five potential taxes at death is outlined below.

1. Estate Taxes

The estate-tax regime has endured a number of changes over the past number of years, making will and trust planning very difficult. However, on January 2, 2013, President Obama signed the American Taxpayer Relief Act, which provided some very favorable changes and likely some permanence to the rules (would that be asking too much?). This will allow much better planning and a more fair and reasonable approach to U.S. estate planning in the years to come.

The IRS manages the estate-tax system, and you have to understand that your worldwide net worth (including all of your assets in Canada) is included in the estate-tax calculation. This includes items such as:

- the value of any life insurance proceeds payable to the estate, or from policies owned or controlled by the deceased, including policies where the deceased transferred ownership and all control within three years prior to death;
- any gifted assets (exceeding any applicable gift tax exemptions) transferred during your life;
- the transfer of any assets where you retain an interest for your life or the right to change or terminate the transfer;
- the commuted value of a monthly corporate pension that continues to your beneficiary at your death;
- assets that are held in joint tenancy with your spouse or any other person;
- your house(s), automobiles, RVs, boats, household and

personal goods, furniture, fixtures, and appliances in the U.S., Canada, and anywhere else in the world; and

- annuities, RRSPs/RRIFs, IRAs, and company-defined contribution plans like 401(k) plans, profit-sharing plans, and money-purchase plans.

To report all of this at your passing, the IRS kindly provides Form 706 — United States Estate (and Generation-Skipping Transfer) Tax Return. For those who prepare these forms (it should be a good estate-planning attorney with a tax designation or an accountant who prepares them on a regular basis), it is clearly understood that you do not mail them to the IRS in an envelope — they are in a box. The documentation (including copies of your wills and trusts), schedules, evaluations, appraisals, and so on required by the IRS make this tax return a major undertaking.

Estate tax rates start at 18% and rise to 40% at just U$1 million in taxable net worth above the exemption (see discussion below). Everything above $1 million in taxable net worth is taxed at the flat rate of 40%. Specifically, the estate tax is calculated in Table 7.2.

TABLE 7.2

CURRENT U.S. ESTATE TAX RATES

Taxable Estate (U$)	Tax Rate	Cumulative Tax Owing (U$)
0–10,000	18%	1,800
10,001–20,000	20%	3,800
20,001–40,000	22%	8,200
40,001–60,000	24%	13,000
60,001–80,000	26%	18,200
80,001–100,000	28%	23,800
100,001–150,000	30%	38,800
150,001–250,000	32%	70,800
250,001–500,000	34%	155,800
500,001–750,000	37%	248,300
750,001–1,000,000	39%	345,800
1,000,001+	40%	345,800+

To protect some (or potentially all) of your estate, Congress gives you a "unified" gift and estate-tax exemption (a "coupon" or the "unified credit") that can be used during your lifetime or at your passing (you don't get both). For 2015, the gift and estate-tax exemptions are U$5.43 million per person over your lifetime, or at your passing, and now adjusted annually for inflation (unified credit of U$2,117,800). This is a welcome relief to many farmers, investment property owners, and small-business owners who, in the past, found themselves in a cash crunch to pay the estate taxes owing on the value of the estate when it consists of just illiquid assets! This has made the U.S. estate tax much less of an issue except for the largest of estates. Previously, to take full advantage of the unified credit for a married couple (U$5.43 million for each) required complex trust and estate planning. This has been greatly simplified with the "portability of the estate-tax exemption." In order for a married couple to take full advantage of the estate-tax exemption, spousal "A" and bypass "B" trusts were needed. Now portability means the unused portion of the decedent spouse's exemption automatically gets added to the surviving spouse's exemption without the need for a trust. The only requirement is to file an estate tax return when the first spouse becomes an angel using Form 706 with the IRS, even if there is no taxable estate, to port the remaining exemption to the surviving spouse. An example may help.

TABLE 7.3
OWNERSHIP AND VALUE OF ASSETS

Asset Titling	Fair Market Value (C$)
Solely owned — husband	5,000,000
Life insurance — husband	1,000,000
Solely owned — wife	1,000,000
Jointly owned — husband and wife	3,000,000
Total	10,000,000

FIGURE 7.1

OLD "AB" TRUST PLANNING

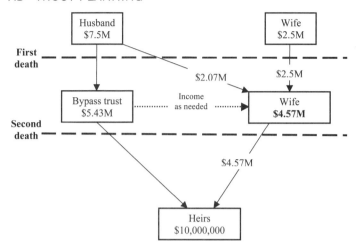

FIGURE 7.2

NEW PORTABILITY OF ESTATE TAX EXEMPTION

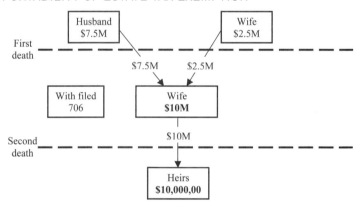

UNLIMITED MARITAL DEDUCTION

One subject that seems to come up frequently is confusion surrounding the "unlimited marital deduction" at the first spouse's passing. American citizens can pass an estate of any size to their U.S. citizen spouses without incurring any U.S. estate taxes because of the unlimited marital deduction available at the first spouse's passing. This means the deceased spouse's entire estate (assets titled in his/her name alone or jointly with the spouse) passes to the survivor with no estate tax, no matter how big the estate is. Likewise, a Canadian citizen only, married to a U.S. citizen and passing first, also has an unlimited marital deduction that permits him/her to pass the entire estate to the U.S. citizen with no estate tax. The confusion comes in when a U.S. citizen married to a Canadian-only citizen tries to pass the estate to the survivor . . . there is no unlimited marital deduction in this case. The reason is that the U.S. government fears the surviving noncitizen spouse can take the excess assets (the amount above the permitted exemption) out of the country without paying any estate taxes due at the American citizen's death. However, given the estate tax exemption portability, even a noncitizen spouse automatically gets to inherit U$5.43M from the U.S.-citizen spouse. Alternatively, the U.S. citizen's estate may elect to take a marital credit under the Canada-U.S. Tax Treaty to shelter an additional amount of the estate equal to almost a whole second exemption.

FIGURE 7.3

UNLIMITED MARITAL DEDUCTION EXAMPLES

	Unlimited	
Dual Canada-U.S. citizen	⟵————→	U.S.-citizen spouse
	Unlimited	
U.S. citizen	⟵————	Non-citizen spouse
	U$5.43M	
U.S. citizen	————→	Non-citizen spouse

It's important to note that a specifically designed U.S. estate plan may be required for Canadians living in the U.S. This is especially true if your estate is greater than the current allowable exemption as estate tax is typically due at the death of the U.S. citizen passing assets to a noncitizen, unless the IRS has some way of "attaching" itself to the assets. One way to do this is to establish a Qualified Domestic Trust (QDOT) in the U.S. estate plan. This trust holds the excess amount of the estate above the exemption that would be subject to estate taxes at the U.S. citizen's passing and delays the estate-tax liability until the Canadian citizen passes. A QDOT provides estate-tax deferral at the first death because the trust is considered resident in the U.S., and the IRS can require the trustee to pay any estate taxes owing (attach itself). The use of this has been reduced greatly with "portability of the exemption" but you need to determine the best course of action for your unique circumstances.

You should note that estate taxes are in addition to any professional fees, court costs, and probate fees that could consume another 3–10% or more of your estate. The complexity and time required to settle an estate via probate are different for every state and province. Some states and provinces have streamlined probate processes that are very inexpensive to settle even with an attorney, while other jurisdictions are much more complex and lengthy. Paying just a few thousand dollars to get an estate plan will pay off in hard savings, never mind the peace of mind that will come from knowing that what has taken a lifetime to accumulate will pass to your heirs according to your wishes. Once your basic estate plan is in place, other estate planning strategies and techniques can be employed to potentially bring your estate-tax liability down to zero. It depends a lot on your unique situation (heirs in both Canada and the U.S.) and your wishes (passing your estate outright or protecting it with a trust). There are strategies using trusts to keep your assets out of your estate for U.S. estate-tax purposes (but still retaining access to them as needed) — if you do the requisite planning before you leave Canada.

ADVANCED TECHNIQUES FOR LARGE ESTATES

If you have had the good fortune of accumulating an estate in excess of the federal estate-tax exemption (greater than U$10.86 million), more sophisticated estate planning techniques can be used to reduce your estate taxes at your passing (like the QDOT mentioned previously). These techniques are unique to each person's situation and go beyond the scope of this book. The time to plan is now because, if your estate is big enough and you just want to leave it all to your heirs, you automatically cut the government in on a piece of it whether you want to or not. In our experience, most of our clients desire greater control over their estates than playing a game of Russian roulette with the IRS or CRA. However, determining which technique to use and how to implement it in your situation so it will withstand the scrutiny of an IRS estate-tax audit will require competent counsel, someone who should be interviewed and selected carefully. Contact our office if you want assistance with this.

2. Gift Taxes

To prevent you from avoiding estate taxes entirely at your death by gifting away your estate on your deathbed, Congress countered with the gift tax. In general, any gift is a taxable gift unless it meets one of the exclusions. See the "Gifting" section later in this chapter for more details.

3. Generation-Skipping Transfer Taxes

To ensure the government gets paid its estate taxes at every generation, it instituted generation-skipping transfer taxes to prevent you from passing your estate too far down the "family tree." The generation skipping transfer tax (GSTT) kicks in at the highest marginal estate-tax rate (currently 40%) on any amount that passes directly from you to your grandchildren, and is in addition to any estate taxes above. Once again, the government is kind enough to allow you to exclude U$5.43 million from the GSTT to pass to the next generation. This means that, without the proper planning, for every dollar in excess of $5.43 million that is passed, 40¢ must be paid to the IRS in GSTT. Since you are in the 40% estate-tax bracket as well, you could see 80¢ in taxes for every dollar transferred to the next generation!

4. State Death Taxes

In general, there can be up to three different death taxes paid to your state of domicile. They include inheritance taxes and estate taxes. An inheritance tax is levied on the right to receive property by inheritance and is in addition to federal estate taxes. The beneficiaries are typically divided into classes according to their relationship to the deceased, and different tax rates/exemptions are applied to each class. Some states have their own "stand-alone" estate taxes that operate like the federal estate-tax system but are in addition to federal estate taxes.

5. Income Taxes

Like the deemed disposition tax in Canada, the U.S. deceased person's executor or executrix must file a final federal Form 1040 and the appropriate state income tax return to report any income in the year of death on behalf of the decedent. If not structured properly, things such as IRAs might have to be declared on your final return along with the taxable portion of your RRSPs. In addition, you will have to declare any interest, dividends, or realized capital gains in the year up to the point of passing as well. These federal income taxes (don't forget state taxes as well) are in addition to any federal (or state) estate taxes owing. As you can see, the total taxes owing when you become an angel can be unbelievable if the requisite planning hasn't been done.

SAME-SEX MARRIAGES

Canada recognizes same-sex marriages as an official tax filing status in Canada under "married," and gives all of the same estate-tax treatment of traditional marriages to common-law marriages and same-sex marriages as well. With the Defense of Marriage Act overturned by the Supreme Court in the U.S., the IRS now recognizes same-sex couples, legally married in jurisdictions that recognize such marriages, as being married for federal estate and income tax purposes. Further, these rules apply even if the same-sex married couple are living in a jurisdiction that does not recognize same-sex marriage! This means the IRS extends all of the same estate and income tax laws given to heterosexual couples to "legal" same-sex marriages. This will simplify estate planning greatly for these nontraditional marriages. The Supreme Court has taken up the debate on same-sex marriage and is expected to rule on this after the publication of this book. It is expected that same-sex couples will be recognized nationally in the U.S. as having the same status as heterosexual couples today.

THE DOUBLE ESTATE-TAX CONUNDRUM

For Canadians residing in the U.S. with assets remaining in Canada, there is the potential for double taxation at death on some assets. For example, you are subject to Canada's withholding tax at death on any RRSPs/RRIFs and the deemed disposition on real estate. In addition, you may be subject to estate and/or income taxes in the U.S. on those same assets.

Fortunately, there are provisions in the Canada-U.S. Tax Treaty that allow a credit against income, profits, and gains paid on Canadian real estate, or other appreciated assets, as a credit for U.S. estate taxes even though the two taxes are different — an estate tax versus a capital gains/income tax. The recently updated treaty now formally allows the 25% withholding tax on RRSPs and other similar plans at the second spouse's death to offset any U.S. estate tax. However, you may not be out of the woods yet on the double taxation issue because the governments may still be able to double dip. You may still be subject to double income tax on your final IRS tax return because it is highly doubtful you could use the same Canadian withholding twice against both your U.S. estate and income taxes owing on the RRSP. In addition, you may also be subject to estate and/or income tax by your state of domicile because the treaty provisions don't apply at the state level. There may also be "income in respect of the decedent" (IRD), depending on your circumstances. Needless to say, there are many gray areas that have yet to play out in tax court. One thing you can do for estate planning purposes in both Canada and the U.S. is review the beneficiaries on your RRSPs (and other registered plans in Canada) to ensure they pass according to your wishes, or collapse them and move them to the U.S. (see Chapter 10). The other is to hire a competent, experienced Canada-U.S. estate planning attorney (hard to come by) to draft your estate plan, taking into account these assets in Canada.

Of equal importance is the fact that the IRS does not recognize common-law marriages in the U.S. These situations typically require additional sophisticated planning to ensure that your wishes are implemented and to mitigate, wherever possible, court costs, attorney fees, and taxes.

THE TRUST-CENTERED ESTATE PLAN

To garner the most control of your estate, we typically recommend a full trust-centered estate plan. There are typically four documents that make up a trust-centered estate plan.

REVOCABLE LIVING TRUST

A living trust provides instructions to the person(s) of your choice (your trustee) on how to handle your financial affairs in the event of your death or incapacity. While you are alive, you and your spouse can be the trustee(s) of your living trust, and you can change the trust at any time (it is revocable). However, at the first death, the surviving spouse continues as trustee, but the trust generally becomes irrevocable and may be limited in what can be changed. A living trust becomes a "receptacle" for all of your assets and governs how this portion of your estate is administered during your lifetime — and how it is to be passed on to your heirs at your death. This document outlines in detail your wishes in a variety of events and circumstances that could befall you. Overall, a living trust offers you the following benefits.

- It allows you to avoid the probate process with its corresponding costs and delays.
- It allows you as much, or as little, control as possible over your estate in a variety of circumstances.
- Your estate is kept private and does not become a matter of public record, reducing the likelihood of it being challenged in court by an ex-spouse or discontent heir.
- While you are noncitizens of the U.S. with a very large estate, the QDOT (Qualified Domestic Trust) allows you to defer any estate taxes until the second death.
- It eliminates the need for a court hearing to determine who is to administer your estate in the event of your death or incapacity (with its attendant costs and delays).
- It alleviates your heirs from making difficult decisions about your money at an already difficult time.
- May provide some level of asset protection.

There are three key roles in any living trust.

1. The grantor puts the assets into the trust (also known as the settlor, trustor, or trust maker).

2. The trustee governs the trust and manages the assets.

3. The beneficiary receives the income and assets from the trust as dictated by the terms of the trust.

When you are alive, you generally occupy all three roles in the trust because you put the assets into the trust, you manage it, and any income or distributions from the trust go to you. However, in the event of death or incapacity, the person you have specified as trustee steps in to manage your assets and to distribute the assets to the beneficiaries you have specified. There can be great difficulties if you have your contingent trustee and/or beneficiaries residing in Canada. For example, the trust could be considered "resident" in Canada for income tax purposes, if your trustee lives in Canada.

For most Canadians, a living trust is a new, potentially frightening topic because the use of trusts in Canada is not near what it is in the U.S. The primary reason is that in Canada trusts are taxed as a separate entity and are subject to the punishing Canadian trust tax rates (top marginal tax rate on the first dollar of undistributed income while you are alive). Further, there is a deemed disposition when assets are moved into, or out of, a Canadian trust, and the trust generally has a life of 21 years after the second spouse dies and then it ends. In the U.S., the taxation of revocable trusts is much different because they are "flow-through" entities that are taxed on your personal return at your respective individual rate. This makes them much more popular and effective as an estate planning tool in the U.S. However, one note of caution: if you moved to the U.S. in the past five years, you have to be careful of the Canadian non-resident trust rules and how they may apply to your situation. Under these rules, if one of the beneficiaries of the newly created U.S. trust is a resident of Canada, the U.S. trust could also be considered a trust in Canada and is, therefore, taxable in Canada. This is where a competent Canada-U.S. transition planner to coordinate your estate planning is critical.

LAST WILL

A last will and testament provides instructions to the person of your choice (your executor or personal representative) on what to do with your financial affairs in the event of your death. If you make your will part of an overall trust-centered estate plan, your Canadian will would simply be replaced with a "pour-over" will, which would "pour" any assets left accidentally or intentionally out of your trust into the trust to be settled by its terms.

Many people have asked us if their Canadian wills are valid in the U.S. To be valid in U.S. probate court, your will simply needs to be presented and be properly signed and witnessed. However, if the provisions in your will are unclear or missing, or violate U.S. law, it may be valid, but the provisions may not be enforceable in the U.S. For example, there are differences in domestic law in who takes custody of your children or the disinheriting of heirs. In some states, a child born after a will has been executed will automatically revoke your existing will. If the witnesses to your Canadian will are not valid, or are unavailable to validate their signatures, then your will may not be valid in a court of law. In some states, if you are both the witness and a beneficiary, then the will is invalid. If your original Canadian will cannot be located or you fail to follow the formalities of a will in your particular state, it could cause your will to be invalid. Further, despite popular opinion, a will does not avoid probate (which means "to prove") and so is more easily challenged by ex-spouses or children from a previous marriage. As long as they can create doubt that your intentions were not as articulated in your will, they can cause long delays in court, and your estate will incur thousands in legal fees to sort it out. During this time period, accounts can be frozen, leaving heirs struggling to meet daily living expenses. In Canada-U.S. situations, you can have double the problems because you may have to settle Canadian "situs" investments, such as real estate (a summer home in Canada), in the Canadian probate court first before going through probate in the U.S. on the same property.

GENERAL POWER OF ATTORNEY (POA)

This document outlines your wishes in managing your financial affairs in the event of your incapacity and gives the person of your choice (your agent or attorney-in-fact) the power to implement your wishes. Such powers may include the ability to pay your bills, vote on corporate stock, file your tax returns, open your mail, care for your pets, conduct routine banking, converse with your financial or legal advisors, and so on when you are unable to do so. Given that these documents are unique to most states, we typically recommend your Canadian POAs be replaced with properly drafted documents in your state of domicile.

HEALTH-CARE DIRECTIVES

Typically, these documents include your living will, health-care, and mental power of attorney documents. Your living will outlines your wishes regarding your health care to physicians and other health-care workers, your family, and the courts in the event you are unable to communicate such wishes because you are brain-dead, unconscious, under the influence of analgesics, or terminally ill. This document provides as much or as little control in how far you want life-prolonging procedures to go, specifies which medical procedures you want administered in which circumstances, and alleviates your loved ones from having to make these difficult decisions in such tragic circumstances.

A health-care/mental power of attorney gives the person of your choice (your agent or attorney-in-fact) the power to implement your health-care wishes as outlined. If you go to the U.S. with Canadian health-care directives, you should have them replaced with documents suited to your state of domicile.

ESTATE PLAN IMPLEMENTATION

As mentioned earlier, getting the estate plan documents drafted and executed is only the beginning. You must implement your estate plan properly if your wishes are to be followed. Unfortunately, a spouse does not automatically have the legal authority to undertake these actions on behalf of the incapacitated spouse on his or her solely named account (this is where proper implementation of your estate plan is important). You must fund your trust, and unless you carry your POAs in your back pocket wherever you go, filing them with a digital retrieval service is recommended. This is important so they are available as necessary for any medical staff to implement your wishes at the time they are needed.

There are a few things to consider in the "titling" of your assets. In the U.S., there are several ways to hold property, including sole and separate property, joint tenancy with rights of survivorship, tenancy in common, tenancy by the entirety, community property, etc. How your assets are titled can have an effect on your estate plan because, with certain titling, your assets pass by law versus your estate plan. For example, joint tenants with rights of survivorship means that such a titled asset passes automatically to the surviving tenant at the first person's death. There are also community property states versus separate property states in the U.S. Separate property states have fewer income tax advantages at the first spouse's death than community property states, so the appropriate counsel should be sought in your state of domicile. The community property states in the U.S. are the following.

- Arizona
- California
- Idaho
- Louisiana
- Nevada
- New Mexico
- Texas
- Washington
- Wisconsin

GIFTING

Most Canadians living in the U.S. are unaware of the rules surrounding gifting in the U.S. In Canada, Canadians can gift cash or assets to spouses, children, or others with no gift tax repercussions because that form of tax does not exist in Canada. There are other Canadian tax rules, such as the income tax "attribution rules," when gifting to spouses or children in lower tax brackets and the deemed disposition when gifting to a trust. You should familiarize yourself with the information below before arbitrarily making any gifts once a tax resident in the U.S.

GIFTING TO A NONCITIZEN SPOUSE

If you and/or your spouse are not U.S. citizens, specific gifting rules apply. U.S. citizen spouses have an "unlimited" gifting exemption between them, which means that, during their lifetimes, they can transfer assets back and forth between themselves with no gift tax consequences. However, for non-U.S.-citizen spouses, there is an annual limit of U$147,000 in 2015 (adjusted for inflation), as outlined below.

FIGURE 7.4
NONCITIZEN GIFTING

	U$147,000	
Non-citizen spouse	←————→	Noncitizen spouse
	Unlimited	
U.S. citizen	←————	Noncitizen spouse
	U$147,000	
U.S. citizen	————→	Noncitizen spouse

If this limit is exceeded, the IRS has again kindly provided for your convenience Form 709 — United States Gift (and Generation-Skipping Transfer) Tax Return, and you end up using some of your lifetime exemption or paying an attorney to devise other legal means of remaining in compliance. These gifts can occur very innocently, so care must be taken in coordinating your transfer of assets from Canada to the U.S. For example, if you collapse and withdraw your RRSP from Canada and deposit the funds in a joint account in Canada or the U.S., you may have just made a gift.

GIFTING TO OTHERS

As mentioned previously, the IRS also has a gift tax of which many Canadians are unaware. U.S. residents are able to gift up to U$14,000 to any one person annually in 2015 (indexed annually for inflation but only in U$500 increments). Any gifts in excess of this amount require taxes to be paid or a portion of your U$5.43 million lifetime gift exemption to be used up (e.g., giving an automobile) as filed on Form 709. The reason behind the gift tax is to prevent U.S. residents with large estates from giving away all of their estates during their lifetime or on their death-beds to avoid estate taxes. The gift tax often catches many Canadians by surprise because of interest-free loans they may have given to family, friends, or associates. You need to determine up front if it is a gift or a loan. If it is a gift, it must be below the annual exemption, or Form 709 must be filed. If it is a loan, the IRS deems an "imputed interest rate" to the lender at prevailing interest rates required on any amount lent. This must be realized as "phantom income" on your tax return even if no cash is received (interest is gifted to the child using the annual exemption). If the interest exceeds U$14,000 annually in 2015, a gift tax return has to be filed to pay the gift tax or "split" the gift with your spouse. One final point: the gift is not considered income to the recipient, so you don't have to worry about handing a big income tax bill along with your gift.

RECEIVING AN INHERITANCE OR GIFT FROM CANADA

We have received countless calls and emails from people desperately thinking that they would lose the inheritance they just received from a Canadian relative due to U.S. income or estate/gift taxes. Nothing could be further from the truth. A gift or an inheritance is exactly that; it isn't "earned income," so it is exempt from U.S. income tax. However, if you receive a gift of appreciated securities or property, the cost basis carries over to you in the U.S. This means while you own the investment, you pay any income taxes owing on that investment and when you sell it, you will be required to pay any capital gains taxes as well. Furthermore, as long as the requisite deemed disposition taxes were paid in Canada when the estate was settled, the inheritance should pass to you free of any Canadian or U.S. death taxes. However, there is one caveat: you should understand the impact of taking possession of the inheritance on your own estate if you live in the U.S. at your passing. Otherwise, you may want to disclaim any inherited amounts to keep them out of your estate for U.S. estate planning purposes. You will also need to report the inheritance to the IRS on Form 3520 — Annual Return to Report Transactions with Foreign Trusts and Receipt of Certain Foreign Gifts if the gift or inheritance exceeds U$100,000 (much less if a gift from a foreign corporation or partnership). Note that this is not a taxable event but simply a reporting requirement of the IRS. Depending on your situation, there are strategies that can be employed using trusts, disclaimers, or other techniques to ensure the inheritance is kept out of your U.S. estate.

TAXATION OF TRUSTS

With the increased use of trusts in the U.S. for estate planning purposes, the following will allow you to familiarize yourself with the differences in the taxation of trusts between Canada and the U.S. In the U.S., the taxation of a trust depends a lot on whether the trust is revocable (changeable) or irrevocable (not changeable). If it is revocable, it is simply a "flow-through" entity and taxed at your individual income tax rates. If it is irrevocable, it is a stand-alone entity that must obtain its own Employer Identification Number (EIN) and is required to file IRS Form 1041 — U.S. Income Tax Return for Estates and Trusts. Trusts are subject to the following tax rates (Table 7.5).

TABLE 7.4

2015 U.S. TRUST TAX RATES

Taxable Income (U$)	Rate
0–2,500	15%
2,501–5,900	25%
5,901–9,050	28%
9,051–12,300	33%
12,301 +	39.6%

In Canada, trusts are always taxed as a stand-alone entity whether you are alive or not. Each trust has its own trust account number and is required to file a T3 trust tax return. If the trust income is retained within the trust, the taxation is simple: all of it is taxed at the highest marginal rate (29% federal plus that of your province, which can total up to 48%+). If the trust income is distributed to its beneficiaries, it is declared on the beneficiaries' tax returns and is subject to their marginal Canadian income tax rates. Moreover, there is a deemed disposition if you move assets into, or out of, a Canadian trust, which means there will be an early collection of capital gains tax for appreciated assets.

Despite their complexity, the use of trusts in Canadian departure and U.S. pre-entry planning may be beneficial and, depending on your circumstances, can produce great income, estate, and gift tax savings. It is a complex procedure and should be undertaken only by attorneys and advisors well versed in Canada-U.S. estate planning.

REAL-LIFE EXAMPLE

We received a desperate call from a woman in California who was the sole trustee on her mentally incapacitated mother's Revocable Living Trust. The investment advisor for the account told her to move the account within 90 days, or it would be frozen (see Chapter 10 for a continuation of this example). Since we are registered to manage investments in both Canada and the U.S., she contacted us to provide help. The problem arose because the trustee had a sibling in Canada who disputed the management of the trust and took the sister/trustee to court. In the process, the Canadian resident sibling was appointed as a co-trustee on the mother's trust, at the suggestion of the attorneys to provide further oversight. A red flag immediately went up for me as the attorneys on both sides of the dispute likely had no idea they perhaps had just made this trust taxable in Canada as well, which would have had some very negative tax and compliance consequences for the mother, who needed these funds to sustain her! When a resident of Canada is placed as a trustee on a U.S. trust, the trust tax residency generally comes to Canada as well, which means the trust is now a foreign trust for IRS purposes. After reviewing the details and fact pattern with our network of professionals, by sheer luck the attorneys avoided having this trust become taxable in Canada, because the trust likely did not meet the Canadian trust residency rules of where "mind and management" of the trust still takes place. However, if the U.S. trustee decides to resign because she can't co-manage the trust with her sibling, or she becomes an angel, mind and management will move to Canada, and the trust will be subject to the punitive Canadian trust tax rates and the cumbersome IRS foreign trust rules. This will result in potentially higher taxes and professional fees, leaving fewer funds for the mother's care.

8 FINANCIAL FREEDOM

And I'll say to myself, "You have plenty of good things laid
up for many years. Take life easy; eat, drink and be merry."
— LUKE 12:19

In our firm, we use the term "independence planning" in place of the more common term "retirement planning" because of the connotations associated with the term "retirement." We are all saving so we can become financially independent, but the question becomes, "Independent to do what?" Retirement is often thought of as stopping work and pursuing an unscheduled life of whatever your heart desires that day. In our experience working with clients, this becomes mundane fairly quickly. In fact, we view retirement not as the closing of a book but as a turning of the page to a new chapter in life. Fortunately, that chapter is blank, and we encourage you to write it so that it is exciting, vibrant, and energizing for years to come.

A big part of our transition process is aimed at determining when you might become independent of work and helping you to understand what you want to do for the balance of your life. This approach creates excitement about the future and enables you to sacrifice now in order to achieve the goals you have set for your future. For you to gain these insights, any transition planning firm should spend ample time understanding what your current and future lifestyle looks like and then determining the cost of that lifestyle on an inflation-adjusted basis over your life expectancy. The financial projections should incorporate the various sources of income you have, make a number of conservative assumptions, add the volatility of returns in financial markets, and then determine how your unique financial situation projects into the future once you are residing in the U.S. From there, you can begin to make these critical decisions based on numerical insights, not on opinions, conjecture, or notions.

In Canada, the primary vehicle used to become financially independent is the RRSP. It allows Canadian taxpayers to contribute up to 18% of their past tax year's salary up to a 2015 maximum amount of C$24,930 (less any pension amounts made by an employer, which means you have to earn C$138,500+ to max out your RRSP contribution). Other savings alternatives include Registered Pension Plans, which allow C$25,370 in contributions in 2015, and Tax-Free Savings Accounts, which allow contributions of $5,500. The questions we are most often asked are "How do we save for our future in the U.S.?" and "Will we still qualify for some form of Canadian government or company pension when we are living in the U.S.?" These questions can be perplexing because you may have short earning histories in both Canada and the U.S. because of your move, which may mean you do not meet the minimum work history in either country to qualify for any government benefits. Once again, proper transition planning can set you on a course that will maximize your benefits because you lived in both countries. Following are some of the independence planning issues you should consider in making your move to the U.S.

CANADA PENSION PLAN/OLD AGE SECURITY

Many people have contacted us concerned that if they move to the U.S. they will lose their Canadian government pension benefits. If you qualify for benefits, you will receive them simply by applying for them no matter where you live in the world. In fact, the Canadian government can deposit your CPP/QPP or OAS benefits directly into your U.S. checking account if requested to do so. The exchange rates used are competitive, and the convenience is tough to beat. For the taxation of CPP/QPP and OAS in the U.S., see Chapter 5.

QUALIFYING FOR CPP/QPP

If you have made contributions into the system, you qualify for CPP/QPP at age 60 at the earliest (full benefits are received at age 65). You can obtain an estimate of your future CPP/QPP benefit by asking the Social Development Canada branch in your province of residence for a statement (1-800-277-9914) or creating a My Service Canada Account and obtaining your Statement of Contributions to ensure all of your earnings are captured. In 2015, the maximum CPP payment you can receive is C$1,065 per month (C$12,780 annually) at age 65 (adjusted every January for CPI).

Determining when to collect your benefits can be tricky now that new rules have been brought in that increase the penalty if you collect before age 65, but you get a retirement "credit" if you delay collecting until after age 65. If you collect your CPP early (at age 60), starting in 2015, it is reduced by 0.58% per month and, in 2016, will reach the maximum of 0.60% reduction per month. Full retirement age is 65, so you will end up with a 34.8% reduction in 2015, and 36% in 2016. There is also a retirement credit added to your benefits if you delay taking CPP after age 65. For each month you delay payment, your benefit will increase by 0.70% per month (that's 8.4% per year!). This means that, if you wait until age 70 to collect CPP, you will receive 42% more than if you collect it at age 65. You can see the Canadian government is trying to incent people to wait on collecting CPP by penalizing them 36% if they collect early but rewarding them 42% if they wait. As a result, if you don't need the money and have longevity in your family tree, it may be worthwhile to wait before collecting. Either way, it is worthwhile having a financial advisor run some numbers with an understanding of your other sources of income to determine the best age to maximize your CPP benefits.

QUALIFYING FOR OAS

To qualify for full OAS benefits at age 65, you must have lived in Canada for at least 40 years after reaching the age of 18 (until age 58), and no contributions to the plan are required. In 2015, the maximum OAS payment per person is C$6,764.88 annually (adjusted quarterly for the CPI) per person. But what happens if you make the transition to the U.S. before age 58? You still qualify for partial OAS benefits, but you must have lived in Canada for at least 20 years after reaching the age of 18 (until age 38). If you left Canada without living 20 years after reaching the age of 18 (left before age 38), the Canada-U.S. Social Security (Totalization) Agreement comes into play and qualifies you for benefits. For each year you live in the U.S., it counts as one year of eligibility toward OAS in Canada. Your benefits are based on the actual amount of time you spent in Canada, but you are now eligible for some benefits instead of losing them altogether because you decided to move to the U.S. There is a two-step process at work here: first, determining if you are eligible for any benefits at all; second, determining what your benefit amount is.

As with CPP, the government is providing incentives to collect OAS later in life to keep the system solvent. As a result, for each month you delay taking OAS after age 65, your benefit increases by 0.6% per month (that's 7.2% per year!). This means that, if you wait until age 70 to collect OAS, you will receive 36% more than if you collect it at age 65. Again, we recommend you sit down with someone who looks at your entire tax liability, cash flow, family history, and retirement situation to see if it makes sense to wait to collect OAS and CPP.

The Totalization Agreement is an executive agreement between the U.S. and Canada signed on August 1, 1984. An executive agreement is different from the Canada-U.S. Tax Treaty because it does not require the formal approval of Congress. The purpose of the Totalization Agreement is to provide employers and employees with relief from double payroll taxes, and to "totalize" the payroll taxes you paid in both Canada and the U.S. in order to receive partial benefits in both countries for which you may not otherwise qualify. The U.S. currently has totalization agreements with 17 other countries. To apply for Canadian CPP or OAS benefits while living in the U.S., you should use Form SC-ISP5054-USA — United States/Canada Agreement — Application for Canadian Old Age, Retirement and Survivor Benefits and send it to International Operations, Service Canada in Ottawa, ON, K1A 0L4.

Be aware of the difficulty in proving you lived in Canada to qualify for OAS. With CPP, the government has a record of how much you paid into the system and can calculate your benefits. OAS, however, does not require payment into the system — it is simply based on the amount of time you have lived in Canada. To keep people who do not qualify for OAS from defrauding the system, the proof of residency standards have increased. In one case, we had a stay-at-home mother who applied for benefits but couldn't prove she had lived in Canada. We helped her to gather some further documents so she would qualify. Some things you may want to consider using as proof include:

- your spouse's tax returns (if divorced) since they will have your name and SIN;
- old passports showing exit from and entry to Canada;
- driver's license records;
- utility bills/records that have your name on them; and
- property tax bills that have your name on them.

U.S. SOCIAL SECURITY

In making the transition to the U.S., you may wonder if you are eligible for any U.S. Social Security benefits. The initial answer is "no" unless you establish the necessary "quarters of coverage" that make you eligible. Since you are splitting your earning years between Canada and the U.S., it is rare that you will qualify for the maximum Social Security benefits. However, similar to CPP/QPP, if you pay into U.S. Social Security, you will receive some benefits. For the taxation of U.S. Social Security, see Chapter 5.

One of the political "hot potatoes" being juggled in the U.S. is what to do with Social Security. Based on the latest projections, the U.S. Social Security system is set to run out of money around 2042. Some subtle changes have been made to extend the life of Social Security. Until 2001, the age when you could receive full retirement benefits was 65. Now the full retirement age is based on the year you were born, as outlined in Table 8.1.

TABLE 8.1

SOCIAL SECURITY FULL RETIREMENT AGE

Year of Birth	Full Retirement Age	% Benefits Reduced if Collected at Age 62
1937 or before	65	20.0
1938	65 and 2 months	20.8
1939	65 and 4 months	21.7
1940	65 and 6 months	22.5

1941	65 and 8 months	23.3
1942	65 and 10 months	24.2
1943 to 1954	66	25.0
1955	66 and 2 months	25.8
1956	66 and 4 months	26.7
1957	66 and 6 months	27.5
1958	66 and 8 months	28.3
1959	66 and 10 months	29.2
1960 or later	67	30.0

Your benefits are reduced by 5/9ths of 1% for each month you collect Social Security before your full retirement age. As the table above illustrates, extending the age to receive full benefits had the effect of penalizing folks in the year of birth by 30% if collected early. The general consensus is that both the Medicare and Social Security systems in the U.S. need significant change to make them sustainable for the next generation. As outlined in Chapter 2, Medicare Part B is now a "means tested" premium (the more you make, the more you pay). We believe that a means tested Social Security benefit may be on its way in the U.S., similar to the OAS recovery tax ("the clawback") in Canada, where the more you make the less you'll get. In addition, we expect the contributions into the system to be increased as well.

To qualify for Social Security retirement benefits, you must have established at least 40 quarters of eligibility in the U.S. To establish four quarters of eligibility in 2015, you must have earned income of U$4,880. If you earn the minimum income amount for at least 10 years, you'll establish the 40 quarters of eligibility and can begin collecting U.S. Social Security. The question then becomes, "What if I can't establish the 40 quarters?" This is where the Canada-U.S. Totalization Agreement can get you qualified for benefits provided you have at least six quarters of eligibility established in the U.S. For each year you lived in Canada, it counts as one year toward U.S. Social Security. Your benefits are still based on the amount you paid into the U.S. Social Security system, and this amount will be nominal given your short earning history in the U.S. In 2015, the maximum Social Security payment you can receive is U$2,663 per month (U$31,956 annually).

Unlike Canada Pension Plan, Social Security offers a spousal benefit. If only one spouse qualifies for a Social Security pension benefit, the other spouse receives half of the spouse's pension benefit automatically (the reward for the stay-at-home parent). Some effective planning can be done with those moving to the U.S. whereby one spouse pays into the Social Security system and qualifies for benefits while the other spouse automatically qualifies for half of the amount without having contributed one nickel to the system.

WINDFALL ELIMINATION PROVISION

When it comes time to apply for your Social Security benefits, you may be surprised to find out that, because you are collecting CPP, your U.S. Social Security benefits will be reduced due to the "Windfall Elimination Provision" (WEP). This is a confusing set of rules that can affect your benefits, but it depends on your individual circumstances.

Here's how it works. To calculate your Social Security benefit, Social Security uses a percentage of your average earnings over the past 35 years. Since most Canadians moving to the U.S. have a much shorter earning history in the U.S., they qualify for a smaller Social Security benefit (because a number of your 35 years have zero as your earnings amount because you were in Canada). Now here's the rub: the smaller your average earnings over your 35-year history, the more Social Security aims to replace those average earnings (the smaller your average earnings, the more Social Security benefits will replace them). Generally, lower-paid workers get a Social Security benefit that equals about 60% of their pre-retirement earnings, while the average replacement rate for highly paid workers is only about 28%. For example, the lowest-earning workers (up to U$9,000 per year) receive a Social Security benefit that equals 90% of pre-retirement-covered earnings, while the average replacement rate for the highest-earning workers (up to U$95,000 per year) is about 25%. You, however, will have unusually low average earnings for U.S. Social Security purposes because you did not contribute for most of the 35-year "look back" period, so you can see where the problem comes in. Why? Because you were working in Canada, contributing to CPP, and becoming qualified for CPP benefits. CPP aims to replace about 25% of pensionable earnings on which your contributions are based. Again, CPP will drop about five of your lowest years in calculating your average contributions. As a result, the Social Security administration calls this a "windfall" that accounts for the fact that you are getting full CPP benefits and are not entitled to the more generous Social Security benefits provided for those with lower average earnings over the 35-year period (some don't think this is fair treatment, but we have to disagree). The Social Security agent then declares the Windfall Elimination Provision and reduces your Social Security benefits to take this "rub" into account (see Figure 8.1).

Currently, the Social Security Administration does not apply WEP if you have 30 or more years of substantial earnings in the Social Security system. However, they are inconsistent in the application of the years worked in Canada because, in some situations, they will count the years worked in Canada toward the determination of benefits, and, in other situations, they won't. As outlined earlier, years worked in Canada are allowed when qualifying for the 10-year minimum working period for Social Security eligibility. However, when it comes time to count the years you worked in Canada towards exempting you from WEP (requires 30 years of substantial earnings), the Social Security Administration suddenly doesn't acknowledge those years. This inconsistency in applying your time worked in Canada is the crux of the issue and it's why we believe the issue will be clarified through the court system at some point.

However, before accepting the agent's declaration that your Social Security benefits are reduced, there are a few things you should know to make sure the Windfall Elimination Provision is properly applied to your situation. First, the provision was written for U.S. federal government workers and some state workers (e.g., police officers) who did not have to contribute to the U.S. Social Security system (it was voluntary). Even though it was written for these folks, like it or not, the Social Security Administration has made it official policy, giving it broader application to those who work abroad. Second, the provision does not apply if you use the Canada-U.S. Totalization Agreement to qualify for either CPP or Social Security benefits. Section 215a(7)(A)(ii) of the Social Security Act contains this rule, which is little known among frontline Social Security staff. In fact, for most agents, your application may be their first (and last) to take into account CPP benefits (but don't let them include OAS or any other company pensions!). You need to ensure the proper application of this rule to your situation, or you could find your benefits unnecessarily reduced. One way to ensure the rules are being applied properly to your situation is to file for Social Security benefits using Form SSA-2490-BK — Application for Benefits under a U.S. International Social Security Agreement. This form will be routed through the Office of International Programs and ensure a higher level of processing. At this writing, the form wasn't available online, so you will have to call the Social Security Administration or visit a local office to obtain a copy but we provide a copy in Figure 8.2. Finally, if you fully qualify for CPP benefits in Canada and Social Security benefits in the U.S., the Windfall Elimination Provision applies, and only your U.S. Social Security benefits will be reduced. Take heart, however; you still come out ahead of someone who qualifies in either the U.S. Social Security system or the Canada Pension Plan system because both systems aim to replace more of the lower earner's wages . . . another advantage for those moving between Canada and the U.S.

FIGURE 8.1
HOW THE WEP RULES APPLY

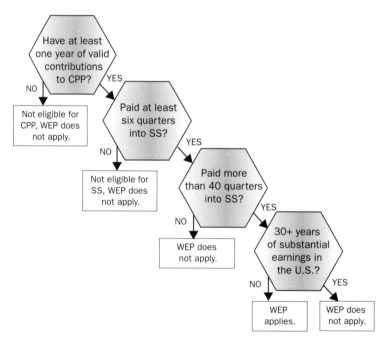

FIGURE 8.2

SOCIAL SECURITY ADMINISTRATION FORM SSA-2490-BK

SOCIAL SECURITY ADMINISTRATION		Form Approved OMB No. 0960-0448

APPLICATION FOR BENEFITS UNDER A U.S. **INTERNATIONAL SOCIAL SECURITY AGREEMENT**	(Do not write in this space)

If the worker is living, this application should be completed by or on behalf of the worker. If the worker is deceased, this application should be completed by one of the worker's survivors who is claiming benefits under the provisions of the international social security agreement.

PART I

Complete Part I in all cases.

1. (a) Print name of worker (First name, middle initial, last name)

   (b) U.S. Social Security Number

   __ __ __ / __ __ / __ __ __ __

2. Provide the following information about the worker's social security credits (coverage) and last place of residence in the foreign country.

   (a) Use columns (1) - (5) to enter information about the worker's periods of employment or self-employment in the foreign country. *(If additional space is required, enter the information in Remarks -- item 19.)*

(1) Dates Worked (From - To)	(2) Name and *Address of* employer or self-employment activity	(3) Type of Industry or business	(4) Social Insurance Number used while working	(5) Name of Agency to which contributions paid

(b) Use columns (1) - (4) to enter information about the worker's periods of coverage under the foreign social insurance system which are not based on employment or self-employment (e.g., coverage for voluntary contributions, deemed or equivalent coverage, periods of military service, illness, etc.)

(1) Dates Covered (From - To)	(2) Type of coverage	(3) Social Insurance Number used for this coverage if different than shown in item 2(a)(4)	(4) Name of Agency to which contributions paid (if any)

(c) Enter the worker's last place of residence in the foreign country:

(City and State or Province)

PLEASE REMOVE PAGE 1 OF THIS FORM BEFORE COMPLETING THE REST OF THE APPLICATION. AFTER APPLICATION IS COMPLETED AND SIGNED, STAPLE DETACHED PAGE TO APPLICATION.

Form **SSA-2490-BK** (4-2004) EF (8-2006) (Formerly SSA-2490-F4)
Destroy Prior Editions   Page 1

SOCIAL SECURITY ADMINISTRATION FORM SSA-2490-BK

SOCIAL SECURITY ADMINISTRATION

Form Approved
OMB No. 0960-0448

APPLICATION FOR BENEFITS UNDER A U.S.
INTERNATIONAL SOCIAL SECURITY AGREEMENT

(Do not write in this space)

If the worker is living, this application should be completed by or on behalf of the worker. If the worker is deceased, this application should be completed by one of the worker's survivors who is claiming benefits under the provisions of the international social security agreement.

PART I

Complete Part I in all cases.

1. (a) Print name of worker (First name, middle initial, last name)

   (b) U.S. Social Security Number

   _ _ _ / _ _ / _ _ _ _

2. Provide the following information about the worker's social security credits (coverage) and last place of residence in the foreign country.

   (a) Use columns (1) - (5) to enter information about the worker's periods of employment or self-employment in the foreign country. *(If additional space is required, enter the information in Remarks -- item 19.)*

(1) Dates Worked (From - To)	(2) Name and *Address of* employer or self-employment activity	(3) Type of Industry or business	(4) Social Insurance Number used while working	(5) Name of Agency to which contributions paid

   (b) Use columns (1) - (4) to enter information about the worker's periods of coverage under the foreign social insurance system which are not based on employment or self-employment (e.g., coverage for voluntary contributions, deemed or equivalent coverage, periods of military service, illness, etc.)

(1) Dates Covered (From - To)	(2) Type of coverage	(3) Social Insurance Number used for this coverage if different than shown in item 2(a)(4)	(4) Name of Agency to which contributions paid (if any)

   (c) Enter the worker's last place of residence in the foreign country:

   (City and State or Province)

Form **SSA-2490-BK** (4-2004) EF (8-2006) (Formerly SSA-2490-F4)
Destroy Prior Editions

Page 2

196 THE CANADIAN IN AMERICA

SOCIAL SECURITY ADMINISTRATION FORM SSA-2490-BK

3.	I apply for all benefits for which I am eligible under the provisions of the social security agreement between the United States and ⟶	Name of country

4.	This application may be used to claim benefits from the U.S. and/or the foreign country shown in item 3. Check (X) the block(s) indicating the type of benefit(s) for which you are applying under the country(ies) from which you are claiming the benefit(s).

BENEFIT CLAIMED FROM FOREIGN COUNTRY

Type of Benefit Claimed From Foreign Country:

☐ Retirement/Old-Age   ☐ Survivors   ☐ None

☐ Disability or Sickness/Invalidity   ☐ Other (Specify) _____

BENEFIT CLAIMED FROM THE UNITED STATES

(a) Are you presently receiving benefits from the United States? ⟶	☐ Yes *(If "Yes" answer (b) below.)*	☐ No *(If "No" answer (c) below.)*
(b) If you are already receiving U.S. benefits, do you wish to file for a different type of U.S. benefit? ⟶	☐ Yes *(If "Yes" answer (d) below.)*	☐ No *(If "No" go on to item 5.)*
(c) If you are not presently receiving U.S. benefits, do you wish to file for U.S. benefits at this time? ⟶	☐ Yes *(If "Yes" answer (d) below.)*	☐ No *(If "No" go on to item 5.)*
(d) Indicate the type of benefit you wish to claim from the United States:		

☐ Retirement   ☐ Disability   ☐ Survivors

INFORMATION ABOUT THE WORKER

5.	(a) Print worker's name at birth, if different from item 1(a)

(b) Check (X) one for the worker ☐ Male ☐ Female	(c) Enter worker's social insurance number in the foreign country if different than shown in items 2(a)(4) or 2(b)(3)

(d) If the worker's Social Security number in either the United States or the foreign country is not known, enter the worker's parents' names:

Mother's name (First name, middle initial, last name, maiden name)

Father's name (First name, middle initial, last name)

(e) Enter the worker's citizenship (Enter name of country)

6.	Do you want this application to protect an eligible spouse's and/or child's right to Social Security benefits? ⟶	☐ Yes	☐ No

7.	(a) Was the worker or any other person claiming benefits on this application a refugee or stateless person at any time?	☐ Yes *(If "Yes" answer (b) below.)*	☐ No *(If "No" go on to item 8.)*
	(b) If "Yes" enter the following information about the person:		

Name	Dates of refugee or stateless status

SOCIAL SECURITY ADMINISTRATION FORM SSA-2490-BK

PART II

Complete Part II ONLY if you are claiming benefits from a foreign country.

8.	If you are applying for sickness or disability/invalidity benefits, enter the date you became disabled. Otherwise enter "N/A." ⟶	Date *(Month, day, year)*
9.	(a) If you are applying for retirement/old-age benefits, have you stopped or do you plan to stop working? ⟶	☐ Yes *(If "Yes" answer (b) below.)* ☐ No *(If "No" go on to item 10.)*
	(b) If "Yes," enter the date you stopped or plan to stop working.	Date *(Month, day, year)*
10.	(a) Are you applying for foreign social security benefits under a special system that covers a specific occupation (e.g., miners, seamen, farmers)? ⟶	☐ Yes *(If "Yes" answer (b) and (c) below.)* ☐ No *(If "No" go on to item 11.)*
	(b) What was your occupation in the foreign country? ⟶	
	(c) Did you perform the same type of work in the U.S? ⟶	☐ Yes ☐ No

INFORMATION ABOUT THE APPLICANT

Complete item 11 ONLY if you are not the worker. If you are the worker, leave this question blank and go on to item 12.

11.	(a) Print your name (First name, middle initial, last name, maiden name)	(b) What is your relationship to the worker?
	(c) Enter your U.S. Social Security number	(d) Enter your social insurance number in the foreign country *(if none or unknown, so indicate)*

ADDITIONAL INFORMATION ABOUT THE WORKER

12.	(a) Enter worker's date of birth (Month, day, year)	(b) Enter worker's place of birth *(City, state, province, country)*
13.	If the worker is deceased, enter the date and place of death ⟶	(a) Date (Month, day, year) — (b) Place *(City, state, province, country)*
14.	(a) Was the worker in the active military or naval service of the U.S. (including U.S. reserve or U.S. National Guard active duty for training) or a foreign country after September 7, 1939? ⟶	☐ Yes *(If "Yes" answer (b) thru (c) below.)* ☐ No *(If "No" go on to item 15.)*
	(b) Enter the name of country served and dates of service: ⟶ Country	Dates of Service — FROM: *(Month, day, year)* TO: *(Month, day, year)*
	(c) Has anyone (living or deceased) received, or does anyone expect to receive, a benefit from any U.S. Federal agency based on the worker's military or naval service? ⟶	☐ Yes *(If "Yes" answer (d) below* ☐ No *(If "No" go on to item 15*
	(d) If "Yes" enter the following information for each person: (If additional space is required, enter the information in Remarks -- item 19)	

Name	U. S. Agency	Claim No.

SOCIAL SECURITY ADMINISTRATION FORM SSA-2490-BK

15.	(a) During the past 24 months, did the worker engage in employment or self-employment covered by the U.S. Social Security system?	☐ Yes *(If "Yes" answer (b) and (c) below.)*	☐ No *(If "No" go on to item 16.)*

List the periods of work covered by the U.S. Social Security system and the name and address of the employer or self-employment activity

(b) Name and address of employer or self-employment activity	Work Began (Month-Year)	Work Ended (Month-Year)

(c) May we ask any employer listed above for wage information needed to process this claim?	☐ Yes	☐ No

INFORMATION ABOUT DEPENDENTS FOR WHOM BENEFITS ARE CLAIMED

16.	(a) Are there any children of the worker who are now, or were in the past 12 months, unmarried and:	Under age 18	☐ Yes ☐ No
		—OR— Age 18 or over and a student or disabled	☐ Yes ☐ No

If either block is checked "Yes", enter the information for each child. NOTE: Children include natural children, step-children and adopted children plus grandchildren living in the same household as the worker.

(b) Name of child	(c) Relationship to worker	(d) Sex (M or F)	(e) Date of birth (Month, day, year)

17. The spouse, widow or widower of the worker may be eligible for a benefit. In addition, a former spouse of the worker may be eligible as a divorced spouse, widow or widower. Provide the following information about any spouse or former spouse of the worker.

	SPOUSE	FORMER SPOUSE	FORMER SPOUSE
(a) Name (including maiden name)			
(b) Date of Birth (Mo., day, yr.)			
(c) Date of Marriage (Mo., day, yr.)			
(d) Date of Divorce (if any) (Mo., day, yr.)			
(e) Country of Citizenship			
(f) Social Insurance Number in foreign country			
(g) U. S. Social Security Number (if any)			

Form **SSA-2490-BK** (4-2004)　　EF (8-2006)　　　　Page 5

SOCIAL SECURITY ADMINISTRATION FORM SSA-2490-BK

18.	(a) Has the worker, or any other person listed on this application, ever previously applied for U.S. Social Security benefits or social insurance benefits from the country shown in item 3 of this application?	☐ Yes (If "Yes" answer (b) thru (f) below.)	☐ No (If "No" go on to item 19.)

If "Yes" enter the information requested for each person. I(If additional space is required, enter the information in Remarks -- item 19.)

(b) Name	(c) Type of benefit (e.g., Retirement)

(d) Claim Number	(e) Amount of benefit (if benefit awarded)	(f) Agency which approved or denied claim

19. REMARKS (You may use this space for any explanations. If you need more space, attach a separate sheet.)

Form **SSA-2490-BK** (4-2004)   EF (8-2006)   Page 6

SOCIAL SECURITY ADMINISTRATION FORM SSA-2490-BK

PRIVACY ACT NOTICE

Statutory Authority: This form requests information under the authority of Section 203(a) and 233 (d) of the Social Security Act as amended (42 USC 405(a) and 433 (d)).

Mandatory or Voluntary: While it is not mandatory, except in circumstances explained below, for you to furnish the information on this form to Social Security, no benefits may be paid under an international agreement on social security unless an application has been received. Your response is mandatory where the refusal to disclose certain information affecting your right to payment would reflect a fraudulent intent to secure benefits not authorized by the Social Security Act.

Purpose: The information on this form is needed to enable Social Security authorities in the U.S. and the foreign country you listed on page 3 of this application to determine if you are entitled to benefits under an international agreement on social security.

Effect: Failure to provide all or part of this information could prevent an accurate and timely decision on your claim and could result in the loss of some benefits.

Use of information: Information from this form will be forwarded to the Social Security authorities of the foreign country you listed on page 3 of this application to help them locate information about the worker's periods of coverage under that system. It will also serve as an application for benefits payable under the foreign laws as well as under U.S. laws if the intent to claim benefits under that system has been indicated in item 4 of this application form. The Social Security Administration cannot be responsible for assuring the confidentiality of information provided to a foreign social insurance agency. In general, that country's rules of confidentiality will apply. The information may also be used (1) to facilitate statistical research and audit activities necessary to assure the integrity and improvement of the Social Security programs, and (2) to comply with Federal laws requiring the exchange of information between the Social Security Administration and another U.S. government agency.

We may also use the information you give us when we match records by computer. Matching programs compare our records with those of other Federal, State or local government agencies. Many agencies may use matching programs to find or prove that a person qualifies for benefits paid by the Federal government. The law allows us to do this even if you do not agree to it.

Explanations about these and other reasons why information you provide us may be used or given out are available in Social Security offices. If you want to learn more about this, contact any Social Security office.

I hereby authorize the United States to furnish to the competent social insurance agency of the other country all of the information and evidence in its possession which relates or could relate to this application for benefits. I also authorize the agency(ies) of the other country to furnish the Social Security Administration or a United States Foreign Service post all of the information and evidence in its possession which relates to this application for benefits.

I declare under penalty of perjury that I have examined all the information on this form, and on any accompanying statements or forms, and it is true and correct to the best of my knowledge. I understand that anyone who knowingly gives a false or misleading statement about a material fact in this information, or causes someone else to do so, commits a crime and may be sent to prison, or may face other penalties, or both.

SIGNATURE OF APPLICANT	Date *(Month, day, year)*
Signature *(First name, middle initial, last name) (Write in ink)*	
SIGN HERE ▶	Telephone number(s) at which you may be contacted during the day ___ ___ ___ *(Area Code)*

Mailing Address *(Number and street, Apt. No., P.O. Box, or Rural Route)* (Enter resident address in "Remarks" if different)

City and State	ZIP Code	Country *(if any)* in which you now live

Witnesses are required ONLY if this application has been signed by mark (X) above. If signed by mark (X), two witnesses to the signing who know the applicant must sign below, giving their full addresses. Also, print the applicant's name in the Signature block.

1. Signature of Witness	2. Signature of Witness
Address (Number and street, City, State, and ZIP Code)	Address (Number and street, City, State, and ZIP Code)

INDIVIDUAL RETIREMENT ACCOUNTS (IRAS)

In the U.S., the closest thing you will find to an RRSP is an IRA. Do not mistake them for RRSPs, because the latter are treated differently from a tax standpoint in the U.S. Many clients are asked by their U.S. accountants what an RRSP is, and the typical response is "It's like an IRA." The accountant then wrongly assumes that it is an IRA and as a result does not prepare your tax return correctly, thereby potentially creating tax and compliance issues with the IRS, and potentially your state of residence, as discussed in Chapter 5.

There are several types of IRAs, and which one to use depends on your unique situation and what you are trying to achieve (your goals and objectives). Traditional plans may be deductible or nondeductible depending on your adjusted gross income. There are SEP-IRAs and SIMPLE IRAs for those who have self-employment income, and Rollover IRAs for those who are leaving their U.S. employers. The Roth IRA allows you to put away after-tax dollars and withdraw them tax free after age 59 1/2 (note: this is tax free versus tax deferred, mirroring the Tax-Free Savings Account in Canada).

The rules surrounding these plans are complex and must be carefully considered before choosing the plan that is right for you. There are rules on how much you can defer each year, additional catch-up amounts if you are over 50, and penalties if you take them out too soon. There are other rules on when you must start taking funds out (age 70 1/2 compared to age 71 for an RRIF), and different rules that apply in the event of your death. There are even more rules on when you can make contributions and when the time has passed (typically you have to contribute by the time you file your tax return on April 15th, whereas RRSPs allow contributions within the first 60 days after year end). There are ways of passing your IRAs on to your heirs and allowing them to continue the tax deferral for the balance of their lives as well (not an option in Canada). Of course, all of this requires the appropriate planning based on what you are trying to achieve.

Table 8.2 shows the maximum contributions you can make to a traditional or Roth IRA (if you qualify).

TABLE 8.2

CONTRIBUTIONS TO AN IRA

Year	Maximum Contribution (U$)	Catch-up Amount (U$)	Total Contribution (U$)
2015	5,500	1,000	6,500
2016	Indexed	Indexed	TBD

CANADIAN COMPANY PENSIONS

Fewer and fewer people ask us how a move to the U.S. will affect their current company pension plans, as less than 30% of Canadian workers are eligible for such plans. Again, if you have paid into the plan and are eligible for benefits, you do not suddenly become ineligible (unvested) for benefits because you move to another country. Your pension benefit amount remains, and in fact you may even get it paid directly into your U.S. bank account if you wish. The taxation of this pension is discussed in greater detail in Chapter 5. The problem with these "defined benefit" pensions is they are paid in Canadian loonies and are most likely not adjusted for inflation. You are thus exposed to a couple of risks. First, you introduce currency risk into your financial situation because, when you move to the U.S., you need U.S. dollars to fund your retirement expenses. Since your Canadian pension is paid in Canadian loonies, your pension amount will fluctuate based on the currency exchange rate, leaving you short one year and with an excess in another year. Some of our clients had their pension incomes drop significantly when the loonie was worth U$0.6199 in January of 2002, for example. Second, you face inflation risk since many defined benefit pensions are not adjusted for inflation; they pay the same fixed dollar amount or only partially adjust it to inflation. As a result, you see a gradual decline in your spending power over your lifetime. By the time it starts to affect you, you are generally unable to return to work to supplement it.

U.S. RETIREMENT PLANS

In the U.S., there is a proliferation of "qualified" plans (versus "registered" plans in Canada) that you can take advantage of to save toward your financial independence. The Employee Retirement Income Security Act of 1974 (ERISA) typically governs these plans. The rules surrounding these plans are amazingly complex, and we have experts who deal with nothing but setting up and administering these types of plans. There are rules on how much you can defer each year and penalties if you take it out too soon. There are rules on when you must start taking funds out and different rules in the event of your death. Which plan you use depends on your individual goals and objectives and what you are trying to accomplish. You can contribute to an IRA in addition to the qualified plans listed below, which means you may be able to put away more pre-tax money in the U.S. than in Canada. Following is a brief description of the most popular plans.

401(K) PLAN

This is by far the most popular retirement plan in the U.S. Its unusual name is due to that section of the Internal Revenue Code that permits these plans. They are used by most corporations and are considered a "defined contribution" plan because it defines how much you can put in (you bear the investment risk versus a defined benefit plan — see below). These plans allow you to defer some or all of your salary pre-tax up to the IRS specified limits (see the table below), and your employer may match a portion of it. However, if you are still a tax resident of Canada, you can't deduct your 401(k) contribution on your Canadian return and must declare and pay tax on your gross salary. If you leave your employer, you are able to roll your 401(k) plan into a Rollover IRA or another employer's 401(k) plan, but you should seek advice before doing so since it can be tricky, and there are some opportunities with company stock available to you. It is important to note that contributions to a 401(k) (and the plans listed below) are on a payroll basis only. So if you are looking to make a large contribution to your 401(k) at the end of the year to save tax, this will not be permitted; contributions must be withheld from your paycheck over the course of the year.

403(B) PLAN

These plans are similar to 401(k) plans but are used exclusively by non-profit organizations (e.g., some hospitals and schools). The administrative expenses associated with these plans can be higher, but they still offer a good opportunity to defer income in a tax-deferred environment. Again, the unusual name is due to the particular section of the Internal Revenue Code that permits these plans.

457 PLAN

These plans are used exclusively by state or federal government employees. There is usually some form of matching by the state, but it varies by state. The maximum contributions you can make to the 401(k), 403(b), or 457 plans are as follows.

TABLE 8.3

CONTRIBUTIONS TO 401(K), 403(B), AND 457 PLANS

Year	Maximum Contribution (U$)	Catch-Up Amount (U$)	Total Contribution (U$)
2015	18,000	6,000	24,000
2016	Indexed	In 500 increments	TBD

DEFINED BENEFIT PLANS

Unlike the plans outlined above that define the amount you contribute to the plan each year (you bear the investment risk), defined benefit plans specify how much must be contributed to produce a defined benefit at a certain age. Recent changes in law have made these plans very attractive in small business situations because they allow over U$200,000 in income to be deferred each year. However, these plans have become less popular for major corporations with the recent changes in law. Overall, these used to be the plans of choice for most large corporations, but over the years they have dwindled (less than 17% of employees) in favor of defined contribution plans because of the cost of funding, administering, and maintaining them. Further, many defined benefit plans had a cost of living allowance on the benefit that has all but been eliminated (it is seen more often in Canadian plans).

SEP-IRA, SIMPLE PLANS

These plans are available for self-employed individuals who don't have the opportunity to shelter their net income with one of the other plans because of the expense to set up and administer them. These plans are easy to set up and inexpensive to administer and can be arranged at most discount brokerage firms.

EMPLOYEE BENEFIT PLANS

Several employee benefits may be available to you if you leave Canada to work with a larger employer in the U.S. Similar to Canada, the U.S. has stock option plans and deferred compensation arrangements. We provide a brief discussion below so you can familiarize yourself with them.

RESTRICTED STOCK UNITS

To retain key people, many companies now use restricted stock units (RSUs). Employees are granted RSUs but cannot do anything with them until certain conditions are met (e.g., partial vesting occurs every six months over a two-year period). After the "trigger" is met, the employee vests in the RSUs. At that point, the stock is no longer restricted, and the employee can keep the stock or sell it. Since the "risk of forfeiture" is now gone, the stock is immediately taxable as ordinary income based on the market value of the stock at the time of vesting. As a result, there is little incentive to keep the stock after vesting. In some cases, an 83(b) election can be taken in the U.S. to recognize the income at the time of the grant, versus the time of the vesting, if the stock has appreciated significantly. This may offer some better tax results in the U.S., but in Canada it is still taxed as employment income included on your T4. Restricted stock awards are another less common form of executive compensation with rules different from RSUs. For example, in Canada RSAs are immediately taxable at the time of grant, versus the time of vesting, which can put a cash flow strain on the employee because there is tax due but no stock vested to sell.

STOCK OPTIONS

Stock options once were a common form of compensation for employees in both Canada and the U.S. because they allow employees to participate in the movement of the employer's stock without having to commit any of their own funds. However, with securities regulators fining many companies for illegal activities surrounding stock options (e.g., back-dating), many companies have abandoned them in favor of RSUs with the advent of mandatory stock option expensing by the corporation. Taxation of these options is complex when moving to the U.S., and it is beyond the scope of this book since each situation is unique with regard to granting and vesting in the option prior to, or after relocating to, the U.S. Following are a few general insights into stock options that may be helpful.

In Canada, stock options are allowed a 50% deduction of the amount between the exercise price and the fair market value of the stock at exercise. This means only half of the gain is taxed at the higher Canadian personal tax rates. In the U.S., there are two types of stock options, and the difference between them is related to how they are taxed in the U.S.

- Non-qualified stock options (NQs): the primary difference from the incentive stock options below is that, when the NQ is exercised, the difference between the exercise price and the fair market value of the stock is considered ordinary wage income.
- Incentive stock options (ISOs): they offer some terrific tax opportunities if circumstances permit. When the ISO is exercised, the difference between the exercise price and the fair market value of the stock is considered ordinary, short-term capital gain income if the stock is sold within a year of exercising. However, if the ISO is exercised and the stock is held for longer than one year, all of the gains are considered long-term capital gains and are taxed at the long-term capital gains rate of 15 or 20% (depending on your tax bracket). However, you have to be careful of the alternative minimum tax (AMT) because the exercise of an ISO is considered income for AMT purposes. This means you could owe a boatload of tax even

though you haven't sold a single share of stock. We highly recommend you exercise options with great caution, or you could cause devastating tax effects.

The Fifth Protocol of the Canada-U.S. Tax Treaty provides clarification on the taxation of stock options. The stock option benefit will now be sourced proportionally between the two countries based on the amount of time spent in each country from the time the option was granted and the time it was exercised. This will help reduce any double taxation and clarifies the old treaty language. Depending on your circumstances, it may be better to exercise all of your options in Canada at the lower tax rates before taking up tax residency in the U.S. Stock options have come under legal and regulatory scrutiny since the tech bubble of the late 1990s and, as a result, are coming increasingly under fire for their reporting on company financial statements. Many companies, including Microsoft and Intel, are moving away from these plans and instead instituting restricted stock programs to reward and retain their employees.

DEFERRED COMPENSATION/RETIREMENT COMPENSATION ARRANGEMENTS

Deferred comp plans, for short, are usually offered to senior level executives to allow them to defer a portion of their salaries (in addition to any retirement plans the company may have) into a plan they can collect after they retire from the company. The idea is to reduce the amount of taxable income now, when the executive is in a high tax bracket, until later, when the executive is assumed to be in a lower tax bracket. There are different types of deferred compensation arrangements in the U.S. depending on the company and its objectives for the plan. Most have the executive pay the payroll taxes up front, and when the plan distributes the income it is taxed just like wages. These plans may be subject to the company's creditors, so there are some risks associated with the tax deferral provided.

Similar to deferred comp plans in the U.S., Canada has the Retirement Compensation Arrangement (RCA). With these plans, the employer typically puts an amount into the employee's RCA. At the time of the contribution, the contribution (and any future earnings) is subject to a 50% refundable tax that must be remitted to CRA. Once the employee has retired from the firm and begins taking withdrawals out of the RCA, the distributions are taxable as ordinary income to the employee. In addition, CRA returns $1 of tax for every $2 withdrawn from the RCA. Although the RCA allows for some tax deferral, 50% of all contributions to the plan (and ensuing income) stay with CRA. When they are returned to the employee, there is no interest paid. In essence, CRA gets an interest-free loan. If you wait until you leave Canada to begin collecting your CRA, Canada-U.S. Tax Treaty rates will apply at a rate of 15% on periodic payments. You could withdraw amounts at a flat 25% withholding rate per the Income Tax Act versus the higher ordinary income tax rates (48% or more) as a resident of Canada. However, in the U.S., all amounts withdrawn are fully taxable, but proper tax planning can ensure that offsetting foreign tax credits mitigate your tax liability.

REAL-LIFE EXAMPLE

We had a client that exited Canada but had an RCA remaining in Canada that would be paid out over a number of years after exit. As a non-resident of Canada, distributions from the RCA were subject to withholding at source. The accountant for the RCA claimed that each payment was subject to a 15% withholding as the payments were coming from a trust. Per the Canada-U.S. Tax Treaty, trust income is subject to a 15% withholding. We stated that this was incorrect because although RCAs are considered to be trusts (like RRSPs), they are retirement arrangements or pensions first. Since the "pension" payments were not periodic payments as defined in the Treaty under Article XVIII, paragraph 2, they were subject to a 25% withholding at source. Sure enough, CRA agreed with us and an additional 10% withholding had to be remitted by the accountant. This also meant all of our client's U.S. tax returns had to be amended to take the additional foreign tax credits being paid to CRA. One final note: the Canadian investment manager managing these funds exposed our client to currency risk because they kept this substantial sum in Canadian loonies. Thankfully, the Canada-U.S. exchange rate maintained near parity throughout the years the RCA was paid out, allowing our client to convert those RCA payments to U.S. dollars without a significant decline. Overall, it was not a risk the client needed to take.

SMARTEN 9 UP!

An investment in knowledge
always pays the best interest.
— BENJAMIN FRANKLIN

In Canada, the primary means of saving for your family's educational needs is the Registered Education Savings Plan (RESP). You can contribute a one-time, maximum amount of C$50,000 to this plan (after tax). If you contribute C$2,500 or more, the Government of Canada will contribute another C$500 to the account (20% match) through the Canada Education Savings Grant (CESG), up to a lifetime maximum of C$7,200. If your income is below C$44,701 in 2015 (adjusted annually), your grant is C$600; if your income is between C$44,701 and C$89,401, your grant is C$550. There is no annual limit to your contributions (C$50,000 maximum) but the maximum CESG available for contributions is C$2,500. This registered plan will allow you to begin accumulating funds toward education expenses. In addition to the RESP, there are other tax credits for the tuition amount, education amount, and student loan interest that can reduce taxes on your annual Canadian tax return. However, when you move to the U.S., complications can arise with these plans. Following are some things to consider in planning for your educational needs when moving to the U.S.

WHAT HAPPENS TO MY RESP?

Similar to RRSPs, there are varying opinions on the taxation of RESPs in the U.S. In our opinion, RESPs do not automatically retain their tax-deferred status with the IRS or the state in which you are resident. Further, unlike RRSPs/RRIFs, there are no specific treaty provisions or revenue procedures for the continued deferral of these plans. As a result, you have to declare the income inside the RESPs each year on your U.S. tax return until collapsed — along with the filing of IRS form 3520 — because an RESP in Canada is considered a foreign trust. Fortunately, CRA will permit non-residents to withdraw funds for "qualified education expenses," including those at a qualified U.S. university. From a Canadian standpoint, funds inside RESPs grow tax deferred until needed for education expenses, and any withdrawals of the gains/income and grant amounts are taxed as ordinary income to the student (who is typically in a lower tax bracket than the contributor). Your original contributions are withdrawn tax-free. From a U.S. standpoint, any withdrawals should be tax free as well because you have been declaring the income annually on your U.S. tax return. However, this asset will be included in your estate for estate tax purposes and could be subjected to estate tax at your death as outlined in Chapter 7.

One thorny issue arises if you become a U.S. resident but leave an RESP in Canada and are unable to use it for education expenses. CRA rules state that as a non-resident you cannot withdraw any earnings on your original contributions to an RESP for any purpose other than "qualified education expenses." This means that, even if you are willing to pay the Canadian taxes and penalties, you still can't get the earnings out — only your original principal can be withdrawn (tax free), and you will have to return all of the grant money received back to the Government of Canada. RESPs require some planning to ensure there will be someone in your family (or among your relatives) who can benefit from these plans; otherwise, the earnings can be left on "Island Canada" indefinitely. We believe this rule was an oversight by CRA in drafting the laws surrounding RESPs and non-residents of Canada, but we are not sure when, or if, it will be addressed.

There are no provisions to roll your RESP into any education savings account in the U.S. and maintain the tax deferral from a Canadian or U.S. perspective. Further, if you have young children who won't be attending a postsecondary institution any time soon, there is the requirement to report the income as taxable in the U.S., and you also have to comply with a number of IRS reporting requirements, such as U.S. Department of the Treasury Form FinCEN — Foreign Bank Account Report, Form 3520 — Annual Return to Report Transactions with Foreign Trusts and Receipt of Certain Foreign Gifts, and Form 3520a — Annual Information Return of Foreign Trust with a U.S. Owner on your U.S. federal tax return when you leave your RESPs in Canada. You may also be required to file IRS Form 8938 — Statement of Specified Foreign Financial Assets. Which compliance requirements your state of domicile will have is another matter. Finally, it will be difficult to manage the investments in your RESP because your financial institution will only allow you to sell investments to avoid the ire of the U.S. Securities and Exchange Commission (see Chapter 10 for more details).

EDUCATION SAVING ACCOUNTS IN THE U.S.

In the U.S., there are several different ways of saving for your child's education and tax benefits to support those improving themselves through education. An assessment of your tax situation needs to be completed to see which alternatives you are eligible for and fit with your overall financial plan. You then have to decide how much control you want to give your child over these funds. Following is a review of the major plans available in the U.S. to fund education expenses.

COVERDELL EDUCATION SAVINGS ACCOUNT
This plan allows you to put U$2,000 after tax away annually per beneficiary. Withdrawals of principal or earnings for qualified education expenses are tax free. These funds can be used for expenses such as tuition, books, computers, internet connections, and actual living expenses, and applies from kindergarten through to university.

UTMA

A Uniform Transfer to Minors Act account can be set up at most brokerage firms in your child's name. You are the custodian on the account. You can then put an unlimited amount of funds in this account, but be aware of the gift tax implications (see Chapter 7). From a tax standpoint, the first U$1,050 in income in 2015 from the account is tax free, with the next U$1,050 taxed at your child's marginal tax rate of 10%. When the income in the account exceeds U$2,100, the excess income is taxed at your highest marginal tax rate (as much as 39.6%) until each child reaches age 18, and while college students are under the age of 24. This is known as the "kiddie tax" and is intended to prevent people from avoiding taxes by simply giving their money to their children to be taxed at their lower tax bracket (similar to the attribution rules on capital gains in Canada). Funds can be taken out for the benefit of the child only and must not be used for "normal" expenses that you as a parent are expected to provide (food or rent). Also be aware that your child gets unrestricted access to the entire UTMA account at the age of majority for the state in which you reside (normally 21), so if they choose to buy a Corvette don't blame us!

STATE COLLEGE SAVINGS PLANS

Known as Section 529 plans in the U.S. after their section in the Internal Revenue Code, these state-sponsored programs have become very popular. Most every state now has a plan. These plans allow you to make after-tax contributions that can be invested in a wide range of mutual funds. When it comes time for withdrawals for education expenses (room, board, books, tuition), everything (dividends, interest, capital gains) is withdrawn tax free at the U.S. federal level, and possibly in your state of residence as well. In addition, there are some great estate tax planning advantages that may be applicable in your situation, as these assets are not considered a part of your estate. Most importantly, you retain full control of the funds and can change beneficiaries at any time with no tax or other implications.

AMERICAN TAX INCENTIVES FOR EDUCATION

When you move to the U.S., you should familiarize yourself with the various income tax credits and deductions that may be available to you, or your child, to offset some of your education expenses.

AMERICAN OPPORTUNITY CREDIT

Through 2017, this tax credit is worth a total of U$2,500 for each of your children in the current tax year. You are eligible to take this credit for up to four years of undergraduate studies for a maximum credit of U$10,000 per child. You are eligible for a U$2,500 tax credit if you pay at least U$2,500 in college expenses each year, which is relatively easy to do. There are income restrictions to be aware of in qualifying for this credit, and it is available only for up to four years of undergraduate studies. You use IRS Form 8863 to claim the American Opportunity Credit, but you'd better hurry, as Congress has approved this credit only to 2017, after which it will expire.

LIFETIME LEARNING CREDIT

This tax credit is worth U$2,000 annually for each tax-paying family as long as there is a child or parent in school full or part time upgrading his or her skills. There are income restrictions in qualifying for this credit, and you can select only between the American Opportunity Credit and the Lifetime Learning Credit in any one year.

There is some coordination that needs to take place between these credits and withdrawals from a Section 529 plan, so it is prudent to seek some advice when freeing up the cash to pay college expenses. For example, you can take either the American Opportunity Credit or the Lifetime Learning Credit but not both in one year. However, if you pay all college expenses with tax-free funds from a Section 529 plan, those are not eligible expenses for either credit.

STUDENT LOAN INTEREST DEDUCTION

As in Canada, in the U.S. there is an "above the line" deduction (don't have to itemize) on your tax return for any interest paid on student loans.

The maximum deduction is U$2,500, but there are income restrictions on your eligibility for this deduction.

TUITION AND FEES DEDUCTION

Similar to Canada's tuition and education amounts, in the U.S. there is a deduction of up to U$4,000 for college tuition and related expenses, but there are income restrictions on whether you qualify or not. Furthermore, you can't take the deduction if you take one of the credits outlined above.

As you can see, there are many alternatives and tax-favorable strategies in the U.S. to save for education expenses. Which options you are eligible for — and the pros and cons of each plan — depend on your individual financial situation and the level of control you want over the funds.

KEY DIFFERENCES

There are several key differences in the school systems between Canada and the U.S.

- In Canada, junior high runs from grades 7 to 9. In the U.S., it is typically grades 7 and 8 and is called middle school.
- In the U.S., K–12 school generally starts in early or mid-August and runs through May, with longer breaks in between. In Canada, school generally starts in early September and runs through June, with shorter breaks.
- Based on our experience and feedback from others, U.S. undergraduate classes tend to be easier than Canadian undergraduate classes, but U.S. graduate classes tend to be more difficult than Canadian graduate classes.

There are some linguistic differences in education circles you should be aware of as well (see Table 9.1).

TABLE 9.1

LINGUISTIC DIFFERENCES IN EDUCATION

Canada	United States
Grade 9 or first year of university	Freshman
Grade 10 or second year of university	Sophomore
Grade 11 or third year of university	Junior
Grade 12 or fourth year of university	Senior
Junior high	Middle school
University	College
Diploma	Associate's degree
Marks	Grades

10 MONEY DOESN'T GROW ON TREES

Fortunes are made by being highly concentrated,
but fortunes are preserved by being highly diversified.
— ANONYMOUS

Canadians making the transition to the U.S. typically leave some investment accounts or RRSPs/RRIFs in Canada, thinking they will just continue managing their accounts as they always have. The reason most often given for leaving these investments in Canada is they will lose money if loonies are converted to U.S. dollars now (see Chapter 6). What folks don't realize is that it's not "business as usual," and there are complications with the accounts in Canada when they are residing in the U.S. If you decide to move the investment assets to the U.S., there are other complications and unforeseen obstacles to overcome. Following are some of the things you should consider in the area of investment planning.

KEEPING ACCOUNTS IN CANADA

Relocating to the U.S. is often followed shortly by a notice from your brokerage firm saying that it can no longer hold your accounts and that you must move them immediately because you are no longer a resident of Canada. This notice may be due to an overzealous compliance officer who doesn't know what to do with a U.S. address on a Canadian account or a brokerage firm that is not registered in your state of residence. In reality, there is no legal reason for you to move your registered accounts anywhere since Canadian financial institutions can continue to hold these accounts for Canadian non-residents. However, securities rules cause more complications with regular, taxable brokerage accounts (as well as with RESPs), so you may find that you can't place any "buy" trades in the account (only sales are permitted). In some cases, you may be forced to liquidate the entire account and close it.

To get around this issue, some Canadian expatriates attempt to "trick" their financial institutions and the securities regulators by providing a Canadian address of a family member or friend, or a post office box number. This tactic can lead to several problems.

- Your financial institution or broker, if proven to be aware of your U.S. residency, could be subject to fines and penalties (under the "Know Your Client" rules) for putting a Canadian address on your account when you are residing in the U.S.
- For any dividends paid into your brokerage account, likely no withholding tax can be taken on this "Canadian-source" income, as required under the Canada-U.S. Tax Treaty, because your custodian believes you are still living in Canada. This creates a compliance issue with the Canada Revenue Agency because they will have T3 and T5 slips with no accompanying tax return (versus NR4 slips). They will reach out to you to file a tax return, and you will have to admit to non-residency and remit the correct withholding on a Part XIII tax return to Canada. Further, if you are being issued Canadian T3 and T5 slips for this income instead of the required NR4 slips, you could compromise your position with CRA that you are truly a non-resident of Canada. Further, any Canadian source investment income must also be declared and is taxable on your U.S. return at the prevailing exchange rates, adding to your tax prep time (see Chapter 5).
- Lump-sum RRSP withdrawals or RRIF payments will most likely have the incorrect withholding taken as outlined in Chapter 5, and you will be then be required to remit the correct withholding on a tax return back to Canada.

- You will not receive your monthly investment statements or other important information (proxy voting, notification of annual meetings, splits or stock dividends, etc.) in a timely fashion because you will be reliant on your family/friends to send them to you when it's convenient for them.
- Your confidentiality could be compromised if your information ends up at a "trusted" friend's or relative's house.

Also overlooked are the restrictions on trading in your Canadian RRSPs and other registered accounts while you are resident in the U.S. Until recently, the Securities and Exchange Commission prohibited Canadian brokerage firms from making trades in these accounts for U.S. residents because of fears of insider trading and proper accounting of the income in these accounts. The Investment Dealers Association in Canada successfully lobbied the SEC, which agreed to allow trading in these accounts (but not RESPs!). However, the states did not readily follow along, but now almost all the states have some form of approval in place, but it depends on the state and on which resolution it has adopted. Before making trades in your account, inquire with your Canadian investment manager to make sure the firm, and the individual, is registered with the SEC and licensed with the state you reside in (your state must have adopted one of the appropriate legislative models to permit that trading). Alternatively, you can hire our firm to manage your RRSPs for you as we are registered to manage investments in both Canada and the U.S.

If you are able to keep your brokerage accounts in Canada (most brokerage firms are no longer permitting U.S. residents to hold brokerage accounts because of SEC rules and oversight), be aware of a couple of difficulties. First, as a U.S. resident, you are subject to U.S. taxes on your worldwide income. Your Canadian investment manager/broker likely doesn't know the U.S. tax implications of the transactions he is undertaking and as a result could be conducting investment trades and handing you an unnecessary tax bill on your U.S. return in the process (short-term capital gains and PFICs as outlined in Chapter 5). Investment research has shown that the costs of investing (internal expenses, commissions and fees) and tax efficiency of investment income are the two largest determinants of overall investment returns. We recommend that you retain an investment manager well versed in the tax rules in both countries and who understands how the Canada-U.S. Tax Treaty applies to your situation to ensure your tax liability is mitigated wherever possible. Another common area overlooked is the difficulty experienced with brokerage accounts in Canada if the account holder dies while resident in the U.S. Typically, the probate process has to be endured twice, once in Canada and once in the U.S., and there is the potential for double taxation (see Chapter 7 for more details). This is where coordination among your investment manager, tax advisor, estate planning attorney, and tax preparer becomes critical.

REAL-LIFE EXAMPLE

We received a desperate call from a woman in California who was the sole trustee on her mentally incapacitated mother's account. The investment advisor for the account told her to move the account within 90 days, or it would be frozen. This was a big problem because as trustee she was using the account to pay her mother's bills and in 90 days would no longer be able to do so! Since we are registered to manage investments in both Canada and the U.S., she contacted us to provide help. The problem arose because the trustee had a sibling in Canada who disputed the management of the trust and took the sister/trustee to court. In the process, the Canadian resident sibling was appointed as a co-trustee of her mother's trust, at the suggestion of the attorneys involved, to provide further oversight despite no discrepancies being found. When the investment advisor was asked to provide duplicate statements to the co-trustee/sibling in Canada, it realized there was a "Canadian control person" on the brokerage account and immediately issued the notice to move the account. Unfortunately, we were unable to assist her in this situation for the same reason, which meant the only option was to remove the Canadian resident sibling as a trustee or have the account frozen. This meant more attorney fees and delays as the 90 days were counting down quickly.

SETTING UP ACCOUNTS IN THE U.S.

When you begin moving your investments to the U.S., you need to select a financial institution. You may approach an institution in your local area that you may never have heard of about setting up an account. Without a doubt, it will be more than happy to get you set up and recommend several "great" investments (review Chapter 13, "Mayday! Mayday!"). Following are some things to consider.

WHERE TO SET ACCOUNTS UP

A common question our firm fields is, "Where should I set up an investment account in the U.S.?" We believe the best value for the dollar is at one of the large discount brokerage firms. They offer low commission rates, a wide array of lower-cost mutual funds, and exceptional internet-based services. The custodian of choice for our clients' investments in the U.S. is TD Ameritrade Institutional, the second-largest discount brokerage firm in the world. It offers discounted transaction and trading rates and virtually every institutional mutual fund available, and it has fixed-income and stock desks. For our clients in Canada or those with investments remaining there, we use National Bank Correspondent Network Institutional (NBCN, which bought TD Waterhouse Institutional). Again, it offers discounted transaction and trading rates as well as a wide range of institutional mutual funds and an experienced fixed-income desk. There are other financial institutions available, but we encourage you to do your research and select a firm that upholds the fiduciary responsibility to you (see Chapter 12).

TEMPORARY VISA

Another issue our firm has been dealing with more often lately is the unwillingness of U.S. financial institutions to open up brokerage accounts to "temporary residents" (e.g., those holding a TN visa). A TN visa is considered a temporary visa typically renewed every three years, so you are not viewed as a permanent resident of the U.S. This means that, for regulatory purposes, many financial institutions are refusing to open up brokerage accounts because of the tragic events of 9/11. Ironically, it's no problem to open up a 401(k) plan with your new employer at those same brokerage firms. This can be a thorny exercise demanding patience.

SOCIAL SECURITY NUMBER/ITIN

For those making the transition to the U.S. and wanting to open an account as a U.S. resident, they must have a Social Security number to put on the account application form (institutions generally won't accept an individual taxpayer identification number [ITIN] because you are considered a non-resident). This number ensures any income from the account can be tracked for income tax purposes. For spouses not eligible to work, they need to apply for an ITIN before opening a joint account with the spouse who has a Social Security number (see Chapter 5 on how to apply). With the tragic events of 9/11, the federal government has determined the best way to fight terrorism is to restrict the access terrorists have to money. As a result, you will find a lot of scrutiny and paperwork to contend with before opening an account. The institution will ask for your employment status, employer's name and address, passport number, and country to determine exactly who is opening the account. In our experience, if you have a nonimmigrant visa, you may find it difficult to open an account with most brokerage firms in the U.S.

TITLING YOUR ACCOUNT

The other question you will see on the account application form asks how you want the account titled: joint tenancy with rights of survivorship, tenancy in common, tenancy in the entirety, community property, sole and separate property, etc. Most Canadians have no idea, so they check any box or don't check one at all, and the brokerage firm uses its default (normally joint tenancy with rights of survivorship). In reality, the option selected can have profound and possibly costly estate planning effects on your family in the event that one of you dies or becomes incapacitated. This is not a decision that should be taken lightly, and the answer is probably none of the options provided but an ownership option that never appears on the form. See Chapter 7 for further details on this issue.

CANADIAN-LOONIE ACCOUNTS

Another big question we get is, "Can I set up a Canadian-dollar account in the U.S.?" At the heart of this question is the issue of losing money when exchanging Canadian loonies into U.S. dollars, which we address in Chapter 6. The answer is, essentially, no. You cannot open a Canadian-dollar account in the U.S. or even exchange Canadian loonies for U.S. dollars at the local bank, whereas in Canada, these are common occurrences. We succeeded once a long time ago in opening a Canadian-dollar account for a persistent client at a U.S. brokerage firm, but that was a very unique situation. Some of the many problems we encountered are listed below.

- It was very difficult to even find a brokerage firm in the U.S. to set up a Canadian-loonie account.
- There was no end of paperwork to set up the Canadian-loonie account, and once submitted we had to follow up to explain to the firm what the client was doing, and the standard answer was, "We can't do that."
- The investment holdings were still reported on the monthly statement in U.S. dollars, so the client still had the "discomfort" of seeing the portfolio in U.S. dollars. It required a monthly call to tell the brokerage firm of the error and asking them to issue a new statement. By then, next month's statement was already received, and we had to start the process all over again.
- When interest or dividends were paid or a bond matured, the Canadian loonies were automatically converted to U.S. dollars at the prevailing rate plus whatever "shaded" amount the brokerage firm decided on, and everything was swept into a U.S. money market fund as a default. To get this converted back to Canadian loonies required many calls and much paperwork.

The bottom line is that U.S. brokerage firms are just not capable of opening and managing Canadian-loonie-denominated accounts effectively because there just isn't sufficient demand for them. With all of the factors listed above, why would you want to try this? It just ends up causing a lot of complexity and frustration in your life.

MOVING INVESTMENTS TO THE U.S.

Another confusing and potentially frustrating area often encountered is moving your Canadian investments to the U.S. Let's dispel a common myth right off — yes, it's possible to move Canadian investments to the U.S. without having to sell them first. However, as we have personally experienced, the simplest transfers can take months for the unwary. Following is some information to consider when moving your investments to the U.S.

MOVING YOUR RRSP/RRIF

Some of the most popular questions our firm fields are, "How should I move my RRSP/RRIF to the U.S.? In a lump sum? In stages? Using the annual minimum withdrawal amount? Spouse's first? This year or next?" Unfortunately, the answers to these questions require considerable thought, a current understanding of financial markets, and a thorough understanding of your unique financial situation to determine the Canadian tax implications, U.S. tax implications, and which RRSP(s) to withdraw first. The other question to consider is, "When a prudent withdrawal strategy is developed, what will be done with the money?" There simply is no easy answer for everyone, but generally it is better to transfer these assets to the U.S. for purposes of estate planning, tax planning, currency exchange, and simplification of life. The answers depend, again, on your individual financial situation and your overall goals and objectives. However, proceed with caution. A C$100,000 lump-sum RRSP withdrawal means at least C$25,000 in Canadian tax — that's a lot of money where we come from. Some proper planning is certainly in order.

MYTH: MOVE YOUR RRSP TO AN IRA

One common myth we often have to dispel is the ability to move a Canadian RRSP to a U.S. IRA. The current rules and regulations simply do not allow a Canadian RRSP to be rolled over to an IRA while maintaining the tax-deferred status in both countries. Your only alternative is to collapse the RRSP and transfer the cash to the U.S. and then make an IRA contribution or leave your RRSP in Canada. Of course, be aware of the tax implications before doing so since you can end up ultimately being double taxed.

Given all these complexities, some people become overwhelmed and simply decide to leave their RRSP in Canada and forget about them. This is akin to an "ostrich putting its head in the sand." Before doing so, consider the following.

- Under current rules, the maximum tax rate on your RRSPs is only 25%, about half of the tax rate if you had withdrawn it when you lived in Canada. Further, solid foreign tax credit planning can reduce the effective withholding rate on your RRSP withdrawal to less than 25% (see Chapter 5). Even if you are planning on going back to Canada, it can still be a good deal.
- As outlined in Chapter 7, there is the potential for double taxes between CRA, the IRS, and your local state. Further, the overall settlement costs of your estate will be higher, and these RRSPs will create an extra burden for your executor.
- As outlined above, there are U.S. Securities and Exchange Commission and state regulatory requirements restricting Canadian financial institutions from trading in your RRSPs/RRIFs unless registered in your state of residence.
- There are several tax-filing administrative duties you must fulfill every year as long as you keep any RRSP/RRIF accounts in Canada (see Chapter 5). These duties should not be missed under any circumstances since the penalties for doing so can be severe. Further, your state of residence usually has separate rules for dealing with these accounts that you will need to investigate. Overall, this means added complexity and added tax preparation fees . . . every year.
- If you are intent on retiring to the U.S., your future expenses will need to be met with U.S. dollars. If you leave a large part of your investments back in Canada held in Canadian

loonies, you could face a decline in your purchasing power in the U.S. due to a declining currency exchange. This is called currency risk, and it introduces unnecessary fluctuations in the future value of your retirement income.

- To cope with the currency exchange issues raised above, your RRSPs should be invested to hedge the U.S. currency and begin generating U.S. income to meet your future expenses in the U.S. The relaxing of the foreign content rules along with the availability of more U.S.-dollar-based investments in Canada has gone a long way to protect you from the potential currency exchange issues. In fact, there are even RRSP and RRIF accounts that have the U.S. dollar as the default currency. However, with the limited number of low-cost investment alternatives in Canada versus those in the U.S., it's more of a challenge to create a low-cost, properly diversified investment portfolio to maintain your desired level of risk and return. If you add up world financial markets, the U.S. is about 40%, while Canada is about 5%. Investing all of your savings in only 45% of the world's markets, or investing in mutual funds with huge expenses, can directly affect your investment return. David Denison, the CEO of CPP stated, "Canada as a single market cannot accommodate the future growth of our organization." As a result, CPP is increasing its current 33% allocation to foreign markets and will begin including emerging markets.

- Investment research has shown that there is a direct correlation between the expenses in your portfolio and investment returns. The higher the expenses, the lower your returns. In general, Canadian investment managers, custodians, and mutual funds cost you multiples more than the management and fees of comparable mutual funds in the U.S. Therefore, a substantial annual reduction in your portfolio expenses is generally available for your portfolio on the U.S. side of the border (see "Investing in the U.S." below).

- Another risk you take by leaving your RRSP/RRIF in Canada is that you are at the mercy of the Canadian government's ability to change, for example, the withholding or other rules relating to your registered accounts. Long ago, non-residents could collapse their RRIFs in a lump sum at a net withholding rate of 15%. Now the withholding rate is 25% on amounts not considered periodic payments. What it will be in the future is uncertain at best, as evidenced by the Canadian government's overnight tax treatment of income trusts a few years back.

- As you have probably noticed throughout this book, we are big on simplifying your life by consolidating all of your assets in the U.S. at one financial institution. Doing so has benefits most people don't realize at first. A simplified financial situation leads to a better understanding of your overall financial picture, which in turn allows you to have more control, which tends to reduce your stress and bring greater peace of mind. Further, it reduces complexity at tax time, which can save you quite a few dollars on tax preparation.

- Finally, you have to deal with it someday. You may be turning 71 and are forced to convert your RRSP to a RRIF to commence the required minimum withdrawals. You may have an unexpected cash need and decide to pull some of it out. Alternatively, your visa came through, and you've decided to stay in the U.S. longer than expected. Or you may just be tired of the complex tax returns and nuisance they cause each year. Whatever the reason, your first withdrawal will cause you to deal with all the above issues. However, the longer the passage of time, the more record keeping required, and the more you have to pay someone to determine the taxable amount of your RRSP/RRIF withdrawal in the U.S. Alternatively, you can just declare it all as income in the U.S. and pay the tax accordingly even though you don't need to.

Despite all of the reasons above, there may be a situation where leaving your RRSPs/RRIFs in Canada is the most prudent thing to do. For example, your RRSP may be in mutual funds with deferred sales charges that will expire soon, or you unexpectedly lose your immigration status and need to return to Canada shortly after moving to the U.S. Or it may make sense to do staged withdrawals of your RRSPs/RRIFs over a longer period of time for foreign tax credit planning purposes or to take advantage of tax-reduced withdrawals using the section 217 filing (see Chapter 5). Our point here is you shouldn't just collapse and move these registered accounts to the U.S. without thinking the process through from beginning to end.

LOCKED-IN RETIREMENT ACCOUNTS

Once you decide to move your investments to the U.S., you come across the thorny issue of how to collapse your Locked-In Retirement Account (LIRA). LIRAs are created when you roll your registered pension plan into a self-administered LIRA. LIRAs are exactly that, "locked-in," because the federal or provincial governments don't trust you to roll it into an RRSP and leave it there for your retirement. They feel the need to "help" you leave your retirement funds intact even though they don't provide any restrictions on how you invest them, and if it is a company such as Bre-X, Worldcom, or Enron you could lose all your funds anyway. We have seen hardship caused by these rules because retirees living in Canada are restricted in the amounts they can withdraw from their Life Income Funds (LIFs) — it's particularly hard for those who don't have other sources of income. For example, someone in her mid-50s who has saved in the company pension all her life and wants to spend more money while she is young and healthy may not be able to support her desired lifestyle because the maximum LIF payment isn't sufficient (and she isn't eligible for CPP or OAS either).

When you tell your financial institution that you want to deregister the funds and withdraw everything to move it to the U.S., the standard answer is, "You can't." You have to wait until the appropriate retirement age (usually 55), when you can convert your LIRA to a LIF (or a Locked-In Retirement Income Fund [LRIF] in certain provinces) and begin taking out the required distributions (there are both minimum and maximum amounts). The problem is the financial institution may still consider you a resident of Canada because you still have a Canadian address on the account. Collapsing your LIRA is a relatively easy process now if you are considered a non-resident of Canada.

The first item you must contend with is determining whether your employer pension plan falls under federal or provincial rules. If your LIRA falls under provincial rules, you will likely be able to withdraw the entire balance depending on which province governs the employer pension plan from which the LIRA was derived. Currently, most provinces allow you to collapse your entire LIRA if you have been a non-resident of Canada for two calendar years or more, and your spouse agrees to give up their rights to the funds. Alberta does not have a time requirement, but they do need an approved NR73 addressed later.

If your plan falls under the federal rules (federally regulated industries, such as telecommunications, television, airlines, or railroads), you have to be out of the country for at least two calendar years before you can withdraw all of your LIRA. The starting point in withdrawing your provincial or federal LIRA from Canada is filling out and filing Form NR73 — Determination of Residency Status (Leaving Canada) with CRA. This form is intentionally tricky so you must be careful when filling it out to avoid CRA determining that you are still a resident of Canada. If CRA agrees you are a non-resident of Canada, they will provide you with a letter in about six weeks confirming your non-residency for the required period. You will need to present that letter to your financial institution along with that province's form (with your spouse's attestation to forgo their rights) to request the collapse and withdrawal of your LIRA. It should take a couple of weeks to process your paperwork and you will have a check, in Canadian dollars, for the full amount of your LIRA. It is important to note that you cannot make partial withdrawals from your LIRA — generally, it has to be the entire account balance or nothing. If you have a substantial sum in your LIRA, you may want to consider collapsing it in a low tax year or at least understand the tax implications of your withdrawal.

TAX-FREE SAVINGS ACCOUNTS

Canada has a Tax-Free Savings Account (TFSA) that is similar to the Roth IRA in the U.S. You are able to contribute $5,500 after-tax to both a TFSA and a Roth IRA, but the Roth requires at least U$5,500 in earned income while a TFSA does not. All withdrawals of interest, capital gains, or dividends are tax free (versus tax deferred). Although Roth IRAs are tax free in

Canada due to the most recent treaty protocol, TFSAs are considered regular, taxable accounts in the U.S. with the income needing to be declared every year on your U.S. income tax return. It may be advisable for you to collapse these accounts tax free in Canada prior to taking up tax residency in the U.S. Obviously, each individual's situation will warrant special attention and ultimately the correct planning recommendation.

SPECIFIC TYPES OF INVESTMENTS

Following are some of the things you need to consider in moving specific types of investments to the U.S.

- **Stocks:** most individual stocks traded on an exchange in Canada can be moved to a U.S. brokerage firm and sold when requested. It usually means big savings in your pockets because the transaction costs in the U.S. versus those in Canada are typically lower. Stocks listed on both a Canadian and a U.S. stock exchange (e.g., Bell Canada, Telus) will be sold on the U.S. exchange, and the proceeds of the sale will be in U.S. dollars. Likewise, any dividends paid will be issued in U.S. dollars.
- **Bonds:** again, most individual Canadian bonds can be transferred wholesale into a U.S. brokerage account and sold when requested. However, these bonds will appear on your statement in U.S. dollars. As with stocks, the proceeds of the sale or any interest paid will be in U.S. dollars.
- **Mutual funds:** despite valiant efforts, we have been unable to transfer a single mutual fund from Canada to a U.S. financial institution or mutual fund company. Even U.S.-based mutual fund companies will not permit you to transfer their mutual funds from Canadian subsidiaries to their U.S. headquarters (e.g., Dimensional Fund Advisors). I personally tried to move the Templeton International Stock fund and the Templeton International Growth fund (both denominated in U.S. dollars) from Templeton's Canadian subsidiary to the U.S. headquarters to no avail. After countless phone calls and written requests, I gave up, sold the mutual funds, and moved the cash to the U.S. Before selling, analyze and understand the tax

implications of doing so as well as the deferred sales charges that may be involved. Without proper planning, moving mutual funds can cost you dearly.

- **Exchange Traded Funds (ETFs):** these mutual funds that trade like stocks have taken the investment world by storm because of their low expenses, tax efficiency and the ability to trade throughout the day. There is a proliferation of ETFs in the U.S. and some in Canada. We have found it possible to move U$ ETFs to a U$ account in the U.S. However, it is impossible to move a C$ ETF to the U.S.

- **Cash:** moving cash is the easiest way to bring your investment portfolio to the U.S. Liquidation of the portfolio avoids a myriad of issues, but you should analyze and understand the tax implications of doing so first. The quickest way to move your cash to the U.S. is to wire it from your bank or brokerage firm using a discount currency exchange firm that will convert your loonies into U.S. dollars and wire it into your U.S. brokerage or bank account as desired. Whatever you do, don't attempt to take a large amount of cash with you when you leave Canada through a border crossing (see Chapter 4 for more details).

- **Partnerships/unit trusts:** these investments offer you a double whammy because generally you can't move them to the U.S., and they tend to be difficult to sell. You end up stuck with this investment orphaned in Canada, which forces you to keep an account open there, and any income it produces is subject to Canadian withholding as well as U.S. taxes, foreign asset and account reporting, and so on. Overall, they add a lot of complexity to your life.

LOBBYING YOUR BROKER

Occasionally, we have witnessed shameful behavior when your broker/investment manager turns from being "Dr. Jekyll" when your investments are under his or her management to being "Mr. Hyde" when you tell him that it's in your best interest to move them to the U.S. Typically, these are people with whom you have had a long relationship and have treated you well, but when it no longer suits them they suddenly forget that your interests need to come first (that's the difference between a fiduciary standard versus a suitability standard as outlined in Chapter 13). They just don't understand that they cannot render investment advice to a resident of the U.S. without their firm being a Registered Investment Advisor, and they themselves being Investment Advisor Representatives by the SEC. On the other hand, we have also seen top-notch investment managers cooperate with their clients to help them meet their needs in expeditiously moving these assets to the U.S., particularly if there are regulatory compliance requirements they are no longer able to meet. In fact, many financial advisors have simply referred out the relationship to us because they knew the client would be better served by our unique specialty. You need to be cognizant of any changes in your investment manager and understand what is going on so you can be proactive in expediting the process of moving your assets to the U.S.

First, your broker may be compensated for the assets housed with the firm. Typically, at the end of the month, a "snapshot" is taken for purposes of compensation, so the broker will try to delay the transfer of assets at least until then. Second, investment managers typically get compensated more for stock holdings in your portfolio or loaded mutual funds, and they don't want to lose that recurring revenue stream! No doubt you'll see some foot dragging. Third, your investment manager simply will not understand why it's in your best interests to withdraw your RRSPs/RRIFs or move your other investments to the U.S. As Canadians, we are trained from birth to put money into an RRSP and never take it out, so when the request is made it's very "countercultural." To ensure the expeditious movement of your investments, we recommend the following.

1. If possible, initiate the transfer from your U.S. brokerage firm, not your Canadian investment manager. You want to use your U.S. firm to initiate a "pull" strategy versus relying on your Canadian manager to initiate a "push" strategy.

2. If necessary, have a nice but firm conversation with your investment manager; make it clear that you are doing this and that there's no changing your mind.

3. Follow up, follow up, follow up. Create a sense of urgency about this move, and keep hounding your investment manager for an update/the status of the transfer so the message is clearly sent.

4. Be sure to obtain the name of your investment manager's supervisor so that, if your investment manager is suddenly "on vacation" or "out of the office," you have a backup person to keep moving the transfer forward.

5. Document, document, document. Keep track of all phone calls, the date and time, the subject, the person you talked to, and the outcome.

6. Email your broker, and if necessary cc his manager, so that everything is documented. Investment management firms are required to maintain all email records for regulatory purposes, so a clear history is built and can be referred to in resolving disputes.

INVESTING IN THE U.S.

There are several differences between Canada and the U.S. when it comes to investing your money. Unfortunately, for most Canadians making the transition to the U.S., they are unaware of these differences and end up making some costly mistakes or paying too much. This is typically the result of an overzealous broker, a smooth-talking mutual fund salesperson, or an annuity provider. Following are some of the things you need to consider before investing your hard-earned dollars in the U.S.

INVESTMENT EXPENSES

The U.S. is known as one of the most inexpensive places in the world to invest, far below the expenses seen in Canada. This is important because investment research has shown that investment expenses and tax efficiency are two key determinants of portfolio return. Competition in the financial services industry continues to put pressure on brokerage fees, commission rates, and mutual fund expenses. Coupled with the advent of index funds and exchange-traded funds, these factors have reduced investment expenses far more in the U.S. than in Canada (although that is changing . . . but slowly due to the large industry lobbying efforts). The most insidious thing about these fees is that most investors don't even know they are paying them unless they look at the prospectuses sent to them (most don't because they trust their advisors, who don't voluntarily disclose them!). Most mutual funds in Canada typically have a 2–3.5% expense ratio compared with an average 0.15–0.50% in the U.S. For example, C$100,000 in Canadian mutual funds can cost you easily 2–3.5% or C$2,000 to C$3,500 per year (on top of any deferred sales charge), whereas a no-load U.S. mutual fund has expense ratios of approximately 0.15–0.50% or U$150 to U$500 per year or less. In addition, there is a much larger selection of low-cost mutual funds in the U.S. that we can use with expense ratios around 0.07% for an S&P 500 Index fund. Not only are the costs of the mutual funds much higher, but the cost to hire an investment manager is also much higher in Canada than in the U.S. In the U.S., the typical investment manager will charge 1% of the first $1 million in assets under management, with a declining percentage for each additional million. In Canada, we have seen the same fees start at 1.25% and go as high as 2% on the first $2 million in assets under management. Canada's high investment costs relative to the world have been publicly condemned by the World Trade Organization, but lobbying efforts in the industry have left much unchanged and investors paying the price. In the U.S., you will find you keep more of your money so it can earn you more.

TAX-PREFERENCE INVESTMENTS

There are several tax-preference investment alternatives available in the U.S. that are not generally available in Canada. These may or may not be appropriate for you.

- Municipal bonds: if you purchase bonds issued by the municipal governments in your state of residence, the interest is both federal and state tax free (if applicable). As expected, the interest rates on the tax-free bonds are typically lower than those on the fully taxable bonds because of their tax-free status. Interest from municipal bonds purchased from outside your state of residence is tax free federally but taxable on your state return (if applicable).

- Federal U.S. obligations: interest from U.S. government bonds, T-bills, etc. is taxfree at the state level (if applicable) but still taxable at the federal level.
- Exempt money market: these money market mutual funds invest only in federal or municipal government bonds and provide the tax benefits outlined above.
- Annuities: you make a contribution to an annuity on a one-time or ongoing basis, and the earnings grow tax deferred. When you are eligible to make withdrawals, your initial contribution is returned tax free, while the earnings are taxed as ordinary income. You should seek competent advice (someone who doesn't sell annuities for a living) before investing in these annuities since they can lock you in for some time and typically have high expenses (hidden) associated with them. Do not move an IRA into an annuity!
- Life insurance: there are many insurance policies that allow part of your premium to pay for the life insurance with the balance going toward investments. These investments are generally mutual funds that the insurance company offers. The investment income grows tax deferred, and you are able to take out a loan against the cash value that does not have any tax implications. If you withdraw the cash value, any amount above your premium payments made is taxable. Again, you should seek competent advice before investing in these policies, because they typically have high expenses associated with them.
- Roth IRA: if you have earned income, you are eligible to make an after-tax contribution to this Individual Retirement Account, invest it, and watch it grow tax free (versus tax deferred). This may be a wonderful alternative for you depending on your unique circumstances (see Chapter 8 for more details).

We have seen many complex schemes, financial products, and complexities added to people's lives to reduce their income taxes. We are all for legal tax avoidance techniques used to your benefit. However, sometimes the simplest strategies are the best. For example, if you buy a low-cost, tax-efficient, exchange-traded fund and never sell it, how much tax will you pay? What are the expenses associated with this strategy? Correct, none. You just got a tax deferral at a fraction of the expense and complexity of some sophisticated tax strategy concocted by a tax attorney! Good advice from an advisor held to a fiduciary standard is typically your best bet.

OTHER DIFFERENCES

- Money market "sweep": dividends or interest payments, maturing bonds, or investment sales result in cash in your account. In Canada, this cash generally sits in an account earning "savings" account interest rates until you choose to invest the cash in a money market mutual fund. These money market funds in Canada may have a deferred sales charge and/or a high management expense ratio, so understand the instrument before investing. In the U.S., the nice thing is that these are low-cost funds that allow you to take money out at any time, penalty free. As a result, you earn the higher money market rate starting the same day your cash hits the account versus a savings account rate, which can be 1–3% less.

- Mutual funds: some investors in Canada have researched and become familiar with the different mutual fund families in Canada, such as Dynamic, Mackenzie, Phillips Hager & North, RBC Asset Management, MD Management, etc. In the U.S., however, no such funds exist. The question then becomes, "Which mutual fund families should I use in the U.S.?" Vanguard? American? Dimensional Fund Advisors? There are close to 17,000 mutual funds you can select from in the U.S., but it will take you a while to determine which mutual fund is right for your unique circumstances.

FOREIGN TAX CREDIT PLANNING

Once you have collapsed your RRSPs/RRIFs/LIRAs, paid the requisite withholding, and moved your cash to the U.S., it is time to invest it again. What many people don't realize is that, by properly structuring your investment portfolio in the U.S. to produce foreign income, you can begin recouping some of the withholding tax you left in Canada on your U.S. income tax return. We have seen folks implement proper foreign tax credit planning strategies withdraw a C$1 million RRSP, leave C$250,000 in withholding in Canada, and recoup all of it on their U.S. tax returns before the foreign tax credits expired. This means they withdrew their entire RRSP tax free from Canada. Unfortunately, some firms use this tax-free RRSP withdrawal promise to promote their services, but it is definitely not the norm. We include it as an example to show you the power of proper foreign tax credit planning strategies. Considering your situation, wouldn't you rather pay 5 or 10% withholding on your RRSP rather than 25%? Our firm can analyze your situation and, if applicable, show you how.

The ideal investment to consume your passive foreign tax credits would produce a lot of foreign income annually and not have any foreign taxes withheld. There is a myriad of investments we can use, but which one to use depends on your individual situation and what you are trying to achieve. Don't forget that foreign tax credits have a defined "life" before they expire, so it's important to implement your foreign tax credit planning strategies as soon as your RRSPs are collapsed, or at least in a balanced fashion to maximize your benefit (see Chapter 5 for more details).

OUR INVESTMENT PHILOSOPHY

We believe in two simple principles when it comes to investing.

1. Grandma was always right: don't put all of your eggs in one basket. In other words, diversify, diversify, diversify. Why? Because of principle number two.

2. Nobody can predict the future!

Based on these principles, our firm doesn't try to outguess short-term market movements or pick hot managers, stocks, or sectors. We don't try to determine when to be in the market or when to be out of it, because the investment research driven out of the institutional investment world where they manage billions of dollars has concluded that accurate predictions can't be made on a consistent, long-term basis (for those who think they can, is it luck or is it skill, and how can you tell?). Instead, our intention is to capture market returns as efficiently and effectively as possible by remaining invested in a broadly diversified portfolio tailored to meet your investment goals and your tolerance for the ups and downs of financial markets. This approach includes an analysis of your long-term projections, current and projected tax situation, current investment portfolio, foreign tax credit inventory, and of course the lifestyle you want now and in the future. In other words, we manage your investment portfolio in an integrated approach to your comprehensive financial plan.

As mentioned earlier, research has shown that the costs of investing along with the tax efficiency of the portfolio are two key determining factors in portfolio returns. As a result, a combination of tax-efficient index funds, exchange-traded funds, and other low-cost vehicles (read no-load) will form the core of your portfolio, with some asset class adjustments as warranted. Our custom-made tools allow us to analyze your Canadian and U.S. investments, consolidate them in one currency for analysis, and determine the right investment strategy to achieve your desired lifestyle.

Our firm believes in a broadly diversified investment portfolio that starts with the four basic asset classes: cash, stocks, bonds, and hedging strategies. Stocks are further broken down into domestic (U.S. and Canadian) and foreign (the rest of the world, including Europe, Asia, and emerging markets). This is further broken down into large cap and small cap as well as growth and value. Bonds are also broken down into domestic and foreign. They are broken down further to include short-term, medium-term, and long-term bonds. Hedging strategies consist of asset classes that move out of sync with stocks and bonds. They include real estate, natural resources, energy, precious metals, and other strategies that are not correlated to these other asset classes as they become available.

Finally, our firm believes in a disciplined approach, and this is where we help our clients the most. This means investing when you have the money and selling when you need it again. There is a big difference between speculating and investing, and it is important to note the chasm between them. We find that people invest in one of three ways: by fear, by greed, or by objective. When investing by fear, the slightest drop in financial markets has these speculators selling out everything. Investing by greed leads them to buy when the market is up. Investing by objective looks at rate of return your portfolio needs to achieve to reach your objectives and structures the portfolio to achieve those objectives over the long term while taking into account your tolerance for market fluctuations.

Our annual retainer service starts by developing an investment policy statement and current and target asset allocation review. This document uses your transition plan to outline further details of how your portfolio should be structured. It provides the guidelines on how the portfolio will be governed to meet your objectives. Once the policy is agreed to by all involved, the portfolio is implemented. You should never have anyone invest your money unless you have a written investment policy statement beforehand. Of course, any plan must be monitored closely. As a result, we conduct quarterly reviews of the portfolio, rebalancing it and managing taxes as necessary. The portfolio information is downloaded daily into portfolio accounting software used to determine the performance of the portfolio, which in turn enables better decision making. We provide quarterly reporting and rebalancing and are available to answer your questions as the markets move through their natural cycles. If you are interested in having your investments managed in context with your Canada-U.S. transition plan, we'd be happy to assist you. We are able to offer a comprehensive, coordinated approach to investing in both Canada and the U.S. since we are registered investment advisors in the U.S. and investment counselors/portfolio managers in Canada.

THE BUSINESS 11
OF BUSINESS

Today or tomorrow we will go to this or that city,
spend a year there, carry on business and make money.
— JAMES 4:13

For business owners, there are more options under their control when moving to the U.S. than for nonbusiness owners. For example, your business can be a ticket to legal U.S. immigration status, health care, or disability coverage. However, business entities also add a lot of complexity to your situation, and there can be many hazards in leaving Canada without getting the requisite planning done. In our experience, business entity planning requires a longer lead time than individual planning (two to three years) and the proper team in place to adequately design and implement the appropriate strategies before entering the U.S. However, if you do this correctly, you can reap huge rewards from both a Canadian and a U.S. perspective.

EMIGRATE TO THE U.S.

If you have a "substantive" business in Canada that has been operating for at least two years, you can use it to set up a U.S. subsidiary. Once the U.S. location is up and running (generating revenues, hired employees, etc.), you as the owner may be able to use that business to obtain an L-1 visa (intracompany transfer) and transfer yourself and your family to the U.S. location. This visa is designed for companies with a presence in both Canada and the U.S. and the need to transfer executives, managers, or others with specialized knowledge between the two locations. The L-1 visa is issued for one year initially for a new U.S. enterprise and can be renewed for a total of seven years. Most importantly, the L-1 visa issued to executives and managers can be a "shortcut" to a green card. With your L-1 visa in hand, you may be able to file for an "adjustment of status," which means you can apply to USCIS to replace your L-1 visa with a permanent resident green card with the intent of operating your business for the foreseeable future in the U.S. Once you obtain a green card and hold it for five years, you are eligible to apply for U.S. citizenship if that is your desire. As you can see, you could be discarding a golden opportunity to move to the U.S. if you sell or wind up your business beforehand.

Another alternative is to obtain an E-2 treaty investor visa by investing in the U.S. in a business intent on carrying on substantial trade between the U.S. and Canada or where a substantial investment of capital is made. This visa holder is admitted initially for two years, and then the visa can be renewed indefinitely as long as you are overseeing the investment or carrying on a trade, but it does not lead easily to a green card. Since 1990, the "gold card" or EB-5 green card has been made available by USCIS for investors who establish a business in the U.S. with an investment of between U$500,000 and U$1 million in a "targeted employment area." The enterprise needs to show how it will benefit the economy and employ at least 10 U.S. workers full time; however, the investor must have some policy-making role in the firm. The "gold card" is issued on a conditional basis for two years. After two years, and once the full investment has been completed and the 10 U.S. workers are employed, a petition is filed to remove the conditions and make it a permanent resident green card. Approximately 10,000 of these visas are available annually, but in the past few years only about 1,000 were approved annually because the rules and regulations surrounding them are very specific (see Chapter 3 for more details). The gold card is rarely used, but our firm has direct experience in assisting clients in this area and working with attorneys with a high success ratio in these applications. One thing to ask when selecting an attorney to process your EB-5 application is if they "receive a 'kickback' from the business your money will be invested in" to qualify you for the EB-5. Often, these investments are legit for USCIS purposes but a poor business decision overall. Be sure to look at the merits of the investment, not just the fact that it might get you qualified for an EB-5 card. Be sure to ask your attorney to apply any kickback to reducing the fees owed for processing your application. If they won't (hint: they are double-dipping), move on to someone who will.

HEALTH-CARE COVERAGE

As a business owner in the U.S., you have an opportunity to get health-care coverage for you and your family. One alternative is to install a group health-care plan for yourself, your family, and your employees. Typically, this can be done with as few as two employees, such as a husband-wife team, and any premiums are deductible to the business. Depending on the number of employees your firm employs, Obamacare now mandates that you must offer a health-care plan to your employees — or face penalties. A lot depends on which state you relocate to and which medical plans are available in that state, since each state governs its own health-care insurance industry.

Another important benefit you can get with a business is disability coverage. Statistics show that, if you are under the age of 45, you are more likely to become disabled than you are to die. The problem with disability is your income goes down while your expenses typically go up. To cover this risk exposure as a business owner, you can set up a group disability insurance plan for you and your employees and deduct the premiums through the business. This plan will provide you with some income (usually 60% of your insured salary) in the event you are no longer able to work (see Chapter 2 for more details).

INCOME TAX IMPLICATIONS

By now, you have an understanding of the personal tax implications when moving to the U.S. However, when you add a business to the mix, the complexity increases dramatically. It has been our experience that your current, trusted team of advisors, whom you have worked with for many years, are typically incapable of addressing the Canada-U.S. issues adequately when you move to the U.S. In fact, some clients have told us that their advisors said it simply couldn't be done because of the complexity and discouraged them from attempting a move to the U.S. altogether. They were told they should just stay in Canada because the taxes upon their exit would simply consume what has taken them a lifetime to accumulate. A move can be done, though, and depending on your individual circumstances, the savings in time, effort, and money can be significant. You just have to understand that your current advisors will need to join or be replaced by a new team led by a competent Canada-U.S. transition planner to coordinate all the activities of the team. In addition, the sooner you put this team in place in anticipation of your move, the more fruit the planning process can bear. Following are some of the issues to be aware of when moving to the U.S. when you own a business.

CANADIAN TAX IMPLICATIONS

When you leave Canada, the shares of your business are subject to the departure tax mentioned earlier in this book. There is typically very little, if any, "cost basis" (original capital contributions) in these shares, which means, in most cases, the fair market value of your business must be declared on your final Canadian exit return. This declaration can cause incredible hardship if the majority of your net worth is tied up in the business and there are no other liquid assets available to pay the tax upon your exit. One option is to file Form T1244 — Election, under Subsection 220(4.5) of the Income Tax Act, to Defer the Payment of Tax on Income Relating to the Deemed Disposition of Property with CRA. This option will allow you to defer the tax as long as you can provide acceptable security to the Minister of National Revenue to cover any amounts of federal tax owing in excess of C$14,500. This deferral has the dual effect of "freezing" your departure tax if you expect your business to increase in value and avoiding the liquidity issues of the tax owing when you leave Canada.

A unique issue arises with the departure tax if there are assets inside the corporation that have appreciated in value. After you pay the departure tax on the company shares and are comfortably residing in the U.S., if you sell appreciated assets inside the corporation, it needs to declare that income on a T2 tax form and pay Canadian income tax on it again. Another issue is that, if you sell the assets out of the business beforehand instead of the shares, you may be subject to capital cost allowance recapture. The business may face a huge tax bill if the assets inside it have been fully depreciated. The reason is that all of the capital cost allowance you have taken over the years is recaptured in the year of sale, and taxes are owed at that time. You can see that an appreciated or depreciated asset inside a corporation can be subject to double tax — once through the departure tax on the company shares and again when the asset is actually sold.

One alternative is to take advantage of CRA's onetime C$813,600 (indexed annually) lifetime Small Business Capital Gains Exemption on your company shares. If you are able to structure your business and other financial affairs appropriately, you may be able to include your spouse and double the capital gains exemption to offset the first C$1,627,200 in capital gains you face when exiting Canada. Unfortunately, the rules for this exemption are very specific and complex, so competent Canada-U.S. counsel should be retained before such an undertaking.

Being self-employed and owning a sole proprietorship when you leave Canada can cause some complications as well. You could be subject to "depreciation recapture" when you leave Canada if you directly hold assets that have been depreciated. There may be other issues, and they depend on the individual situation, but there is typically very little departure tax to contend with because the primary value of a sole proprietorship is its owner.

As a U.S. resident holding Canadian corporate entities, you quickly face complex tax-filing requirements. First, since the business is located in Canada, you must continue filing Canadian corporate T2 tax returns. Any income withdrawn as wages may have to be declared on a Canadian individual T1 tax return. If the income is paid out as a dividend, you must ensure the appropriate treaty withholding is taken at source, or you will have to file a Part XIII tax letter and Form NR7-R to correct the withholding with CRA. Don't forget, you need to continue to collect and remit Goods and Services Tax (GST) for the federal government or the Harmonized Sales Tax (HST) for your respective province.

We have seen people who have neglected to do the requisite planning before leaving Canada with a substantive business entity and, when they realize their situation, start playing tax tie games with CRA. They live in the U.S. but retain tax ties to Canada, so they are not subject to the nasty departure tax on their corporation. In our experience, this is akin to playing Russian roulette with the tax authorities, and it is inevitable that you will commit tax suicide. We don't recommend maintaining tax ties to both countries without seeking the appropriate counsel beforehand to ensure you understand your risks. We have also seen people undertake tremendous planning where most of the taxable portions of the business can be paid out as a dividend subject to a treaty-reduced withholding tax, which can then be used as a foreign tax credit on their U.S. returns. The key is having the right team in place and enough lead time to get the planning done.

U.S. TAX IMPLICATIONS

When keeping a business entity in Canada as a U.S. tax resident, you must be aware of the IRS Controlled Foreign Corporation (CFC) rules. A common strategy in Canada is to leave retained earnings inside the corporation and invest them as a tax-deferral technique. A problem arises in that the portfolio income is taxed directly in the hands of the shareholder in the U.S. There is a "mismatch" of the foreign tax credits on the U.S. return, which creates a double tax situation. Further, the shareholder does not get the preferred tax rates on income such as dividends and capital gains and instead is taxed at regular marginal tax rates. As a result, the lack of planning can lead to the following accumulation of taxes.

> 13% — Canadian corporate tax
> 39.6% — U.S. federal personal tax
> 3.8% — U.S. net investment tax

All told, the cumulative tax rate could be up to 56.4% on every $1 of income. If you add state tax (like California at 10%), the total could be over 65%!

As a U.S. citizen or resident who is a shareholder, officer, or director of a foreign corporation, you must file Form 5471 — Information Return of U.S. Persons with Respect to Certain Foreign Corporations with your U.S. personal income tax filing, which is due April 15th each year. This is simply a reporting requirement (versus a tax return), but if not completed the penalties can be up to U$10,000 for each year the form was not filed. In fact, if this form is not filed, the IRS will now automatically assess this penalty! The IRS estimates the average time to prepare the form (exclusive of the requisite bookkeeping) at about 50 hours, but the actual time could be much longer for the uninitiated. Form 5471 appears to be deceptively simple since it is only four pages long, but there are also several worksheets and schedules that must be prepared along with 15 pages of instructions that will test your patience.

Any income taken out of the Canadian corporation as wages or dividends must also be reported on your individual 1040 tax return in the U.S. because you are required to declare your worldwide income on your U.S. tax return. Proper tax preparation should allow you to take offsetting foreign tax credits to avoid double taxation, but you still have to be aware of the other effects the income may have on your itemized deductions, personal exemption, and marginal tax bracket.

Another issue to be aware of is that, once a U.S. person has SubPart F income to report from a foreign corporation, the corporation thereafter must switch to a calendar year. This change can cause complications because, if the Canadian corporation has a fiscal year like June 1st, you may have to pick up 18 months of income on that return spread out over five years, whereas it is common to operate on a fiscal year end (mid-year) in Canada. This difference causes complications because you have to reconcile your books twice to get the appropriate numbers together for your tax preparer. In addition, reconciling your personal wages, dividends, and varying currency exchange rates from the corporation to align with the mandatory calendar tax year for your individual tax returns in Canada and the U.S. makes things complicated.

When located in Canada, Canadian private corporations get preferred tax rates on the first C$400,000 in income (generally between 14% and 19% depending on the province of your company). However, many people move to the U.S. without the requisite planning and, as a result, lose the preferential tax rates and are required to pay net corporate tax rates between 29% and 35%, again depending on provincial rules. This is particularly true when the date you move to the U.S. is different from the fiscal year end of the corporation. There are some good planning opportunities here that can assist you in retaining the preferential rates.

In Canada, it is common to carry a lot of "retained earnings" inside the corporation. In essence, they provide a form of tax deferral until distributed as wages or dividends. In the U.S., however, accumulated earnings in excess of U$250,000 for a C corporation (U$150,000 for certain personal service corporations) require a case to be made with the IRS that the accumulated earnings are required for business purposes (e.g., an investment in capital or having cash available for an expected downturn). Otherwise, the retained earnings could be subject to "accumulated earnings tax" of an additional 20% on top of what is already owing. Table 11.1 is a summary of the corporate tax rates in both Canada and the U.S.

TABLE 11.1

2015 FEDERAL CORPORATE TAX BRACKETS

Canadian Taxable Income		U.S. Taxable Income (U$)	
C$0 +	15%	0-50,000	15%
Derived as follows:		50,001–75,000	25%
General corporate rate	38.0%	75,001–100,000	34%
Less federal abatement	(10.0%)	100,001–335,000	39%
Equals	28.0%	335,001–10,000,000	34%
Rate reductions	(13.0%)	10,000,001–15,000,000	35%
Equals	15.0%	15,000,001–18,333,333	38%
		18,333,333 +	35%

U.S. BUSINESS ENTITIES

Compared with Canada, there are more business entities in the U.S. that are "flow-through" for tax purposes. This means any income generated by the company flows through to your personal tax return in the U.S. and avoids the higher corporate income tax rates or being taxed twice, as with corporate dividends. Following are some of the most common business entity types in the U.S.

- **C corporation:** this is a common corporation that files a corporate Form 1120 tax return, is subject to U.S. corporate income tax rates, and offers liability protection. This is how most large "blue-chip" corporations in the U.S. are structured. These organizations have shareholders (common, preferred, etc.), typically issue bonds, and need to file annual meeting minutes to ensure compliance.

- **S corporation:** this is simply a C corporation that has taken an "S corp" election to pass through all income to the individual shareholders. The company still has shareholders, prepares annual meeting minutes, and offers liability protection, but all income is taxed at the individual's personal income tax rates. The S corporation files a Form 1120-S tax return and issues Schedule K-1s to each shareholder to declare on their individual tax returns (similar to the T5013 returns in Canada). Both the "C" and the "S" corporations are more difficult to set up and maintain, but because shares are issued they are easier to transfer in the event of a sale.
- **Limited liability company (LLC):** not a corporation per se, this entity has "members" instead of shareholders, and all income is passed through to the members. This is a very popular business entity in the U.S. because it is inexpensive and easy to set up, does not require annual meeting minutes, offers liability protection, and avoids the federal corporate income tax rates. However, you can elect to have an LLC taxed as a C corporation in the U.S. if that suits your planning needs.
- **Partnerships:** there are many different kinds of partnerships, and which one to use depends on your needs. For example, there are general partnerships, limited partnerships, limited liability partnerships, limited liability limited partnerships, and so on.

Understanding what you are trying to build helps you to determine which of these tools to use in your situation and depends on your individual financial circumstances, the type of business you want to set up, and what you intend to do with the business over the long term. Needless to say, it is best to do some planning beforehand to select the appropriate entity and get it set up appropriately to avoid complications later.

A SIMPLIFIED EXAMPLE

Owning a Canadian corporation when you relocate to the U.S. has its own set of complexities, particularly when entities span the border. We have seen many business entity structures that made sense to the client when presented by a Canadian accountant or attorney but in reality made no sense given a full understanding of the rules in both Canada and the U.S. Figure 11.1 is one business structure we worked on, and it provides a vivid illustration of what the wrong structure can do. A husband and wife living in Canada each owned half of the shares of 1234 Canada Inc., a Canadian corporation. Inside this corporation were three investment properties, one located in Canada and two in the U.S. 1234 Canada Inc. owned U.S. Holdings Inc., an American C corporation. U.S. Holdings owned two investment properties located in the U.S. This structure was recommended by the clients' Canadian attorney to "protect them from U.S. liability issues" while they lived in Canada, but this "cross-border expert" created a multilayered tax situation for the clients that they weren't aware of until it was explained to them.

FIGURE 11.1
SAMPLE BUSINESS STRUCTURE

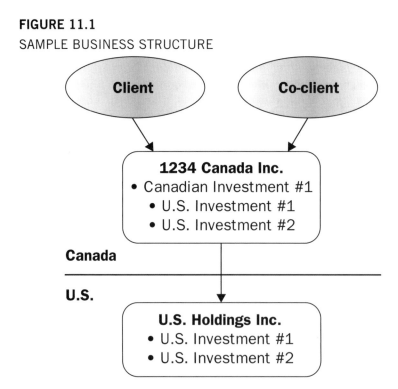

Here is the tax situation for U.S. Holdings Inc.

- **Tax #1:** all income generated by the two investments inside U.S. Holdings Inc. must be declared on IRS Form 1120 — U.S. Corporation Income Tax Return and taxed at U.S. corporate rates, which can be as low as 15% and as high as 39.6% (on taxable income over U$100,000) plus state tax (as high as 12.3%, but it depends on which state[s] the corporation operates in or derives income from).
- **Tax #2:** since U.S. Holdings Inc. is owned by 1234 Canada Inc., all dividends moved up to 1234 Canada Inc. are subject to a 5% non-resident withholding by the IRS.
- **Tax #3:** all the dividends received from U.S. Holdings Inc. will be declared on a Canadian T2 corporate tax return and taxed at Canadian corporate rates at 15%. There will be a foreign tax credit for the 5% withholding but not for the tax paid in the U.S. by U.S. Holdings Inc.
- **Tax #4:** any income from U.S. Holdings Inc. distributed as salary from 1234 Canada Inc. would flow through to the clients' personal tax returns at Canadian rates of 30–45% or more, but 1234 Canada Inc. would get a deduction, so an additional layer of taxes won't occur. However, if distributed as a dividend, the dividend tax credit applies, but no deduction is available to 1234 Canada Inc., so some double taxation still results.

Note that these taxes are primarily cumulative, with little or no offsetting foreign tax credits for an aggregate tax rate of 60–70% or more! For every dollar in income generated inside U.S. Holdings Inc., only 30–40¢ was actually ending up in the clients' pockets. Even more tragic is the fact that the damage was already done, and little could be done to avoid the steep income tax bill on the income and gains already accrued on the U.S. investments. The clients had no clue this was happening, and with the successful investments they had made they were essentially helping to eliminate the annual deficits in both countries! They had a U.S. accountant preparing their U.S. tax returns and their trusted

Canadian accountant preparing their Canadian returns, yet the attorney who devised the structure wasn't coordinating tax preparation on both sides of the border. The clients were trying to do it themselves, but given the complexity it is no surprise they didn't catch the fact that they were paying these levels of tax on the same income either. Further, this entity planning did not take into account the clients' desire to move eventually to the U.S. With the requisite planning, the clients would have realized more of the fruits of their investments and had an appropriate structure for an eventual tax-prudent move to the U.S.

We will briefly explain the taxation of the investments inside 1234 Canada Inc., but as you can see double taxation can be avoided for the most part because offsetting foreign tax credits and deductions are available.

- **Tax #1:** the IRS reserves the right to tax any trade or business income connected to the U.S. (except as exempted by the Canada-U.S. Tax Treaty) plus fixed income such as dividends and interest. Because a Canadian (foreign) corporation held the U.S. investments, any income produced by these two investments must be declared on IRS Form 1120F and taxed at U.S. corporate rates, which can be as low as 15% and as high as 39.6% (on taxable income over U$100,000) plus state tax (as high as 12.3%).
- **Tax #2:** any income generated by any of the properties held by 1234 Canada Inc. is declared on a Canadian T2 corporate tax return and taxed at Canadian corporate rates at 15%. For the two U.S. properties, a foreign tax credit is available for the tax paid on the U.S. corporate tax return.
- **Tax #3:** depending on where the work is performed, any income distributed as salary from 1234 Canada Inc. may be declared as a Canadian source and flows through to the clients' personal tax returns at Canadian rates of 30–45% or more. However, 1234 Canada Inc. would get a deduction for those wages paid, and double taxation is avoided. Yet you have to consider any payroll taxes that you may owe in Canada or the U.S. on those wages. If distributed as a

dividend, however, the dividend tax credit applies, but no deduction is available to 1234 Canada Inc., so some double taxation still results.

TAXATION WHEN MOVING TO THE U.S.

When these folks move to the U.S., their current business structure leaves them in a multilayered tax situation as well. The taxes noted above all remain the same (except as outlined below), and they also have to face the departure taxes.

- **Departure tax:** when the owners of the business left Canada, the shares of 1234 Canada Inc. were "deemed" disposed of. Since there were substantive gains in the shares of 1234 Canada Inc. (reflecting the gains in each of the investments inside U.S. Holdings Inc.), the gains are declared on their Canadian "exit" returns, and a large tax liability is created. The problem with the departure tax is that it occurs on the shares of 1234 Canada Inc., not on the gains in the investments inside the company. When these investments are sold and the gains realized, this income will have to be declared and will be taxed again!
- **Distributions:** any income distributed as salary from 1234 Canada Inc. will be declared as a Canadian source, and tax will be paid on T1 personal tax returns at Canadian rates of 30–45% or more, but 1234 Canada Inc. would get a deduction, so an additional layer of taxes will not occur. Because the IRS requires taxpayers to declare their worldwide income, the wages would have to be declared on a U.S. 1040 tax return and U.S. taxes paid with offsetting foreign tax credits for any Canadian taxes paid. If the income is distributed as a dividend from 1234 Canada Inc., no deduction is available to 1234 Canada Inc., and the dividend would be subject to a 15% withholding per the Canada-U.S. Tax Treaty. The dividend would have to be declared on the taxpayers' U.S. 1040 tax returns and U.S. taxes paid with offsetting foreign tax credits for the 15% withholding left in Canada.

- As mentioned earlier, a U.S. resident who is a shareholder, officer, or director of a foreign corporation must file Form 5471 — Information Return of U.S. Persons with Respect to Certain Foreign Corporations with your U.S. personal income tax filing, which is due April 15th each year.
- **U.S. estate taxes:** as outlined earlier, when you move to the U.S., you are subject to the U.S. estate-tax regime, with punishing tax rates of 40% on amounts over U$3.5 million in net worth in 2015. Unfortunately, the value of your worldwide assets, including your Canadian business, is included in this calculation. This means that, if you move to the U.S. without the requisite planning and perish, your heirs may have to conduct a "fire sale" of your business to pay the 40% U.S. estate taxes. The depletion of your estate can be significant.

As this simplified example vividly illustrates, the taxation of business entities when leaving Canada can become extremely complex. No wonder so many accountants and tax lawyers simply throw up their hands and declare "It just can't be done." We are thankful for the network of professionals proficient in these transactions who have assisted our clients over the years. They have a thorough knowledge of this area and have a number of strategies and techniques that can be deployed as needed to address most business issues. We have personally witnessed this planning save hundreds of thousands of dollars and countless hours of frustration. The best thing you can do? Hire the appropriate team three to four years in advance of your move to start the planning.

ESCAPING THE 12 ENDLESS WINTER

He spreads snow like wool
and scatters the frost like ashes.
He hurls down His hail like pebbles.
Who can withstand His icy blast?
— PSALM 147:16-17

For some folks, remaining in Canada during the summer months before heading south to the U.S. for the warmer winter months suits them just fine. Unlike their "sunbird" counterparts seeking to escape the summer heat in the southern states, these "snowbirds" seek to escape the winter cold, particularly in the prairie provinces where it can get unbearably cold. When arthritis begins to set in, winter sports aren't appealing anymore, and the World Junior Hockey Championships are over, these folks set their sights on heading down to the warm southern states where they can maintain their active lifestyle. Owning property in the U.S. offers many benefits, including a fixed place to go and a potential increase in your investment. Despite these benefits, people aren't generally prepared for the potential tax, estate planning, and paperwork nightmare that comes with having a property in the U.S. This complexity needs to be considered in your overall decision to buy a second home in the U.S. This chapter aims to clear up a lot of confusion surrounding owning property in the U.S. while remaining a resident of Canada.

RECREATIONAL PROPERTY

For properties in the U.S. that are used exclusively for personal use, there are several issues to consider. For example, there are several options in how you title the property, tax implications when buying or selling it, and disposition issues at your death.

TITLE/OWNERSHIP

During the real estate craze of 2008 in the U.S., Canadians were buying up properties in the southern states at a record pace. This rush on U.S. properties at the beginning of the twenty-first century occurred when: (1) the real estate market in the U.S. crashed due to poor mortgage underwriting standards; (2) the Canadian loonie and the U.S. dollar were at parity; and (3) Canadian real estate prices skyrocketed. This allowed many to take out equity from their existing home or sell a second property, convert it at parity to U.S. dollars, and buy a second home at bargain basement prices in the warm climate of their choice. Our office receives a lot of calls that start with, "I am closing on a house tomorrow and the title company is asking me how I want to title the property? Can you help?" It is a simple question, but answering it, unfortunately, requires a full understanding of your financial situation. It sounds harsh but a lack of planning on the part of these folks does not constitute an emergency for us. Hopefully, the following will help you navigate the complexities of how to take title to a U.S. leisure property when a resident of Canada — well in advance of when the title company asks you the question.

There are several ways to take title to personal-use property in the U.S. We will cover the main ones here, with the remaining being addressed in the section on buying investment property later in this chapter.

OWN IT OUTRIGHT

"What?! You mean just take title in my own name? That seems too simple!" Yup, often titling in your own name turns out to be the simplest, easiest solution to the problem of owning personal property in the U.S. Far too often we see U.S. and Canadian accountants and lawyers wanting to complicate something that shouldn't be complicated so they can charge extra fees. Taking title individually or with your spouse (if you are married) is generally the best approach. Often, we hear, "I heard I should add my children to the title because . . ." Our response generally is, "Why?" There is no need to complicate things any further by adding anyone else to the property title. Previously, when the U.S. estate exemption was much smaller, there were many other schemes used to try and reduce the estate tax, like corporations, partnerships, trusts, ownership with kids, nonrecourse mortgages, etc. Now, with the estate-tax exemption increasing to U$5.43 million (as discussed later in this chapter), a lot of this is no longer necessary. However, there are different options in taking title outright depending in which state your property is located.

If your property resides in any of the 41 common law property states (versus 9 community property states outlined below), you have the following choices to take title to your property.

Joint Tenancy With Rights of Survivorship (JTWROS): This is the most common way to take title to property for married (including same-sex) couples or where more than one person is involved. Each spouse (or others) owns their half (or third, or quarter) of the property and, at the first person's passing, that decedent's portion goes automatically to the remaining owner(s) and avoids probate.

Tenancy by the Entirety: Each spouse (or others) owns their equal share of the property and at the first person's passing, that decedent's portion goes automatically to the remaining owner(s) and avoids probate. The problem with this form of ownership is each owner is viewed as owning the entire property. This means that no one can act independently of the others and you all must agree before anyone can sell or gift the property. This method of titling is only available for properties in: Alaska, Arkansas, Delaware, District of Columbia, Florida, Hawaii, Illinois, Indiana, Kentucky, Maryland, Massachusetts, Michigan, Mississippi, Missouri, New Jersey, New York, North Carolina, Oklahoma, Oregon, Pennsylvania, Rhode Island, Tennessee, Vermont, Virginia, and Wyoming.

Tenancy in Common: This method of titling is generally used by unrelated parties to own properties, particularly when ownership of parts isn't equal. This allows for various ownership interests (40%, 40%, 20%), but when an owner dies that portion goes to the deceased's estate, not to the other owners. This means that a new owner — who may or may not get along with the others — can now be involved with the property.

If your property is located in any of the community property states outlined in Chapter 7 (Arizona, California, Idaho, Louisiana, Nevada, New Mexico, Texas, Washington, Wisconsin), you have these two choices as a married (or same-sex) couple.

Community Property: Each spouse owns their half of the property and at the first spouse's passing, the decedent's half goes through probate as directed in their estate plan.

Community Property With Rights of Survivorship: Each spouse owns their half of the property and at the first spouse's passing, the decedent's half goes automatically to the surviving spouse and avoids probate because the property passes title by law, not by an estate plan. This is the preferred method of ownership between married couples because it avoids probate, and you get some income tax benefits at the second spouse's passing. At the first spouse's passing, you get a "full step up in basis," which means all embedded gains (and losses) in the property are eradicated. With joint tenancy, only the decedent's half of the gains in the property are eradicated. Sometimes, at the passing of the first spouse, the survivor may no longer want to make the trip to Florida alone and decides to sell the property. If there is an embedded gain, there will be more tax to pay with joint tenancy than with community property because the surviving spouse will have to pay the capital gains tax on her half of the embedded gain. With community property, all the gains are eradicated when the first spouse becomes an angel.

TAX ISSUES

There are several tax issues to consider when you buy and sell your second home.

BUYING YOUR SECOND HOME

There are no real tax issues to consider in Canada, or the U.S., at the purchase of your second home. However, you may want to start thinking about two important considerations: (1) What are the tax considerations when I sell the property? And (2) What happens to my property if I should become an angel?

SELLING YOUR SECOND HOME

When the time comes to sell your second home in the U.S., there are some tax consequences to consider. The first thing to come to grips with is that selling your second home is a taxable event in both the U.S. and Canada. In the U.S., it is a taxable event because the IRS reserves the right to tax U.S. situs property. It is also taxable in Canada because you are a tax resident of Canada and CRA requires you to declare your worldwide income on your Canadian return. This can lead to a double tax situation.

United States

If your negotiations are going well and you expect, or have received, an offer on your property, the first thing you need to be aware of is you are subject to the Foreign Investment in Real Property Tax Act (FIRPTA) administered by the IRS. This is a way for the IRS to ensure any requisite taxes are paid by non-residents selling property in the U.S. With some exceptions listed below, the buyer of the property must withhold 10% of the gross proceeds (sale price) of the property, not the net gain. For example, if you buy a home for U$350,000 and sell it for U$450,000, FIRPTA will require the buyer to withhold U$45,000. Alternately, if you sell the house for U$305,000, FIRPTA requires the buyer to withhold $30,500 of the sale proceeds. Failing to do so could subject the buyer to FIRPTA as it is the buyer's responsibility to inquire/determine if you are a foreign person.

There are a few exceptions to the FIRPTA withholding rules when Canadians sell their property in the U.S.:

- If the property sells for U$300,000 or less and the new owner intends to make the property their principal residence by living there at least 50% of the time for the first two years of ownership;
- You receive a withholding certificate from the IRS that excuses withholding;
- You provide certification to the buyer, under penalties of perjury, that you are not a foreign person and include your name, taxpayer identification number, and address. This may apply in rare situations if the property is held by a U.S. business entity where you own less than 5%.

You can read more about the exceptions at the IRS website here: irs.gov/Individuals/International-Taxpayers/Exceptions-from-FIRPTA -Withholding

If you don't meet one of the exceptions, there is a way to reduce the FIRPTA withholding by filing Form 8288-B — Application for Withholding Certificate for Dispositions by Foreign Persons of U.S. Real Property Interests with the IRS as soon as possible to ensure it gets processed in a timely fashion. This certificate will state the required withholding (which should be less than the 10% of gross proceeds) the buyer must keep when your sale proceeds are ready to be distributed. The first thing you will notice with this form is that it requires an Identification Number for all parties involved in the transaction. Unless you were issued a Social Security number in your past, you are required to affix a U.S. Individual Taxpayer Identification Number (note: not your Social Insurance Number). Since you don't have an ITIN, you will need to attach IRS Form W-7 — Application for IRS Individual Taxpayer Identification Number to the 8288. You will select box "h" and you qualify under Exception 4 per the instructions to the form. The difficult part is providing the necessary documentation the IRS requires to prove your identity. As the instructions outline, you need your original passport or a certified copy from the issuing agency of your Canadian passport. Another alternative is find an Acceptance Agent authorized by the IRS who can verify the original or certified copies. There is a list of agents listed at irs.gov when you search for "acceptance agent program." The W-7 instructions tell you to allow six weeks for the IRS to notify you of your ITIN, but eight to ten weeks if you submit your documents from January to April.

Once you get the proceeds from the sale of your property, many people think the matter is finished . . . but it's not. You still have a requirement to file IRS Form 1040NR — U.S. Nonresident Alien Income Tax Return with the IRS by June 15th of the year following the year of sale. This will be the final tax reconciliation of the sale and, in all likelihood, you will have a refund coming. If you owned the property for greater than one year, you will generally pay a flat tax rate of 15% on the net gains.

Net gains are calculated as follows:
Sale Proceeds – Original Purchase Price – Improvements – Closing Costs = Net Gains

If, however, you held the property for one year or less, you will be subject to ordinary income tax rates starting at 10% and going up to 39.6% at around U$229,000 in income. Since your second home is not your principal residence, the U$250,000 capital gains exemption is not applicable. Thankfully, the Net Investment Income Tax (NIIT) of 3.8% does not apply to non-residents. We encourage you to "run the numbers" once you have some of the details of your sale pinned down so you can prepare accordingly.

Canada

The sale of your U.S. property needs to be declared on Schedule 3 of your Canadian T1 tax return in Canadian loonies. This means you will have to get the exchange rate from the date of purchase, date of sale, and any improvements made to the property to accurately calculate the gain in Canadian loonies. Since Canada only taxes half of the capital gain, the tax rates in Canada will range from a low of 19.5% in Alberta to as much as 25% in some of the maritime provinces. Thankfully, any tax you end up paying in the U.S. (they get first dibs as the income is sourced in the U.S.) can be used as a foreign tax credit on your Canadian return. As usual, CRA will require proof that you paid the tax, so it is best to attach IRS Form 1040 NR as outlined above.

ESTATE/GIFT PLANNING

After much wrangling over the years, Congress finally settled on a path forward regarding U.S. estate tax and gift laws. As outlined in Chapter 7, the estate tax exemption is U$5.43 million for each spouse, which means U.S. situs assets of U$10.86 million can be sheltered from estate tax in 2015 for those Canadian owners. Many people assume that the exemption is only U$60,000 because that is what applies to countries that don't have a treaty with the U.S. In fact, Article XXIX B — Taxes Imposed by Reason of Death outlines the provision extending a "full unified credit" to non-residents. Later in the article, it appears that a double exemption may be available when the first spouse becomes an angel. Regardless, what used to be a quagmire is now clarified with the exception of the largest estates. If you fall into that category, we highly recommend some professional advice to assist you in navigating the complexities.

In Canada, there is no "gift tax" per se (but watch the attribution rules), so many Canadians think they can just give their U.S. property to their kids. In fact, the U.S. has a gift tax regime to prevent U.S. taxpayers from giving away their entire estate on their deathbed to avoid estate taxes. As outlined in Chapter 7, the annual exemption each person can give to any other person without having to file a gift tax return is U$14,000. However, if you decide to give your property equally to your children because you no longer want to go down to the U.S., you will be required to file Form 709 as outlined in Chapter 7.

A popular question we field is, "What happens to my property when I become an angel?" The answer is, "It depends!" The first thing to consider is who died and how the property is titled. If the property is held as JTWROS and the first spouse dies, the property is now owned completely by the survivor. Usually, the root of the question goes to, "What happens when the second spouse becomes an angel?" Does my Canadian will govern the property? Do I need a U.S. trust to avoid probate? We outline the options, along with the pros and cons of each, below.

Canadian will: Yes, your Canadian will can govern your U.S. property but there are issues, as outlined in Chapter 7. Remember, a will does not avoid probate, and when you have to endure probate in two countries, it makes things much more expensive because you have to pay lawyers on both sides of the border. We generally do not recommend this approach.

U.S. will: One solution is to have a very narrowly drafted U.S. will specifically for the real estate property located in the U.S. However, to avoid conflicts with your Canadian will, it is very important that your U.S. attorney and your Canadian attorney coordinate their respective drafting. The U.S. will should specifically exclude all other assets except the U.S. real estate, and the Canadian will should specifically exclude all U.S. real estate. This should avoid the double probate issue with just a Canadian will — but you endure probate nonetheless with its attendant costs and delays.

U.S. trust: Many times, U.S. estate planning attorneys will go into the "snowbird" communities to put on an estate planning seminar and espouse the horrors of probate. Their solution is a U.S. trust and the requisite fees you pay them to have it drafted. This really annoys me because I have taken a few of these attorneys to task by asking them, "What are the tax implications of having a trust when a resident of Canada?" The answer is, "I don't know anything about Canada," to which I respond, "Then how can you make a recommendation for a trust when you don't know all of the facts?"

Revocable Living Trusts are a common estate planning tool in the U.S., but they make little sense in Canada because they are now considered offshore trusts by CRA and come with a complex set of rules. In the U.S., trusts are considered a "flow-through" entity for tax purposes and are taxed at your personal rates. The problem is you are not a U.S. tax resident, and trusts are taxed much more punitively by CRA (as outlined in Chapter 7).

REAL-LIFE EXAMPLE

We received a call from California where a couple from British Columbia had been recommended a U.S. trust as the solution to their probate problem in an estate planning seminar. This couple had a second home in Palm Springs worth U$650,000 that they'd bought a number of years ago for U$300,000 — so there was an embedded gain of U$350,000 in the property. The attorney suggested they set up the trust and change the title on the property to the name of the trust so that it could be governed by the terms of the trust. The problem doesn't arise in setting up the trust, it arises when the asset is moved into the trust as this is considered a "deemed disposition" for tax purposes in Canada. As a result, they would need to declare U$350,000 (about C$375,000 with the appropriate exchange rates) on their Canadian tax return at a tax rate of 22.9%, or taxes of C$85,875! The couple intended to keep the property, which is an illiquid asset, so they would have had to find some other source of funds to pay the tax.

Canadian Trust: Another alternative is to set up a Canadian trust, but for the same reasons as outlined with U.S. trusts they just don't make a lot of sense. Canadian trusts were used in certain cases to plan around U.S. estate taxes, but with the exemption at U$5.43 million now, these sophisticated techniques are reserved for all but the largest estates.

Beneficiary Deed: One of the most inexpensive and effective ways of passing your property is through a beneficiary deed, also known as a transfer-on-death deed. In a growing number of states, this legal option allows you to name a person(s) or entity to inherit the property when you become an angel. You can change your beneficiary(ies) at any time up to the first spouse's passing, and the property doesn't go to your heirs until the second spouse becomes an angel. The beauty of the beneficiary deed is that it can be done after you purchase the property, it is relatively inexpensive to draft (U$200 or so), and it avoids probate. You don't have to reside in one of the states listed below to use a beneficiary deed; you just need to have real property located in that state. The document needs to be signed, notarized, and recorded to be valid. You can draft it yourself — there are several offers online for do-it-yourself beneficiary deeds.

This legal option is currently only available in these states, but the list is growing so be sure to check with a local real estate attorney if your state is not listed: Alaska, Arizona, Arkansas, Colorado, District of Columbia, Hawaii, Illinois, Indiana, Kansas, Minnesota, Missouri, Montana,

Nebraska, Nevada, New Mexico, North Dakota, Ohio, Oklahoma, Oregon, South Dakota, Virginia, Washington, West Virginia, Wisconsin, and Wyoming.

Despite Canada and the U.S. being neighbors, there are many complexities in owning real property for personal use in the U.S. when a resident of Canada. You need to consider early on how you will take title to the property, the tax implications when you sell and how the property will be governed if you become an angel in the meantime.

INVESTMENT PROPERTY

When you purchase a home in the U.S. for investment purposes (to rent out or to "flip"), you still have to contend with the ownership, tax, and estate planning implications outlined above. There are additional issues to consider with investment property — like liability and tax filing requirements — because the property is generating income.

LIABILITY

The U.S. is a much more litigious society than Canada, particularly since successful lawsuits have made people a lot of money in the U.S. As a result, most U.S. liability attorneys advise landlords to protect themselves against liability. Most recommend forming some sort of business entity — as is common in the U.S. — but doing this can be disastrous from a Canadian tax standpoint. Your first step is to have a good liability insurance policy with high coverage in place, as that is your first line of defense in protecting yourself. If you get a lawsuit filed, you will have a team of experienced liability attorneys ready to jump to your defense because the insurance company doesn't want to pay out a claim. You need to make sure your policy is for a rental property rather than personal use, so that you don't have to go out and hire your own attorney and pay them a retainer, which can be very expensive. The one benefit you have is all of your other assets are resident in Canada, which makes it much more difficult and costly to pursue a lawsuit. Furthermore, federal law in Canada protects certain assets (like RRSPs). Therefore, you may just want to consider holding your investment property outright in your own name. The biggest thing you can do to avoid a lawsuit is to take away the incentive to sue — and, because of the cost and complexity, a multi-jurisdictional lawsuit does just that.

UNITED STATES

There are a variety of business entities used to mitigate liability in the U.S. — but they don't make sense from a Canadian standpoint.

Limited Liability Company (LLC): This is the most common entity used by Americans as it is inexpensive to set up, requires little maintenance, offers liability protection to just the assets inside the entity, and is a flow-through entity for U.S. tax purposes. This means all income from the rental flows through to their personal tax return, to be taxed at the lower personal rates. However, in Canada, this entity is taxed as a corporation only when there are distributions, causing double taxation. You pay personal tax in the U.S. on any income every year and corporate tax in Canada when there are distributions. Now you have a mismatch in the foreign tax credits (personal versus corporate and timing), so the taxes are stacked on top of each other rather than offset. I cannot tell you how many times Canadians get advice from a U.S. attorney and end up in a pickle because of it . . . it's simple malpractice.

C corporation: In the U.S., you can set-up a "C corp" to insulate yourself from the liability but, again, you create a pickle from a Canadian stand-point. C corps require more paperwork and annual maintenance because they issue shares, have shareholders, must publish annual meeting min-utes, have articles of incorporation, etc. These entities are taxed at the higher U.S. corporate tax rates and any income ends up being double taxed — once at the corporate level and again at the personal level when the entity distributes the income to you as the individual. Then don't forget, all of this income needs to be taxed in Canada as well, with some foreign tax credits offsetting on the personal side. When presented with this, some attorneys will suggest you take the "S corp" election, which means the C corp converts to a flow-through entity taxed at your personal rates. The problem with this is the tax code prohibits non-resident aliens from being shareholders in an S corp unless they hold a green card or meet the substantial presence test. Either way, this is just not a good option.

Limited Liability Partnership (LLP): Partnerships are a good alternative for holding investment real estate in the U.S. because it allows the income to flow-through to your personal return, limits your liability, and is fairly straightforward to set up. If you are a married couple, or a group of investors in U.S. real estate as tax residents of Canada, this is probably your best alternative.

Living Trust: Despite the potential tax issues you run into with a living trust, as outlined above, this trust does not provide any liability protection for your investment real estate. An irrevocable trust may be a good liability solution, but you must relinquish ownership of the property and you face new tax issues as a result.

CANADA

Unlimited Liability Companies (ULCs)

Another option many investors are presented with by their Canadian accountants and attorneys is to set up some form of entity resident in Canada to hold their U.S. real estate interests. Similar to the U.S., Canada offers ULCs in BC, Alberta, and Nova Scotia. This entity was an effective way to hold your investment property in the U.S., but then changes to the treaty rendered them ineffective from a tax standpoint.

Corporations, Partnerships, and Trusts

Again, for all the reasons cited above, it is generally best to avoid all of these. One exception might be a Canadian Partnership, as it can serve the purpose of limiting liability, and the income flows through to your personal return. A Canadian irrevocable trust may be a good solution as it can help avoid U.S. estate tax, is taxed at personal rates, and provides liability protection. The downside is it requires you to relinquish ownership and control of the property.

TAX ISSUES

There are several tax issues to consider when owning investment real estate in the U.S. as a resident of Canada. The following aims to provide some clarity with regards to a very complex area.

UNITED STATES

Since your investment property is located in the U.S., the IRS reserves the right to tax it. How the income is taxed depends on how the property is owned/titled. Given that we discussed liability above, we will just address the tax implications of owning the property outright or in a U.S. business entity.

Rental Income

Despite what seems to be popular opinion, any rental income generated from a U.S. property needs to be declared in the U.S. They get first dibs at taxing the income, which, once calculated, becomes a foreign tax credit on your Canadian return. Let's look at the tax filing requirements for the two viable means of owning U.S. investment property.

Owned Outright: There are two ways to pay income tax on rental income that accrues to an individual.

1. The default position of the IRS is that 30% of the gross rents are remitted as soon as collected. This makes it easy and your tax obligation is fulfilled at that time. You don't have to keep track of expenses but, as you'll see below, this is likely more expensive than alternative number two.

2. For each person that has ownership in the property, each will need to file Form 1040NR — U.S. Nonresident Alien Income Tax Return, along with Schedule E, and declare their share of the income and expenses related to the rental activity. This method costs a bit of tax preparation time but you only pay tax on the net income the property generates

(after depreciation) versus the gross rents. Usually, this means paying no tax because the property doesn't generate a profit after taking depreciation, which is mandatory.

Now, don't forget to consider what tax return the state requires as well. Each owner(s) will need to have an ITIN, as outlined earlier, but what is important is you need it starting in your first tax year. You will need to file a W-7 form and select option "h" and then Exception 1, as outlined in the instructions.

Partnership: A partnership needs to file Form 1065 — U.S. Return of Partnership Income annually, which declares all income and expenses related to the property. Since this entity is considered a flow-through, each partner will receive a Schedule K-1, which they need to declare on Form 1040NR. There will also be a K-1 for the state the property is located in, and the requisite return will need to be filed there as well.

CANADA

Again, as tax residents of Canada, you are required to declare the income and expenses on your Canadian return in Canadian loonies. For those with no U.S. estate-tax issues, the following options are two of the best to use.

Outright Ownership: This is the simplest method and requires you to file your T1 tax return with CRA along with Form T776 — Statement of Real Estate Rentals. Taking capital cost allowance is optional and any tax paid in the U.S. at the federal and state levels is permitted as a tax credit against your Canadian tax liability.

U.S. Partnership: You will need to declare all K-1 income on your T1 tax return on Form T776 after converting it to Canadian loonies. Again, tax paid on your 1040NR, plus any state tax, can be used as a tax credit against your Canadian tax liability. You may want to consider a Canadian partnership to hold the U.S. property as well.

SALE OF THE PROPERTY

When you sell the property (assuming it's at a gain), you will need to contend with FIRPTA and filing a 1040NR, as outlined earlier. For property owned by a partnership, the K-1 will be used to declare the capital gains on your Canadian T1 return on Schedule 3. As described in Chapter 5, capital gains are taxed differently in the U.S. depending on how long the property is held. If you've held the property for greater than one year you will be taxed at a flat 15% capital gains rate.

MORTGAGES

During the real estate bubble in the U.S. that peaked in 2006, Canadians could qualify for a U.S. mortgage on their personal or investment property in the U.S. However, when the real estate market collapsed, the lending standards at most banks rose considerably, shutting most Canadians out of the market. As a result, your best alternative now is to "cash out and refinance" your property in Canada to get the funds needed to purchase in the U.S. Another option is to approach one of the major Canadian banks like RBC or TD, as they have noticed and seized the business opportunity in this arena. Another alternative is to approach one of the U.S. banks owned by a Canadian bank, as they tend to be knowledgeable about pulling Canadian credit reports and performing the necessary underwriting for non-residents.

MAYDAY! 13
MAYDAY!

Plans fail for lack of counsel, but with many
advisors they succeed.
— PROVERBS 15:22

Having read this book, you may feel like crying out, "Mayday!" ("M'aidez!" if you speak French.) Indeed, you may feel overwhelmed with all of the things to consider in your move and the amount of time you have to address them. This feeling should provide you with the motivation to address them. Don't panic; although limited, help is available. You have to decide what you are going to do and where you want help. Some folks want more help and want to delegate most of the tasks involved, while others may want to do it on their own just using this book. We encourage you to determine this up front since it will help to guide you in the relationship you are seeking. Your next step is to go out and find the help you want. This chapter will outline some of the things you need to consider in your search for a Canada-U.S. transition planner, and be sure to use the checklist provided in Appendix C.

SELECTING A TRANSITION PLANNER

Today, it seems, everyone is calling himself or herself a "financial planner" or "financial advisor." In our opinion, no industry has so pillaged a term and created such confusion as the financial services industry and the term "financial planner/advisor." Any relationship has trust as its underpinning. This trust requires a strict upholding of the fiduciary standard to you (versus a suitability standard). The word fiduciary is defined as, "of or relating to a holding of something in trust for another." This means your interests are put ahead of the financial planner's, even if you are leaving the firm. With a suitability standard, the product simply needs to be suitable to you (leaving lots of room for the recommender to serve his or her own needs), not necessarily the best thing for you. Essentially, the financial product salesperson does not have to disclose that she is recommending a particular financial product because she has a quota to meet, a bonus for selling it, or a contest to win — it just has to be suitable. Do you see the chasm between these two standards?

An example may help. We fielded a call from a sales representative in Denver who found our website and needed some help with a Canadian client. The client had C$1 million in an RRSP in Canada that this salesman had convinced the client to withdraw and put into a variable annuity. We explained to the representative that the client would pay C$250,000 in withholding to CRA and that the proceeds should be left in a taxable account for foreign tax credit planning purposes. The salesperson replied, "This is a C$40,000 commission I am not going to forgo." We explained further that there would be tax ramifications on the client's U.S. federal and Colorado returns that should be quantified beforehand as well, but that didn't matter to him. We finally challenged him to do the right thing for the client because a loss of C$250,000+ could devastate the client's financial projections. His response was, "I am doing the best thing for the client with the products I am able to sell." We had tried for an hour to save this client from some bad and costly advice. Now let us be clear that caveat emptor applies because the client did not do the requisite research to find an advisor that met their needs. On the other hand, we believe the salesperson bears the responsibility to fully disclose the hidden fees, expenses, and, yes, his commission to this client. As long as the product is suitable, he is off the hook. But can he honestly say he put his client's interests ahead of his own? Particularly when we pointed out the issues to him?

Our firm believes the best way to fulfill the fiduciary responsibility to you is to be fee-only (no product sales, no commissions, payment only from you, the client). This puts us firmly on your side. The planning process should start by having a conversation about you and what you are trying to achieve, not about a particular product, your investments, or a tax-saving strategy that "fits" into your situation. From there, our role is that of a quarterback to coordinate the bevy of attorneys, insurance agents, accountants, investment managers, and other professionals to ensure your best interests are served at all times. The key is to focus everyone on the achievement of your goals and objectives. As a result, your Canadian stockbroker's interests or your U.S. CPA's preferences should be secondary to your needs when moving to the U.S. Here are the things to consider in selecting a Canada-U.S. transition planner.

COMPETENCE

The first step in hiring any Canada-U.S. transition planner is to look for the Certified Financial Planner™ designation in both Canada and the U.S. The license to use the CFP® designation is issued annually by the Certified Financial Planner Board of Standards in the U.S. and the Financial Planning Standards Council in Canada. To hold these designations, one must complete course requirements and a comprehensive exam. In addition, there are work experience requirements (three years) that must be obtained in the financial services industry before use of the designation will be granted. Maintaining these designations requires meeting ongoing continuing education standards to ensure the licensee is current with the changing rules and regulations. Most important, however, is the requirement to abide by a strict code of ethics. Rule 2.4 of the CFP Board of Standards Rules of Conduct state that "a certificant shall offer advice only in those areas in which he or she is competent to do so." An undergraduate and a graduate degree (preferably on both sides of the border) should be considered an asset, as well as the Tax and Estate Practitioner (TEP) designation given by the Society of Trust and Estate Practitioners.

The next thing to look at is the experience of the transition planner you are considering. You need to ask if they work on a consistent basis in the Canada-U.S. planning arena. Some people call themselves "cross-border" planners, but under further probing it comes to light that they have helped a friend three years ago when he moved to the U.S. or that the bulk of their clients have no international issues at all. Ask about their current clientele and if they themselves have made the move. There is nothing like having someone with the practical experience of having made the move to help you with your move. If they haven't walked in the shoes you are about to put on, run — don't walk — away. We have seen the negative side of so-called experts, and it ends up costing you twice (a good example is tax preparation: you pay once for the initial work and again to adjust or amend your returns to bring you into compliance), plus there is usually little recourse for a job poorly done. When it comes to transition planners, be careful that you are getting what you pay for!

Unfortunately, there is no formal professional training in Canada-U.S. transition planning. It has to come with practical experience, "on-the-job" education, and a comprehensive network of professionals. This means competent Canada-U.S. transition planners are in very short supply, and there are only a handful of people who can competently write a comprehensive financial plan for your transition to the U.S. It often comes down to knowing which questions to ask and how to get effective answers. In addition, there are many potential gray areas to consider in any Canada-U.S. move, and often the judgment and experience of a good transition planner are worth more than the fees paid. In the tax preparation arena, there are a greater number of people who can competently deal with Canada-U.S. tax issues and how the treaty between the two countries applies. As always, we recommend you choose your professionals carefully and demand full disclosure of their compensation.

PLANNING PROCESS

The next thing to focus on is the process the transition planner will follow in developing your financial plan. Lack of a well-defined process typically indicates a poor planning approach and, subsequently, poor results. Our years of experience in Canada-U.S. transition planning have led to a very defined process that has proven itself successful many times. As a result, our process is not something we alter or try to find a shortcut around. There are too many small details in any Canada-U.S. move that can create havoc with your unique financial situation. In considering any transition planner, ask if she has a planning process. If so, is it designed for a Canada-to-U.S. transition? Does the process focus on you and what you are trying to achieve, or is it on a particular product, on tax savings, or on an investment scheme? Any transition plan starts with a thorough exercise setting goals and objectives. This is time consuming but necessary to establish the context in which to place individual Canada-U.S. financial decisions. Ask how much time will be spent understanding your needs and your unique financial situation and how the conversations will be documented. In our experience, this process typically requires two meetings of two to three hours each to fully understand your situation.

Once the process is complete, ask if a custom-tailored, written report will be issued. Ask to see a sample transition plan. It is important to note the difference between a myriad of colored charts produced by most planning, insurance, or investment software and a financial plan containing detailed analysis of every aspect of your financial situation. Be sure that specific recommendations will be given on all aspects outlined above, from cash management and income taxes to Canada-U.S. issues in estate planning.

CLIENT RELATIONSHIP

Another important attribute in selecting advisors is whether you can work with them or not. Ensure that you understand that they know whom they are going to serve (you!). Ask if you will be working directly with a principal of the firm or with an associate. If an associate, how does the company assign one to you? When did that associate make their Canada-to-U.S. move? When you call in, who will take your call? Is this person technically competent, or does he have to ask someone more senior for every answer? Do you share a common heritage? If not, you will find the associate will typically be your "parrot" to someone senior in the firm (who you met in the first meeting and haven't seen since) who really knows the answer. This can be a frustrating, time-consuming process for you. Is this person fun to work with? Are they a "fit" with the way you like to work (in person, via email, etc.)? Ask how long the associate has been with the firm. You should also know, once your plan is complete, who is going to assist you with implementing it and how much that will cost. Be sure you have a detailed understanding of the recommendations being made, the pros and cons of each, and how each will be implemented. Overall, your transition to the U.S. shouldn't be a laborious task, and your consultations should offer healthy interactions that any good relationship is expected to provide.

NATURE OF THE FIRM

It is prudent to ask some difficult questions about the firm you are considering. For example, ask about the number of clients lost and gained in the past couple of years. If you get an answer at all, you should ask why people are leaving the firm to glean further insights into your potential relationship with it. If there have been many new clients, you should ask if the firm is on a big marketing push, for you may be lost in the shuffle.

Another difficult question to ask is whether there has been a high rate of employee turnover. If so, it is difficult to retain someone who has an intimate understanding of you and your financial situation, because new associates constantly need to be brought up to speed (usually by you because the partners are too busy). A lack of consistency in the relationship can lead to things missed. Also, if there is turnover, you need to ask yourself, "Why isn't this firm able to keep its top employees? Are its hiring practices suspect? Is it just desperate to staff up to handle its marketing growth?"

Find out the strategic direction of the firm and what it is trying to achieve; you will gain insights into the motivation of a relationship with you (are you just a fee, or does the company want to help you build a better life?). If there is no limit to its growth, this may indicate a focus on fees rather than on a relationship with you. Get some details about the principals of the firm, such as their ages and retirement/succession plans, and so on. Look for principals who are committed to their business over the long term and certainly for as long as you intend to have a relationship with them. Ask them if they own the firm outright or if they are part of a larger institution. If so, beware of any new conflicts of interest that could be introduced into your relationship. If the firm has new equity partners, ask how long the principals expect to stay on with the firm. Do the new partners have any Canada-U.S. expertise, or are they just looking for a "book of business" that they can consolidate with other firms to increase economies of scale and increase their profit margins? You should ask for two or three references of clients who have been with the firm (for varying time periods, starting with relatively new to several years) to get a broad perspective on what it is like to work with this firm. How big is it, and how many relationships does it currently have? How many relationships does it have per associate? Per principal? The higher the client-associate ratio for relationships, the more difficult it will be to service you. If you visit the firm, is there a sense of organization or chaos? Ask to see the office of the person you will be working with. Are there files stacked all over the floors, desks, and shelves, or is everything relatively clean and in order? A chaotic firm can mean little or no time to service your needs and one focused on fees rather than clients.

Another area to consider is the agreement you will sign with the prospective firm. Ask for a sample agreement, and be sure you understand the details. Is the agreement long and complicated, with the fee buried deep in the agreement or not present at all? Do you understand how the fee is calculated for your situation? Is this an objective or subjective process? Does the fee seem reasonable for services rendered, and how does it compare with other fee quotes? You should also watch for agreements that lock you in for a defined period of time or levy penalties if you want out before the expiration of your agreement. This is all good for the advisor and bad for you. Why would you want to be cemented in a relationship that isn't working? Why can't the advisor earn your business and keep it voluntarily rather than force you into a contractual relationship? Does the financial planner get all or most of your money up front and therefore leave little incentive to continue servicing you afterward? Ask for an estimated completion date for your financial plan. Asking some pointed questions will ensure you have an advisor you can trust to uphold the fiduciary responsibility to you.

REGULATORY COMPLIANCE

By law, anyone rendering financial advice must be registered with the appropriate government authority. In the U.S., this means your transition planning firm must be registered as a registered investment advisor with the Securities and Exchange Commission or with the appropriate authority in the state where it is located. In Canada, any advisor must be registered with the appropriate provincial authority in the province where you'll reside. In the U.S., you should ask for a Client Disclosure Brochure, which is required by the regulator and should be provided when you inquire about the firm's services. This document must be updated and filed annually, and it contains everything about the financial advisory firm you are considering, including the backgrounds of the professionals employed, the services offered, and how they are compensated. You will also be able to check for any disciplinary hearings or other issues that may be important to you.

You should also check with industry regulators and associations for more information on the firm you are considering. Most of this can be done online with the Securities and Exchange Commission (adviserinfo.sec. gov) or for any commission folks at finra.org/Investors/ToolsCalculators/BrokerCheck/. You should also confirm the license to use the CFP® designation at the CFP Board of Standards in the U.S. (www.cfp.net) and the Financial Planning Standards Council (fpsc.ca) in Canada. You can also check the background of the licensee, how long they have held the license, and if there have been any disciplinary hearings (and the outcome). Another thing to consider is the advisor's involvement in professional associations. They are a good source of information on the person you are considering to become your trusted financial advisor. In the U.S. the largest financial planning organization is the Financial Planning Association (fpanet.org). There is also the National Association of Personal Financial Advisors (napfa.org), where you can check membership, involvement, standing, and so on.

COMPENSATION

Another important thing you should know is how your transition planner is compensated. This is a controversial subject in the industry, so our intent here is to arm you with the information you need so you can make an informed decision and pick the right planner for you. Whether they tell you or not, all transition planners get paid . . . nobody works for free. There are basically four methods of compensation.

- Commission-only: the person gets paid commissions and trailers from financial products sold to you; this is the most common method of compensation in the industry and is evidenced by a focus on your investments and the disclaimer that the person can't offer tax advice.

- Fee-offset: advice is rendered for a fee, but if you purchase a financial product afterward the commissions or trailers are reduced by the fee you have paid up front.
- Fee-based: this is a combination of a fixed fee for advice rendered and then commissions and trailers for any products sold to you. In our opinion, it's really "double-dipping," and it's telling how the financial plan typically recommends products for which the person will earn a commission as well.
- Fee-only: you pay a fee for advice rendered, and there is no other source of third-party compensation (no commissions, trailers, etc.), similar to how you work today with an accountant or an attorney.

Let us say up front that our firm is a fee-only financial planning firm, and therefore we are disclosing our bias toward fee-only planning. We believe this method of compensation removes as many conflicts of interest as possible from the relationship with you and puts any firm more solidly on your side in rendering advice in your best interests (upholding the fiduciary responsibility to you). When compensation comes from the sale of financial products to you, it creates an inherent conflict of interest because there is generally a quota to meet or a sales contest to win. Unfortunately, this is perfectly legal in our society because of two very different standards for financial product salespeople versus true financial advisors. In the case of financial product sales, there is a suitability standard, which means the product has to be suitable to your situation in order to avoid the ire of the regulator. With a fiduciary standard, the regulator requires your interests to come ahead of your advisor's, which means the advice rendered should be as conflict-free as possible. We suggest you demand full disclosure and ensure you understand, in dollar terms, how much it will cost to implement any recommendations provided. You should carefully discern between:

- a financial product salesperson, who renders advice about a particular product;
- a financial planner, who renders advice on specific technical topics such as tax or investments;

- a financial advisor, who renders comprehensive financial advice based on an understanding of your entire financial situation and what you are trying to achieve; the focus is on you and your financial goals, not on a particular financial product, technical area, or strategy; and
- a transition planner, who is a financial advisor who specializes in your transition from Canada to the U.S.

We have provided a checklist in Appendix C you can use to help you determine exactly what type of advisor you are considering.

It has been our experience that a transition planner well versed personally and professionally in Canadian and U.S. financial matters is typically the best person to assist you with your move to the U.S. It really takes a comprehensive understanding of both sides of the border and continual practice in this area to render the best advice to you.

To save a few dollars, some people believe their Canadian chartered account (CA) and their U.S. Certified Public Accountant (CPA) are all they need to competently cross the border. We have seen Canadian CAs do things for Canadian tax or liability protection purposes with no idea of the consequences in the U.S. Double or even triple taxation is the result when that person moves to the U.S. (see Chapter 11 or 12 for examples). We have seen U.S. CPAs prepare tax returns with no understanding of the IRS or CRA compliance issues . When the first piece of "hate mail" arrives from the IRS or CRA and is presented to the "cross-border tax professional," suddenly calls are no longer returned, or the response, "We don't deal with Canadian tax issues" is given. We have seen a Canadian CA complete the Canadian exit return and a U.S. CPA complete the U.S. startup return with no coordination between the two returns for income and foreign tax credits. As a result, extra taxes are usually paid.

We have seen immigration attorneys simply file a visa application for an unsuspecting client with no explanation of what it means to take up tax residency in the U.S. and no understanding of the Canadian and U.S. tax or estate planning consequences such a visa brings when issued. We have seen estate planning attorneys create estate plans costing thousands of dollars that pay no regard to registered plans or real estate holdings in Canada, the Canadian non-resident trust rules, and the issues non-U.S.

citizens bring to the estate planning process. We have seen Canadian "investment managers" trading RRSP, RRIF, and brokerage accounts with no understanding of the U.S. tax consequences they are causing their clients who now reside in the U.S. Come tax time, the unsuspecting client is shell-shocked by the tax bill handed out by CRA or the IRS. Likewise, we have seen U.S. investment managers managing a portfolio with no understanding of how to use up foreign tax credits, with the excuse that we don't want the "tax tail wagging the investment dog." And, sadly enough, we have often seen people rely on the advice of their current Canadian financial planners to orchestrate their moves to the U.S., with dire tax and estate planning consequences and little regard for the fiduciary responsibility owed to you . . . even putting clients into deferred sales charge mutual funds before they move to the U.S. to lock in the commissions and trailers before they lose the relationship. Unfortunately, these people are rendering advice in an area they are not capable of practicing in . . . a clear violation of principle three of the CFP® Code of Ethics and Professional Responsibility (if they hold the CFP® at all). All of these folks may be welcome on a well-rounded Canada-U.S. transition planning team, but they require a quarterback to coordinate all of the activities and to ensure that all the right questions are being asked, and answered, along the way. Failure to put in place a well-thought-out plan, unique to your individual situation, and have it coordinated effectively can have many unintended consequences and cause you no end of grief. To assist you in selecting the right transition planner to meet your needs, use the handy checklist we have provided in Appendix C.

OUR FIRM

Transition Financial Advisors Group uses the tagline "Pathways to the U.S." to clarify that we specialize in helping people make a smooth transition from Canada to the U.S. To that end, our firm operates best as a "financial coordinator" of your Canada-U.S. transition planning team. Not only does our firm have the educational background to meet your needs (we hold both Canadian and American financial planning and investment management designations), but we also have the personal experience in moving back and forth across the 49th parallel. One of the most important things our firm brings to any relationship is empathy with you in the many joys and frustrations you will experience in moving to the U.S. Why? Because we have walked in the shoes you are about to put on. In addition, we share a common Canadian heritage and can easily talk about hockey, Canadian politics, or fishing in Alberta. I enjoy many relationships with other professionals across Canada and the U.S. who are competent in Canada-U.S. planning matters and can bring them onto the team as needed. These people include accountants, attorneys, insurance agents, and government contacts. We have chosen this approach over bringing everything in house so we can select the best people to work with you on your Canada-U.S. transition issues.

Our planning fees are typically based on a sliding scale of your net worth and generally start around U$5,000 (may be tax deductible) and go up from there. These financial plans take 50 to 80 hours of time to complete on our part and require an investment of 10 hours of your time participating in the process. This approach falls in line with our comprehensive financial planning philosophy because our firm looks at everything related to your move. This may include rendering advice on the tax implications of selling your home or converting it to a rental property or providing advice on your homeowner's insurance policy. Our fee is made known up front and put into an agreement that both you and we sign. The fee is then fixed until the engagement is fulfilled, giving you peace of mind that there are no hidden fees or expenses to surprise you later. Obviously, this is how we feed our families, so we don't render advice for free! When we do have time, we are committed to helping our community through pro bono work, so any work we do for free is done in this area only (budget counseling, teaching, etc.).

In our experience, folks who meet the following criteria will benefit the most from our services:

- desire a close, long-term working relationship versus just a transaction;
- willing to delegate their financial matters and have done so in the past;
- have a lead time of three to four months to implement the

plan before a move to the U.S. is scheduled (longer with business entities);

- believe in our comprehensive transition planning approach and willing to follow our proven process vs. tax preparation or a spotlight strategy in one specific area;
- willing and able to expediently implement the plan (with our assistance) once completed;
- make friends easily and willing to share of themselves, expecting the same in return;
- comfortable using the internet; and
- have investment assets of at least $500,000, with a net worth approaching $1 million or a high income with a view towards saving and building your future.

You can contact us for a no-obligation review of your situation and the opportunities and obstacles your unique financial situation presents. Just go to our website and click on the green "Get Started" tab to download our "Introductory FactFinder." Fill it out to the best of your ability and send it to us. We will contact you to set up an appointment, and with your "FactFinder" in hand we can be in a better position to discuss your unique situation. It is important to note that with the success of our books and our commitment to our comprehensive financial planning approach, we generally do not extend hourly or project engagements that focus on a particular area of your situation (tax planning/ preparation or estate planning). We are looking for clients that desire a long-term relationship, not customers that want a single transaction. If you have some questions up front you want addressed before submitting your FactFinder, feel free to call or email us at the coordinates below.

Transition Financial Advisors Group, Inc.
— Pathways to the U.S.
Gilbert, AZ
Phone: 480-722-9414
Email: book@transitionfinancial.com
Website: www.transitionfinancial.com

14 REALIZING THE DREAM

. . . I still have a dream. It is a dream
deeply rooted in the American dream.
— MARTIN LUTHER KING, JR.

Now that you have moved, settled in, and begun realizing your lifestyle dream in the U.S., there are some differences from Canada you will notice. Contrary to popular opinion, there are general cultural differences between Canada and the U.S. that you should be aware of since some of them may be harsh realities. Many of these differences are based on our experiences and the experiences of others we have spoken to who have made the transition to the U.S. For example, Canadians typically tend to be more risk averse, conservative in their relationships, and better savers. Americans tend to be greater risk takers, are more comfortable with debt, are more entrepreneurial in business, and overall tend to be more outgoing. As a result, they tend to save less and carry more consumer debt than Canadians, although in our opinion that appears to be changing based on the number of check-cashing/payday loan stores and stores willing to extend credit, creative financing, and increased comfort with debt we are seeing in Canada. Following is a host of other things you will find interesting in comparing Canada and the U.S.

MILITARY

You will need to become comfortable with the constant presence of the military (aircraft overhead, equipment on the roads) and military personnel most everywhere you go. In Canada, we rarely saw the military or knew of anyone who had served except maybe an uncle or a great-grandparent in the great wars in Europe. In the U.S., there are numerous military branches and locations throughout the country. Here is a snapshot to give you a working knowledge. All military resides under the Department of Defense and consists of the Army, Navy, Air Force, and Marines (Canada does not have Marines). You also have the National Guard, but it is a state-run (and funded) military organization. You typically see just the Air National Guard and the Army National Guard. They are local to each state, but these branches can be called to active duty by the federal government as needed. The Coast Guard is not part of the military; rather, it is under the Department of Homeland Security along with the Secret Service and Citizenship and Immigration Services. There is also the Reserve Officer Training Corps (more commonly known as the ROTC), while Canada has Cadets. These are high school and university candidates in training for the military. It is strictly voluntary and is intended to prepare them for the military. Each branch of the military has an ROTC, and when you graduate from university you are commissioned as an officer in that branch. Finally, there are the Reserves, which are also found in Canada. These are people who were in the military, have left it, but can be called back in an emergency. It is interesting to note that all males aged 18 to 25 must register for the Selective Service in the U.S., even if they are only resident aliens (not U.S. citizens).

You will meet people who have served in the military or have children in the military, particularly with the recent Gulf conflict, Afghanistan, and Iraq wars, and military service is done with pride. This relates to another phenomenon with which you will have to become comfortable in the U.S., the profound patriotism here. Canadians could learn a lesson in this area by observing how passionate Americans are about their country. U.S. flags and ribbons are everywhere: hanging from houses, flying on automobiles, hanging in the windows of businesses. Americans' support for their troops is truly amazing. However, it is interesting to note that Americans do not wear a poppy on Remembrance Day (Veterans Day), and when we have worn ours, many Americans have asked us what it stands for. Furthermore, the poem "In Flanders Fields" by Lieutenant Colonel John McCrae is virtually unknown in the U.S., and we haven't heard it recited here.

LAW ENFORCEMENT

It's also interesting to note the differences in law enforcement between the two countries. In Canada, you have your local city police officers or marshals and in their absence the RCMP. Not so in the U.S. Nationally, you have the Secret Service and the Central Intelligence Agency (CIA), which is akin to the Canadian Security Intelligence Service (CSIS); along with the Federal Bureau of Investigation (FBI); the U.S. Marshals Service, the Bureau of Alcohol, Tobacco, Firearms and Explosives (ATF); and the Drug Enforcement Agency (DEA); in Canada, all of these sectors seem to be managed by the RCMP (seems to make sense). You also have the Highway Patrol and State Police in the U.S., and the local Sheriff's Department, which is run and funded by the county. You also have local city police forces that overlap with the Sheriff's Department. It becomes confusing, but rest assured there are many people available to write you tickets!

GOVERNMENT

You will also have to become familiar with the political landscape in the U.S. if you want to engage in an intelligent conversation at parties. There are essentially two political parties at all levels of government in the U.S.: the Republicans (right wing) and the Democrats (left wing), versus four parties in Canada: Conservatives (right wing), Liberals, New Democratic Party (left wing), and Bloc Québécois (separatists). In the U.S. and Canada, it basically comes down to whether you believe in more government, higher taxes, and more social programs (Democratic) or less government, lower taxes, and a more individualistic view of making it in this world (Republican). In the U.S., you register to vote if you are a citizen, and you get a voter's registration card that declares your party allegiance and in which precinct you vote. If you move, you have to update your registration card; it is a valid form of ID that you can carry with you wherever you go. The mayor of your city in Canada is still the mayor in your city in the U.S., but your premier becomes your governor, and your prime minister becomes your president (see the "Encyclopedia" section below). You can't vote in any elections in the U.S. unless you become a U.S. citizen. However, you can still vote in Canadian elections if you are residing in the U.S. and a Canadian citizen.

VOTING IN CANADA

On May 2, 2014, Justice Robert Sharpe of the Ontario Superior Court of Justice overturned certain provisions of the *Canada Elections Act* that prohibited Canadian citizens living abroad for more than five years from voting in federal elections. Now, any Canadian citizens may vote by a special mail-in ballot and shape the political landscape in Canada as long as they resided in Canada at some point. Elections Canada has revised the international elections form (see Figure 14.1 below) to remove the offending statement that "you intend to return back to Canada on this date." Based on this ruling, we believe it is "safe" to vote in Canada without raising the ire of CRA in deeming you a resident of Canada. In fact, the new form asks when you left Canada so that is more confirmation of your non-residency.

FIGURE 14.1

APPLICATION FOR REGISTRATION AND SPECIAL BALLOT

Application for Registration and Special Ballot
For Canadian electors residing **outside** Canada
INSTRUCTIONS AND GENERAL INFORMATION

Deadlines to Register and to Return your Ballot

To be added to the International Register of Electors and vote by special ballot in a federal election, your completed application form and accompanying documents must be received by Elections Canada in Ottawa **no later than 6:00 p.m., Eastern Time on the Tuesday before election day.** Electors who are already registered will automatically be sent a special ballot voting kit at the call of an election.

Apply as early as possible, to allow enough time for the ballot to be sent to you and for your marked ballot to reach Elections Canada in Ottawa **no later than 6:00 p.m., Eastern Time, on election day.**

How to Complete the Application Form

Complete the application form prior to printing

1. Your family name, given name and middle name(s)

2. Your daytime and evening telephone numbers, including country code, city code and/or area code, where you can be reached (optional fields)

3. Your gender (optional field)

4. Your date of birth (year/month/day)

5. Your preferred language for communicating with Elections Canada (English or French)

6. Your e-mail address (optional field)

7. Your Canadian address for voting purposes. This can be:
   • your last home address in Canada; **or**
   • the current home address of your spouse or common-law partner; of a relative of yourself, your spouse or common-law partner; of a person in relation to whom you are a dependant or of a person with whom you would live if you lived in Canada.

   "Common-law partner" means a person who is cohabiting with you in a conjugal relationship and has done so for at least one year.

   Your Canadian address for voting purposes must be a **physical address, not a mailing address.** It determines for which electoral district your vote will be counted and cannot be changed once your name is added to the International Register. You cannot use a post office box or rural route, except in areas where no other physical address is available.

8. The mailing address where you want to receive your special ballot voting kit. You can use the address of a Canadian diplomatic or consular office (embassy, high commission or consulate), but you should make arrangements with that office **before** submitting your application and provide them with your contact information.

9. The date of your departure from Canada

10. If your personal information is not already in the National Register of Electors and you do not want it to be added, check the box.

11. Read, sign and date the declaration.

Optional fields: Elections Canada may use this information to contact you if your application is not complete or to help ensure the timely delivery of your voting kit.

Checklist

Remember to:
✓ Complete and print the application form.
✓ Read, sign and date the declaration.
✓ Include copies of the required proof of identity. **Do not send originals.**
✓ Submit the application form using the quickest method. **Make sure you include both pages.**

APPLICATION FOR REGISTRATION AND SPECIAL BALLOT

Proof of Identity

You must include a copy of one of the following authorized pieces of identification with your application:
- pages 2 and 3 of your Canadian passport; **or**
- your Canadian citizenship certificate or card; **or**
- your birth or baptismal certificate, showing that you were born in Canada.

Photocopy or scan your documents. Ensure they are LEGIBLE. Do not send original documents.

Keep Your Information Up to Date

Once you are listed in the International Register of Electors, you must inform Elections Canada of any changes to your contact information in writing to ensure you receive your voting kit at the next federal election. You must contact Elections Canada to update your information once you return to live in Canada.

How to Return Your Completed Application

In person: You can return your application form and accompanying documents to any Canadian diplomatic or consular office for forwarding to Elections Canada. Please note that they do not process applications or issue voting kits on behalf of Elections Canada.

By fax:

613-998-8393
1-800-363-4796
toll-free in Canada and the United States

By courier:

ELECTIONS CANADA
30 VICTORIA STREET
GATINEAU QC K1A 0M6
CANADA

By mail:

ELECTIONS CANADA
PO BOX 9830 STN T
OTTAWA ON K1G 5W7
CANADA

Privacy Notice

Pursuant to the *Canada Elections Act*, Elections Canada will use the personal information provided to determine the electoral district in which your ballot will be counted and to send you a special ballot voting kit at the call of future federal elections. Providing this information (except for the optional fields) is mandatory and it will be added to the International Register of Electors. We will only use information provided under the optional fields to contact you if your application is not complete or to help ensure the timely delivery of your voting kit. We will also use information provided (except for the optional fields) to maintain the National Register of Electors. We use information contained in the National Register to prepare and share lists of electors with members of Parliament, political parties and candidates for uses authorized under the *Act*. In accordance with information sharing agreements, also authorized under the *Act*, we may also disclose it to provincial and territorial electoral agencies. Inclusion in the National Register is optional and will not impact your inclusion in the International Register. If you choose to opt out from the National Register, your information will not automatically be included on future lists of electors. If you wish to be removed from the National Register or do not wish to have your information shared with your provincial or territorial electoral agency, please contact us. We use the services of third parties to receive applications and issue special ballots who are also bound to protect your personal information.

You have the right to access and correct your personal information, and to have your information protected under the *Privacy Act* and the *Canada Elections Act*. The information is retained under personal information banks CEO PPU 037 and CEO PPU 040. A detailed description can be found at www.infosource.gc.ca or www.elections.ca .

How to Contact Us

By telephone:

613-993-2975 (collect calls are accepted)
1-800-463-6868 toll-free in Canada and the United States
001-800-514-6868 toll-free in Mexico

TTY 1-800-361-8935 toll-free in Canada and the United States

By e-mail:

svrenq@elections.ca
Please note that e-mail is not a secure method of communication.

Visit the Elections Canada Web site at www.elections.ca .

APPLICATION FOR REGISTRATION AND SPECIAL BALLOT

Application for Registration and Special Ballot
For Canadian electors residing **outside** Canada
(See sections 222 and 223 of the Canada Elections Act)

EC 78500-W
(05/2014)

Full Name and Contact Information

(1) Family Name

Given Name

Middle Name(s)

(2) Daytime Phone Number (optional)

Evening Phone Number (optional)

(3) Gender (optional)
Male ☐   Female ☐

(4) Date of Birth (yyyy-mm-dd)

(5) Language
English ☑   French ☐

(6) E-mail address (optional)

Last Address Before Leaving Canada or Current Home Address in Canada of a Person Mentioned in the Attached Instructions
(This address determines for which electoral district your vote will be counted)

(7) Number and Street, or Lot and Concession, or Township and Range

Apt. / Unit

City, Town, Village or Municipality

Province / Territory

Postal Code

Present Mailing Address (Where you want to receive your voting kit)

(8) Number and Street, Apt. or Unit, Rural Route (RR), Post Office (PO) Box or General Delivery (GD)

City, Town, Village or Municipality

Province, Territory or State

Country

Postal / Zip Code

Date You Left Canada

(9) Date I left Canada (yyyy-mm-dd)

Declaration

(10) If you do not want your personal information to be added to the National Register of Electors, check here: ☐

Signature

(11) · I am a Canadian citizen. I am 18 years old or older, or will be 18 years old or older on election day.
· All of the statements made in this application are true and correct.

Signature

2015-05-08

Date

1DCE129F88D90001213814BB620012A6

APPLICATION FOR REGISTRATION AND SPECIAL BALLOT

Application for Registration and Special Ballot
For Canadian electors residing **outside** Canada
(See sections 222 and 223 of the Canada Elections Act)

EC 78500-W
(05/2014)

Family Name

Given Name

Date of Birth (yyyy-mm-dd)

1DCE129F88D90001213814BB620012A6

HERITAGE

Most Americans view their heritage as American, while most Canadians know they are of German, Ukrainian, Polish, etc. descent. Canadians typically know about their family heritage and how their ancestors came to Canada. Ask an American what their heritage is, and they typically won't know or will have to think about it for a while. We attribute this difference to the fact that America is a much older nation and has been settled longer. It is not uncommon to find fifth- and sixth-generation Americans, while it is not uncommon to find first- and second-generation Canadians. I am a second-generation Canadian born to first-generation Canadian parents who in turn were born to my grandparents from Germany. As Canada wanted to settle its land, it opened the doors to many immigrants, who came to homestead in Canada and escape the unrest in Europe. As Canada continues its program of diversity through immigration policies, there is a whole new group of first-generation Canadians emerging, particularly from Asia and India.

Another interesting difference between Canada and the U.S. is Canada holds to a policy of "multiculturalism" whereas the U.S. holds to a "melting pot" philosophy. In Canada, most policies are focused on multiculturalism where there is a real emphasis on preserving the culture you came from when you land in Canada. The view is it leads to more innovation, new ways of thinking, etc. For example, there are two official languages, Quebec has been granted additional rights to preserve their culture, and the RCMP has made uniform and policy changes to accommodate people from different cultures and religions who make it on to the force. In the U.S., English is the only official language and attempts to add Spanish were thwarted. The idea of a melting pot is you come to the U.S. and "melt" your culture into the existing culture; special accommodations are hard to come by. In our observation, multiculturalism often leads to more conflict because to preserve one's culture imposes on the existing culture. It is like they are losing some of their identity in the process, which can lead to animosity, whereas in the U.S., it doesn't seem as big an issue. There are plenty of issues in the U.S., though, as African American and Hispanic cultures grow and take more precedence. It is an interesting phenomenon that is worth watching in both nations.

SPORTS

Another cultural phenomenon is the much different sports scene in the U.S. We grew up when Saturday night was spent watching *Hockey Night in Canada* on CBC with Don Cherry and Ron MacLean bantering back and forth. Hockey was everywhere in the news, on the radio, and on the TV. It was easy to stay abreast of favorite hockey teams or players in Canada. In Arizona, however, hockey news is relegated to the back page or simply not reported at all despite Wayne Gretzky leading the Phoenix Coyotes in the local market for a while. Instead, you have to get used to "football Sunday" from September to January. The NFL rules on Sunday, and it is common for people to wake up at 9 a.m. on Sunday and watch NFL football until 10 p.m. If it's not football (or the culmination of the Super Bowl in January), it will be the NBA (basketball) from January until the summer, when MLB (baseball) takes over until the fall, when the NFL starts again. Then you have to add in college (university) sports, which are huge in the U.S. compared with Canada. The support Americans provide to their college athletes is incredible, and it is typical to have 50,000 people attend a college football game. Again, we think Canadians could learn from Americans in supporting their local university athletes. Saturdays in the U.S. are reserved for college football until "March Madness" hits and the National Collegiate Athletic Association (NCAA) basketball championships are played. We must admit that, during the hockey lockout, we acquired a taste for college basketball and the NFL. And what about you avid curlers? Forget it. You won't even hear about curling until the Winter Olympics coverage starts again.

OTHER

At the suggestion of some of our readers, we thought we would comment a bit on some other differences between Canada and the U.S. In the southern U.S., tornadoes and hurricanes pose a serious threat and are a common problem. In Canada, we experience more threats such as freezing weather, ice storms, "whiteouts," and the like. In the U.S., they have more problems with rogue alligators, poisonous snakes, "killer bees," fire ants, and termites. In Canada (and Alaska), bears of all types pose more of a threat.

FOOD

One of the biggest adjustments we had to make in moving to the U.S. was the difference in food between the two countries. Yes, food. Here are some of our favorites that we have had to learn to do without because they are hard to find in the U.S.

- Perogies, although we have found them occasionally at Trader Joe's
- Montreal smoked meat sandwiches
- Butter tarts and crumpets
- Mincemeat for pies, tapioca pearls for pudding
- Vanilla custard powder
- Watkins spices (their ground cinnamon cannot be beat)
- Ginger beef — thin strips, coated with a sweet sauce
- Japanese mandarin oranges at Christmas
- Pancake mix — Mrs. Nunweiler's or Coyote brand (nice and hearty!)
- Snacks — all Old Dutch potato chips, Humpty Dumpty snacks, Popcorn Twists, Hostess Hickory Sticks and Shoestrings, Hawkins Cheezies
- Chocolate bars — Jersey Milk, Eat-More, Caramilk, Coffee Crisp, Aero, Smarties, Mirage, Wunderbar, Cadbury Bars, Oh Henry!, Glosettes, Maltesers, Crispy Crunch, Crunchie, Big Turk, Mr. Big, Mack Toffee, Malted Milk, Neilson (Coconut Fingers, Golden Buds, Macaroons, Slowpokes, Willocrisp), Bridge Mixture, Cherry Blossoms
- Cookies — Dare (Wagon Wheels, Chocolate Fudge, Coffee Break), Christie (Fudgee-O's, Maple Leaf), Dad's (Oatmeal, Oatmeal Chocolate Chip, Oatmeal Raisin)
- Candy/gum — Thrills, Maynard's Wine Gums

- Sauces/syrups/spreads — Roger's Golden syrup, Summerland Sweets syrups, HP Sauce, E.D. Smith Lemon Spread, Shirriff Caramel Spread, Imperial Cinnamon Spread, Kraft's Sun-Dried Tomato salad dressing
- Cereals — Post Shreddies, Muesli, Red River, Sunny Boy, Quaker Harvest Crunch
- Beverages — Tim Hortons coffee, Red Rose tea, Mott's Clamato juice, SunRype juice, and of course almost all Canadian beers(!)
- 222's pain reliever
- Oh yes, how about poutine! (Even finding fries with gravy is difficult in the U.S.)

Here are some other differences we have found or been told about.

- Fruitcake is considered a delicacy in Canada and is found in most wedding cakes and during the Christmas season. In the U.S., it is considered a social faux pas to give or receive fruitcake.
- You can't find Nanaimo bars anywhere in the U.S!
- Canadian Twizzlers red licorice are better tasting than the U.S. version.
- Dairy Queen Brazier in Canada is far better than in the U.S.
- Dairy Queen ice milk soft serve is creamier tasting in Canada than in the U.S.
- McDonald's offers muffins in Canada, while breakfast burritos are available in the U.S.
- KFC is crispier and better tasting in Canada than in the U.S.
- KFC gravy is much more flavorful in Canada than in the U.S. (fries and gravy are uncommon).
- Tim Hortons coffee is available primarily in the border states in the U.S.
- Earls, Boston Pizza, and The Keg have all opened up restaurants in the U.S.

Here is a list of items we can't find in Canada when we visit there.

- Poore Brothers potato chips
- Chocolate bars — Hershey's milk chocolate, Almond Joy, Mounds, Baby Ruth, Three Musketeers, Payday, 100 Grand, Milk Duds, Mr. Goodbar
- Malt-O-Meal cereal or Wheaties
- Krispy Kreme doughnuts (harder to find)

However, here are some things we, and others, have noted when back in Canada.

- P.F. Chang's Chinese Bistro (Pei Wei is the takeout) is nowhere to be found.
- Ruth's Chris Steakhouse is starting to expand across Canada (Toronto, Vancouver, Calgary, Edmonton).
- Good Mexican food and good southern style barbeque food are hard to find.
- Portions are generally bigger in the U.S., and eating out is cheaper (before the exchange rate).
- The number of restaurants that offer buffet service all day is much greater in the U.S. than we have found in Canada.
- The selection in most grocery and retail stores is far greater in the U.S. than in Canada.
- Most "sin" taxes are higher in Canada than in the U.S. (liquor, wine, beer, cigarettes, cigars, chewing tobacco, gasoline).

If you have something to add to this list, please email us at book@transitionfinancial.com and tell us about it.

THE POSTAL SYSTEM

- It is a postal code in Canada and a zip code in the U.S.
- A first-class stamp costs 49¢ in the U.S. versus 85¢ in Canada in 2015.

- Mailing a postcard costs 34¢ in the U.S. versus 85¢ in Canada.
- First-class postage for a regular #10 envelope from the U.S. to Canada costs U$1.15 versus C$1.20 from Canada to the U.S.
- It takes approximately 7–10 calendar days for first-class mail to reach Canada from the U.S., but it takes approximately 10–14 days for mail in Canada to reach the U.S.
- In the U.S., a letter mailed for delivery in the same city will typically be delivered the next day, whereas in Canada it can be two to three business days.
- In the U.S., mail is delivered on Saturdays. Not so in Canada.
- If you have friends or relatives in Canada who are mailing out wedding invitations to you in the U.S., tell them a U.S. stamp is required for the return postage. Putting a Canadian stamp on a return envelope that originates in the U.S. is not recognized by the U.S. postal system (however, such letters have been known to slip by).

THE ENGLISH LANGUAGE

The American version of English is different from the British version used in Canada, so words such as cheque, labour, harbour, centre, and litre become check, labor, harbor, center, and liter. That is why your computer's spell checker may highlight these words as misspelled. Table 14.1 shows other differences in the way Canadians use the English language versus Americans.

TABLE 14.1
CANADIAN VERSUS AMERICAN ENGLISH

Canada	United States
Pop	Soda or Cokes
Barbecue	Cookout
Housecoat	Robe
Chesterfield	Sofa/couch
Car accident	Car wreck
Holidays	Vacation

Ensuite	Master bath
Dinner	Lunch
Supper	Dinner
Felts	Markers
Chocolate bar	Candy bar
Garbage	Trash
Buns	Rolls
Thongs	Flip flops
Slacks	Pants
Runners	Tennis shoes
Golf shirt	Polo shirt
Squares	Dessert
Garburator	Garbage disposal
Washroom	Restroom
Marks	Grades
Junior high	Middle school
University	College
Floating rate	Adjustable rate
Cutlery	Silverware
Pot holders	Hot pads
Tea towels	Wash towels
Porridge	Oatmeal
Toque	Toboggan hat
Brown bread	Wheat bread
Sucker	Lollipop
Soother	Pacifier
Licking	Spanking
Standard	Stick shift
Needle	Shot
Slippers	House shoes
Eavestrough	Gutter
Cabin	Cottage
Guaranteed investment certificate (GIC)	Certificate of deposit (CD)

THE METRIC SYSTEM

After you move to the U.S. and are settled in, you will start talking in terms of gallons, Fahrenheit, etc. However, when you are talking with your friends and family back home in Canada, they will be talking in terms of liters, Celsius, etc. The following should help you in these conversations.

- Celsius can be converted to Fahrenheit quickly by doubling the Celsius number and adding 30 (e.g., 30°C x 2 = 60 + 30 = approximately 90°F). For negative numbers, the calculation works like this: –30°C x 2 = –60 + 30 = approximately –30°F.
- If you want an exact conversion, use (°F – 32) x 5/9 = °C.
- The boiling point is 212°F versus 100°C.
- Freezing occurs at 32°F versus 0°C.
- Room temperature is 70°F versus 20°C.
- Body temperature is 98.6°F versus 37°C.
- Mr. Fahrenheit was the only glass blower in his day who could blow a symmetrical, thin cylinder (thermometer) to record temperatures. He set 32°F as his starting point because it was the lowest temperature he could record with his device.
- 100 kmph = approximately 60 mph.
- 1 mile = 1.61 km or 1 km = 0.62 mile.
- 1 inch = 2.54 centimeters.
- 1 meter = 3.28 feet.
- The U.S. adheres to the metric system for track and field, while Canada uses yards for football.
- 1 liter = 1.06 quarts.
- 1 ton = 1.1 tonnes (pronounced "tawns").
- 1 imperial gallon = 4.5 liters.
- 1 U.S. gallon = 3.8 liters.
- 1 imperial gallon = 0.84 U.S. gallon.
- 1 kilogram = 2.2 pounds.
- 500 grams = 1.1 pounds.

ENCYCLOPEDIA

GEOGRAPHY

- The Russian Federation is the largest country in the world, Canada is second, China is third, the U.S. is fourth, and Brazil is fifth.
- Canada covers 3,849,674 square miles (9,970,610 square km), of which 291,576 square miles (755,180 square km) are inland water (7.6%), while the U.S. covers 3,717,811 square miles (9,629,091 square km), of which 181,519 square miles (470,131 square km) are inland water (4.9%).
- Quebec is the largest province, and Ontario is second, while Alaska is the largest state, and Texas is second (note that the Yukon, Northwest Territories, and Nunavut are territories, not provinces).
- Texas is 13,314 square miles larger than Alberta.
- The population of Canada is about the same as the population of California (about 38 million). The population of the U.S. crossed 314 million.
- The largest metropolitan populations in the U.S. are New York, with approximately 20 million, and Los Angeles, at approximately 15 million. In Canada, Toronto has approximately 4.3 million, and Montreal has approximately 3.3 million.
- Canada shares a 5,527 mile (8,895 km) border with the U.S. spanning 12 states and is the largest unprotected border in the world.
- The lowest temperature ever recorded in Canada was −81°F (−63°C) in Snag, Yukon, while the highest was 115°F (46°C) at Gleichen, Alberta.
- The lowest temperature ever recorded in the U.S. was −79.8°F (−62.1°C) at Prospect Creek Camp along the Alaska pipeline 20 miles north of the Arctic Circle.
- In the contiguous 48 states, the lowest temperature was −69.7°F (−56.5°C) in Rogers Pass just west of Helena, Montana, while the highest temperature was 134°F (56.7°C) in Death Valley, California.

- It is interesting to note that the record low ever recorded in Hawaii was 12°F (−11.1°C).

GOVERNMENT

- In the U.S., Congress creates the laws governing the land (legislative branch) and is made up of the Senate and the House of Representatives. In Canada, the Parliament is made up of the Senate (upper house), the House of Commons (lower house), and the Sovereign (represented by the governor general).
- Canada is a constitutional monarchy under the queen, while the U.S. is an independent republic.
- Canada has a parliamentary-cabinet government versus a presidential-congressional government in the U.S. This means that in the U.S. the president is both the head of state and the head of government. In Canada, the queen (represented by the governor general) is the head of state, while the prime minister is the head of government.
- The Republicans (the GOP, for Grand Old Party — the elephant) are most akin to the Conservatives in Canada (the Tories).
- The Democrats (whose symbol is the donkey) are akin to the Liberals (Grits) in Canada.
- It is a governor who heads the state government in the U.S., while in Canada it is a premier who heads the provincial government.
- The Canadian equivalent to the CIA (Central Intelligence Agency) in the U.S. is CSIS (Canadian Security Intelligence Service).
- The Canada Pension Plan can be collected as early as age 60, whereas U.S. Social Security can be collected as early as age 62.
- Canada is part of the British Commonwealth (along with Australia, New Zealand, and India, among other countries) while the U.S. is not.
- Unlike in Canada, U.S. health-care coverage (Medicare) does not start until age 65; for those under this age, it is available for the indigent through Medicaid. Many people receive

health insurance as a benefit from their employers, but if you are self-employed or a part-time worker you have to "go bare" or obtain coverage on your own.

- There are 11 statutory holidays in both Canada and the U.S. In the U.S., Thanksgiving is on the last Thursday in November versus the second Monday in October in Canada; Memorial Day in the U.S. is the fourth Monday of May versus Remembrance Day in Canada on November 11th; Victoria Day in Canada is on the Monday lying between May 18th and May 24th; and Independence Day in the U.S. is July 4 versus Canada Day on July 1. There is no holiday for Good Friday or Boxing Day in the U.S.

MISCELLANEOUS TRIVIA

- Both Saskatchewan and Arizona do not change their clocks for daylight savings time. Neither do Hawaii, Puerto Rico, the Virgin Islands, American Samoa, Southampton Island in Nunavut, and parts of Quebec.
- U.S. banks typically do not offer currency exchange services, Canadian banks do.
- Canadian banks charge a fee for each check, while most U.S. banks offer free checking.
- Americans refer to grades 7 and 8 as middle school, while in Canada grades 7, 8, and 9 are known as junior high.
- American high school is grades 9, 10, 11, and 12; the grades are referred to in collegiate fashion as freshman, sophomore, junior, and senior.
- In NFL football, the field is 100 yards long by 53 1/3 wide, and the game has four downs, while the CFL field is 110 yards long by 65 yards wide, and the game has three downs.
- Winnie the Pooh, the zipper, the snow blower, the snow-mobile, the electric car heater, plexiglass, the light bulb, and, of course, the goalie mask were all created in Canada.
- Basketball and hockey were both created in Canada.
- In the U.S., the big shopping day is "Black Friday," the day after Thanksgiving, while in Canada it is Boxing Day (the day

after Christmas per English tradition). However, U.S. retailers are succeeding in making Black Friday a bigger shopping day in Canada now — especially with cyber Monday.

- In the U.S., the biggest newspaper is typically Sunday versus Saturday in Canada.
- In the U.S., making a U-turn at an intersection is legal, whereas in Canada it isn't.
- In Canada, traffic circles are more common, whereas they are very rare in the U.S.

THE TAX SYSTEM

- Tax filing deadlines are April 15th in the U.S. and April 30th in Canada for personal taxes.
- In Canada, you get a Social Insurance Number (SIN), while in the U.S. you get a Social Security number (SSN).
- One return is filed per married couple in the U.S. versus one return per person in Canada.
- A W-2 slip in the U.S. is equivalent to a T4 slip in Canada.
- A 1099-INT or 1099-DIV slip is generally equivalent to a T3 or T5 slip in Canada.
- In Canada, only Quebec has a separate return and collects its own taxes. In the U.S., 43 states have separate returns and collect their own taxes (the other seven do not have state income taxes).
- Both Canada and the U.S. allow a tax deduction for medical expenses but limit it by 3% of net income and 10% of adjusted gross income respectively.
- The closest thing to an RRSP in the U.S. is an Individual Retirement Account (IRA); unlike the IRA, RRSP contributions are always deductible.
- In Canada, lottery winnings are not taxable and are paid out in a lump sum. In the U.S., lottery winnings are taxable and are paid out over a 20-year period unless the cash option is requested in advance.
- Both tax systems have an alternative minimum tax

APPENDIX A

GLOSSARY

AHCCCS: Arizona Health Care Cost Containment System
AMT: Alternative Minimum Tax
ATF: Bureau of Alcohol, Tobacco, Firearms and Explosives (U.S.)
ATM: Automatic Teller Machine
CA: Chartered Accountant (Canada), soon to become CPA
CBC: Canadian Broadcasting Corporation
CBSA: Canada Border Services Agency
CCA: Capital Cost Allowance (Canada)
CFC: Controlled Foreign Corporation
CFP®: Certified Financial Planner™
CIA: Central Intelligence Agency (U.S.)
CMHC: Canada Mortgage and Housing Corporation
COBRA: Consolidated Omnibus Budget Reconciliation Act (U.S.)
CPA: Certified Public Accountant (U.S.)
CPI: Consumer Price Index
CPP: Canada Pension Plan
CRA: Canada Revenue Agency
CSIS: Canadian Security Intelligence Service
DEA: Drug Enforcement Agency

DOT: U.S. Department of Transportation

DPSP: Deferred Profit Sharing Plan

EA: Enrolled Agent with the IRS (U.S.)

EIN: Employer Identification Number

EPA: U.S. Environmental Protection Agency

ERISA: Employee Retirement Income Security Act (U.S.)

FATCA: Foreign Account Tax Compliance Act

FBI: Federal Bureau of Investigation

FHA: Federal Housing Authority

FPA: Financial Planning Association (U.S.)

GST: Goods and Services Tax (Canada)

GSTT: Generation Skipping Transfer Tax (U.S.)

IRA: Individual Retirement Account (U.S.)

IRC: Internal Revenue Code

IRS: Internal Revenue Service

ISO: Incentive Stock Option (U.S.)

ITIN: Individual Taxpayer Identification Number (U.S.)

LIF: Life Income Fund

LIRA: Locked-In Retirement Account

LLC: Limited Liability Company

LRIF: Locked-In Retirement Income Fund

NAFTA: North American Free Trade Agreement

NAPFA: National Association of Personal Financial Advisors

NIIT: Net Investment Income Tax

NQ: Non-Qualified Employee Stock Option (U.S.)

OAS: Old Age Security (Canada)

PBGC: Pension Benefit Guaranty Corporation (U.S.)

PFIC: Passive Foreign Investment Company

POA: Power of Attorney

QDOT: Qualified Domestic Trust (U.S.)

QPP: Quebec Pension Plan

RCA: Retirement Compensation Arrangement (Canada)

RCMP: Royal Canadian Mounted Police

RESP: Registered Education Savings Plan (Canada)

ROTC: Reserve Officer Training Corps

RPP: Registered Pension Plan (Canada)

RRIF: Registered Retirement Income Fund (Canada)

RRSP: Registered Retirement Savings Plan (Canada)

S&P: Standard and Poors (U.S.)

SEC: Securities and Exchange Commission (U.S.)

SEP: Simplified Employee Pension

SIN: Social Insurance Number (Canada)

SS: Social Security

SSA: Social Security Administration

SSN: Social Security number (U.S.)

STEP: Society of Trust and Estate Practitioners

TEP: Trust and Estate Practitioner

TFSA: Tax-Free Savings Account

TN: Trade NAFTA (visa)

U.S.: United States of America

USCIS: U.S. Citizenship and Immigration Services

U.S.-VISIT: United States Visitor and Immigrant Status Indicator Technology

UTMA: Uniform Transfer to Minors Act Account (U.S.)

VA: Veterans Administration (U.S.)

VWP: Visa Waiver Permanent Program Act

WEP: Windfall Elimination Provision (U.S.)

APPENDIX B

RESOURCES YOU CAN USE

In our digital age, there is a multitude of information that can be obtained with the simple click of a button. Following are a host of websites, publications, and firms of relevance to each chapter in this book. If the link is out of date, feel free to email us at book@transitionfinancial.com and let us know.

CHAPTER 1: AMERICAN ASPIRATIONS
Financial Planning Standards Council: fpsc.ca
CFP Board of Standards: cfp.net
Financial Planning Association: fpanet.org
National Association of Personal Financial Advisors: napfa.org
Society of Trust and Estate Practitioners: step.org
Transition Financial Advisors: transitionfinancial.com

CHAPTER 2: COVER YOUR ASSETS
For a list of health-care consultants we recommend, see the risk management section of our website at transitionfinancial.com.
U.S. Medicare: medicare.gov
Life Insurance Quotes: accuquote.com

Auto Insurance Quotes: insweb.com

Homeowners Insurance Quotes: accucoverage.com

Health Insurance Quotes: ehealthinsurance.com or healthcare.gov

All Types of Insurance Quotes: insure.com

Alberta Health Care Insurance Plan: health.alberta.ca

British Columbia Ministry of Health: gov.bc.ca/health

Manitoba Health: gov.mb.ca/health

New Brunswick: gnb.ca

Newfoundland and Labrador: health.gov.nl.ca/health

Nunavut: gov.nu.ca/programs/health

Northwest Territories: hss.gov.nt.ca

Ontario: health.gov.on.ca

PEI: gov.pe.ca/health/index.php3

Quebec: msss.gouv.qc.ca

Saskatchewan Health: health.gov.sk.ca

Yukon: hss.gov.yk.ca

CHAPTER 3: A PLEDGE OF ALLEGIANCE

For a list of immigration attorneys we recommend, see the immigration section of our website at transitionfinancial.com.

U.S. Citizenship and Immigration Services: uscis.gov

U.S. Department of State: travel.state.gov

Citizenship and Immigration Canada: cic.gc.ca

Foreign Affairs and International Trade Canada: dfait-maeci.gc.ca

American Immigration Lawyers Association: aila.org

CHAPTER 4: MOVING YOUR STUFF

U.S. Customs and Border Protection: cbp.gov

Bureau of Alcohol, Tobacco, Firearms and Explosives: atf.gov

U.S. Department of Transportation: dot.gov

U.S. Environmental Protection Agency: epa.gov

Car History: carfax.com

House Valuations: zillow.com

American Moving and Storage Association: moving.org

Canada Border Services Agency: cbsa-asfc.gc.ca

Canadian Import Restrictions: beaware.gc.ca

CHAPTER 5: DOUBLE TAXES, DOUBLE TROUBLE

For a list of Canada-U.S. tax preparers we recommend, see the income tax section of our website at transitionfinancial.com.

IRS: irs.gov

Publication 54: Tax Guide for U.S. Citizens and Resident Aliens

Publication 213: Check Your Withholding

Publication 501: Exemptions, Standard Deductions, and Filing Information

Publication 514: Foreign Tax Credits

Publication 519: U.S. Tax Guide for Aliens

Publication 521: Moving Expenses

Publication 527: Residential Rental Property

Publication 597: Information on the United States-Canada Income Tax Treaty

Publication 733: Rewards for Information Given to the IRS

Publication 901: U.S. Tax Treaties

Publication 1915: Understanding Your Individual Taxpayer Identification Number

Publication 2193: Too Good to Be True Trusts

Publication 4261: Do You Have a Foreign Bank Account?

Publication 4446: IRS Best Websites, Phone Numbers, and Other Useful Info

U.S. Department of the Treasury: treas.gov/Pages/default.aspx

State Income Tax Links: taxsites.com/state.html

State Sales Tax Links: retirementliving.com/taxes-by-state

CRA: cra-arc.gc.ca

Interpretation Bulletins

IT161R3: Non-Residents: Exemption from Tax Deductions at Source on Employment Income

IT171R2: Non-Resident Individuals: Computation of Taxable Income Earned in Canada and Non-Refundable Tax Credits

IT221R3: Determination of Canadian Residency Status

IT262R2: Losses of Non-Residents and Part-Year Residents

IT298: Canada-U.S. Tax Convention: Number of Days "Present"

IT420R2: Non-Residents: Income Earned in Canada

Provincial Income Tax Links: ctf.ca/ctfweb/EN/Pages/Tax_Research_
Links.aspx
Provincial Sales Tax Links: taxtips.ca/salestaxes.htm

CHAPTER 6: SHOW ME THE MONEY
International Salary Calculator: homefair.com
U.S. Salary Calculators: salary.com
Pay Scale Calculator: payscale.com
Currency Exchange Rates: bankofcanada.ca/rates/
exchange/10-year-converter
Western Union: onlinefx.westernunion.ca
Free Credit Report: annualcreditreport.com
FICO Scores: myfico.com

CHAPTER 7: TILL DEATH DO US PART
For a list of competent estate planning attorneys we recommend, see the
estate planning section of our website at transitionfinancial.com.
IRS: irs.gov
Publication 555: Community Property
Publication 559: Guide for Survivors, Executors, and Administrators
Publication 950: Introduction to Estate and Gift Taxes
Estate Planning Information: www.estateplanninglinks.com

Estate Planning Attorneys
Wealth Counsel: wealthcounsel.com
National Network of Estate Planning Attorneys: nnepa.com
American College of Trust and Estate Counsel: actec.org

CHAPTER 8: FINANCIAL FREEDOM
CPP/OAS: sdc.gc.ca/eng/retirement/index.shtml
U.S. Social Security: ssa.gov
IRS: irs.gov
Publication 560: Retirement Plans for Small Business
Publication 575: Pension and Annuity Income
Publication 590: Individual Retirement Accounts
Publication 915: Social Security

Publication 939: General Rules for Pensions and Annuities
Publication 4333: SEP Retirement Plans for Small Business
Publication 4334: SIMPLE IRA Plans for Small Business

Retirement Living: retirementliving.com
Sperling's Best Places to Live: bestplaces.net
Moving.com: moving.com/real-estate/explore-cities-neighborhoods.asp

CHAPTER 9: SMARTEN UP!

U.S. Department of Education: ed.gov
Federal Student Aid Website: studentaid.ed.gov
College Savings Plans Network: collegesavings.org/index.aspx
IRS: irs.gov
Publication 970: Tax Benefits for Education

CHAPTER 10: MONEY DOESN'T GROW ON TREES

Investment Industry Regulatory Organization of Canada: iiroc.ca/Pages/
      default.aspx
Toronto Stock Exchange: tmx.com/en/index.html
Montreal Stock Exchange: m-x.ca/accveil_en/php
NASDAQ Canada: nasdaq.com/markets/global-markets.aspx
Morningstar Canada: www2.morningstar.ca/homepage/h_ca.aspx?
      culture=en-CA
Dimensional Fund Advisors Canada: dfaca.com
Blackrock iShares: ca.ishares.com/home.htm
Securities and Exchange Commission: sec.gov
Financial Industry Regulatory Authority: finra.org/index.htm
American Stock Exchange: usequities.nyx.com/markets/
      nyse-mkt-equities
New York Stock Exchange: nyse.com
NASDAQ: nasdaq.com
Chicago Board of Trade: cmegroup.com
Chicago Board Options Exchange: cboe.com
Index Funds: indexfunds.com
Morningstar U.S.: morningstar.com

Dimensional Fund Advisors: dfaus.com
Blackrock iShares: us.ishares.com/home.htm
IRS: irs.gov
Publication 550:Investment Income and Expenses
Publication 551: Basis of Assets
Publication 564: Mutual Fund Distributions

CHAPTER 11: THE BUSINESS OF BUSINESS
IRS: irs.gov
Publication 541: Partnerships
Publication 542: Corporations
Publication 583: Starting a Business and Keeping Records
Publication 587: Business Use of Your Home
Publication 1635: Understanding Your EIN
Publication 3402: Tax Issues for Limited Liability Companies

CHAPTER 12: ESCAPING THE ENDLESS WINTER
FIRPTA: irs.gov/Individuals/International-Taxpayers/
        Exceptions-from-FIRPTA-Withholding
Taxation of Nonresident Aliens: irs.gov/Individuals/
        International-Taxpayers/Taxation-of-Nonresident-Aliens

CHAPTER 13: MAYDAY! MAYDAY!
Transition Financial Advisors: transitionfinancial.com, or call us at
        480-722-9414
Financial Planning Standards Council: fpsc.ca/, or call 1-800-305-9886
CFP Board of Standards: CFP.net/utility/find-a-cfp-professional, or call
        1-888-237-6275
U.S. Securities and Exchange Commission: adviserinfo.sec.gov/IAPD/
        iapdMain/iapd_SiteMap.aspx
National Association of Personal Financial Advisors: napfa.org, or call
        1-800-366-2732
Financial Planning Association: plannersearch.org/Pages/home.aspx, or
        call 1-800-647-6340
Society of Trust and Estate Practitioners: step.org

CHAPTER 14: REALIZING THE DREAM

Transition Financial Advisors: transitionfinancial.com, or call us at
480-722-9414

Government of Canada: gc.ca

Canadian Embassy Initiative: connect2Canada.com

Elections Canada: elections.ca

Royal Canadian Mounted Police: rcmp-grc.gc.ca/index.htm

Canadian Security Intelligence Service: csis-scrs.gc.ca

Canada Post: canadapost.ca/cpo/mc/languageswitcher.jsf

U.S. Government: usa.gov

Federal Bureau of Investigation: fbi.gov

Bureau of Alcohol, Tobacco, Firearms and Explosives: atf.gov

Drug Enforcement Agency: justice.gov/dea/index.shtml

U.S. Military

    Army: army.mil

    Navy: navy.mil

    Air Force: airforce.com

    Marines: marines.com/home

United States Postal Service: usps.com

APPENDIX C

TRANSITION PLANNER INTERVIEW CHECKLIST

COMPETENCE

1. Do you hold both the Canadian and the U.S. CFP®
   designations?
2. What other designations, degrees, or training do you have in
   transition planning?
3. How long have you been practicing specifically in the area of
   Canada-U.S. transition planning?
4. How long have you been working at the firm? What is your
   next career step in the firm?
5. What percentage of your clients are Canada-U.S. clients
   versus others?
6. Tell me about your own personal experiences in transitioning
   between Canada and the U.S.

PLANNING PROCESS

1. Describe in detail the planning process you have to address
   the needs of my Canada-U.S. transition.

2. How do you determine my goals and objectives for my transition?
3. How do you integrate my goals and objectives into my transition plan?
4. Do you have a written sample plan I can review?

CLIENT RELATIONSHIP

1. Tell me about your firm. How long have you been in business? Please provide me with your Form ADV or other regulatory disclosures.
2. How many employees do you have? How many clients per employee? Per principal?
3. What are your assets or net worth under management?
4. Will I be working directly with a principal or an associate? Why?
5. How do you determine the person I will be working with in the firm?
6. How much employee turnover have you had in the past two years? Why?
7. What is your typical client? What is his or her net worth?
8. What are the principals' goals and objectives for the firm in the next five to ten years?
9. How old are the principals? What are their plans for retirement and succession? When will that take place?
10. What personalities work best with you? Your firm? Why?
11. How many clients have left the firm over the past two years? Why?
12. How many clients have you gained in the past two years? Why?
13. Where do you custody investment accounts? Why? Are there any conflicts of interest I need to be aware of?
14. What are your personal interests?

COMPENSATION

1. How are you paid? When are you paid?
2. How do you calculate your fees? What is my fee in dollars? Specifically, show me the calculations for my fee.
3. How do you ensure that your fiduciary responsibility to me is given the highest priority?
4. Can I see a sample agreement? How long does my agreement last? How can I terminate it?

PROFESSIONAL AFFILIATIONS AND ASSOCIATIONS

You can consult with the following professional organizations to confirm any credentials or affiliations for the transition planner you have interviewed.

1. Financial Planning Standards Council: the organization that licenses and governs the Canadian CFP designation (fpsc-canada.org, or you can call 1-800-305-9886).
2. CFP Board of Standards: the organization that licenses and governs the CFP® designation in the U.S. (cfp.net/search/, or call 1-888-237-6275).
3. U.S. Securities and Exchange Commission: this is the regulatory body in the U.S. that governs financial advisors (adviser-info.sec.gov).
4. National Association of Personal Financial Advisors: the only organization in the U.S. and Canada comprised of fee-only financial advisors (fee-only.org, or call 1-800-366-2732).
5. Financial Planning Association: the largest association of financial planners in the U.S. (plannersearch.org, or call 1-800-647-6340).
6. Society of Trust and Estate Practitioners: the global organization for those practicing advanced trust and estate matters (step.org).

APPENDIX D

100 QUESTIONS TYPICALLY ASKED BY THE USCIS EXAMINER

A. PRINCIPLES OF AMERICAN DEMOCRACY

1. What is the supreme law of the land?
2. What does the Constitution do?
3. The idea of self-government is in the first three words of the Constitution. What are these words?
4. What is an amendment?
5. What do we call the first ten amendments to the Constitution?
6. What is one right or freedom from the First Amendment? *
7. How many amendments does the Constitution have?
8. What did the Declaration of Independence do?
9. What are two rights in the Declaration of Independence?
10. What is freedom of religion?
11. What is the economic system in the United States?
12. What is the "rule of law"?

B. SYSTEM OF GOVERNMENT

13. Name one branch or part of the government.
14. What stops one branch of government from becoming too powerful?
15. Who is in charge of the executive branch?
16. Who makes federal laws?
17. What are the two parts of the United States Congress? *
18. How many United States Senators are there?
19. We elect a U.S. Senator for how many years?
20. What is one of your state's U.S. Senators?
21. The House of Representatives has how many voting members?
22. We elect a U.S. Representative for how many years?
23. Name your U.S. Representative.
24. Who does a U.S. Senator represent?
25. Why do some states have more Representatives than other states?
26. We elect a President for how many years?
27. In what month do we vote for President? *
28. What is the name of the President of the United States now? *
29. What is the name of the Vice President of the United States now?
30. If the President can no longer serve, who becomes President?
31. If both the President and the Vice President can no longer serve, who becomes President?
32. Who is the Commander-in-Chief of the military?
33. Who signs bills to become laws?
34. Who vetoes bills?
35. What does the President's Cabinet do?
36. What are two Cabinet-level positions?
37. What does the judicial branch do?
38. What is the highest court in the United States?
39. How many justices are on the Supreme Court?
40. Who is the Chief Justice of the United States?

41. Under our Constitution, some powers belong to the federal government. What is one power of the federal government?
42. Under our Constitution, some powers belong to the states. What is one power of the states?
43. Who is the governor of your state?
44. What is the capital of your state? *
45. What are the two major political parties in the United States? *
46. What is the political party of the President now?
47. What is the name of the Speaker of the House of Representatives now?

C. RIGHTS AND RESPONSIBILITIES

48. There are four amendments to the Constitution about who can vote. Describe one of them.
49. What is one responsibility that is only for United States citizens? *
50. What are two rights only for United States citizens?
51. What are two rights of everyone living in the United States?
52. What do we show loyalty to when we say the Pledge of Allegiance?
53. What is one promise you make when you become a United States citizen?
54. How old do citizens have to be to vote for President? *
55. What are two ways that Americans can participate in their democracy?
56. What is the last day you can send in federal income tax forms? *
57. When must all men register for the Selective Service?

D. AMERICAN HISTORY
a) Colonial Period and Independence

58. What is one reason colonists came to America?
59. Who lived in America before the Europeans arrived?

60. What group of people was taken to America and sold as slaves?
61. Why did the colonists fight the British?
62. Who wrote the Declaration of Independence?
63. When was the Declaration of Independence adopted?
64. There were 13 original states. Name three.
65. What happened at the Constitutional Convention?
66. When was the Constitution written?
67. The Federalist Papers supported the passage of the U.S. Constitution. Name one of the writers.
68. What is one thing Benjamin Franklin is famous for?
69. Who is the "Father of Our Country"?
70. Who was the first President? *

b) 1800s

71. What territory did the United States buy from France in 1803?
72. Name one war fought by the United States in the 1800s.
73. Name the U.S. war between the North and the South.
74. Name one problem that led to the Civil War.
75. What was one important thing that Abraham Lincoln did? *
76. What did the Emancipation Proclamation do?
77. What did Susan B. Anthony do?

c) Recent American History and Other Important Historical Information

78. Name one war fought by the United States in the 1900s. *
79. Who was President during World War I?
80. Who was President during the Great Depression and World War II?
81. Who did the United States fight in World War II?
82. Before he was President, Eisenhower was a general. What war was he in?
83. During the Cold War, what was the main concern of the United States?
84. What movement tried to end racial discrimination?

85. What did Martin Luther King, Jr. do? *
86. What major event happened on September 11, 2001, in the United States?
87. Name one American Indian tribe in the United States.

E. INTEGRATED CIVICS

a) Geography

88. Name one of the two longest rivers in the United States.
89. What ocean is on the West Coast of the United States?
90. What ocean is on the East Coast of the United States?
91. Name one U.S. territory.
92. Name one state that borders Canada.
93. Name one state that borders on Mexico.
94. What is the capital of the U.S.? *
95. Where is the Statue of Liberty?

b) Symbols

96. Why does the flag have 13 stripes?
97. Why does the flag have 50 stars? *
98. What is the name of the National Anthem?

c) Holidays

99. When do we celebrate Independence Day? *
100. Name two national U.S. holidays. *

* Those aged 65+ that have been permanent residents in the U.S. for 20+ years just have to study these questions.

APPENDIX E

John and Jenny Movers hired Transition Financial Advisors to assist them in making a smooth transition to the U.S. (this account is based on a real-life fact pattern, but all names and numbers have been changed). Following are the financial planning issues, obstacles, and opportunities our proven planning process revealed for the Movers. This is intended not to be blanket advice applicable to all situations but to increase your understanding of the many things that must be taken into account when considering a move to the U.S. Each person's situation is unique and requires a custom analysis to determine the best course of action. As any good transition planner should, we review the following eight areas of planning: customs, immigration, cash management, income tax, financial independence, risk management, estates, and investments; each is part of a comprehensive transition plan.

BACKGROUND

On April 30th, John and Jenny received good news. John's U.S.-based employer accepted his transfer request to move him down to Arizona from Ontario. Better yet, his employer agreed to pay his current salary of C\$100,000 (bonus averaging C\$40,000) in U.S. dollars (U\$100,000 +

323

U$40,000 bonus). Aged 53 and 52 respectively, married, with no children, both John and Jenny are Canadian citizens only. Jenny will resign from her current position as a marketing manager to pursue employment in the U.S. The Movers have a net worth of C$3,650,000 comprised as follows.

TABLE E.1

THE MOVERS' NET WORTH

Asset	Fair Market Value (C$)	Cost Basis (C$)	Titling
Canadian brokerage account	750,000	500,000	Joint
RRSP	450,000	—	John
RRSP	300,000	—	Jenny
LIRA	100,000	—	Jenny
Checking/savings accounts	50,000	50,000	Joint
Vested stock options exercise	450,000	200,000	John
Employee stock purchase plan	100,000	30,000	John
Principal residence	1,600,000	375,000	John
Mortgage	-100,000		
Autos (x2)	50,000	75,000	One each
Personal/ household/jewelry	100,000	200,000	Joint
Total	C$3,650,000		
	C$2,325,000		John
	C$425,000		Jenny
	C$900,000		Joint

LIFE PLANNING

We started by determining where John and Jenny were "going," where they "were" now (net worth, financial circumstances), and how they were going to get "there." The "plan" allowed individual financial decisions to be placed in context and ensured limited resources are channeled toward achieving their plan. Following is a summary of their intentions.

- John and Jenny would like to remain in the U.S. for five to seven years and then return to Canada.
- They would like to take advantage of John's employment opportunities and the lower tax rates in the U.S. to build their net worth and then move back to Canada.
- The Movers would like to be financially independent by the time John is 60 through a combination of work in Canada and the U.S.
- When they are independent, they would like to purchase a five-acre piece of land in Ontario near family with a modest home and a guest retreat.
- When independent of work, the Movers would like to be involved in full-time charitable work and offer their home and retreat at no charge to charity workers.
- They might "snowbird" two to three months per year in the U.S. after becoming financially independent and moving back to Canada.
- They would simplify their lives wherever possible and lead a relatively simple life.
- The bulk of their estate would go to their respective parents who survive them, some to siblings, and the balance to charitable organizations (they have no children).

CUSTOMS PLANNING

The Movers wanted to take their Lexus with them to the U.S. to replace it there later. They were going to sell their Mercedes. We pointed out that their Lexus might not meet the Department of Transportation (DOT) Motor Vehicle Safety Standards and Environmental Protection Agency (EPA) standards to import. We advised the Movers to write to Lexus Canada and Mercedes Canada to obtain letters that clearly stated that their respective vehicles meet the U.S. EPA exhaust emission standards for their year of vehicles as well as the DOT motor vehicle safety standards. To their surprise, Mercedes Benz sent a letter that clearly stated it met the U.S. standards in both areas, but Lexus could not confirm their vehicle met the DOT safety standards. As a result, it would cost over U\$2,400 for them to hire an importer to bring the Lexus with them to the U.S. They changed their plan and brought the Mercedes down and sold the Lexus in Canada. They also completed a full inventory of their personal goods when packing and donated a host of items to charity. Because they decided to sell their home, most of their sweaters, winter clothing, and sporting goods were stored with family until their return at Christmas. We informed them that they had to pass the written portion of the Arizona driving exam and provide a valid Canadian driver's license in order to get an Arizona driver's license.

IMMIGRATION PLANNING

John's company sponsored him for an L-1 visa (intra-company transfer), while Jenny would enter on an L-2 visa (dependent of an L-1). However, at the time of their transition, we pointed out that Jenny's visa did not offer work authorization, and the loss of her salary would seriously retard achievement of their independence goals. The Movers began negotiations with John's employer in an attempt to get some sponsorship for Jenny that would permit her to work, but the negotiation process had gone too far to include that. The Movers made the transition to the U.S., and Jenny remained dormant for 18 months before she got a break . . . the U.S. Immigration and Naturalization Service changed the rules for L-2 visa holders, enabling her to work and resolving a key issue for the Movers' financial situation.

We assured Jenny in particular that in moving to the U.S. she would not lose her Canadian citizenship and that dual Canada-U.S. citizenship was a possibility if they wanted it. The L-1 visa, when issued to executives or managers, is a "shortcut" to a green card, and once a green card was held for five years they would be eligible to become naturalized citizens of the U.S. However, in looking at the Movers' intention to reside back in Canada permanently, we pointed out that U.S. citizens must file a U.S. tax return no matter where they live in the world. To avoid this nuisance, we recommended that John and Jenny retain their current L-1 and L-2 visas (can be renewed for a maximum of seven years). If they proceeded to obtain a green card and stayed longer than eight years in the U.S., we cautioned them that they could be subject to the new expatriation rules for green card holders. Based on their current plan, if they move back to Canada in five to seven years, they simply hand in their visas or green cards at the border, and typically their tax-filing obligation ceases.

CASH MANAGEMENT PLANNING

In moving to the U.S., the Movers had concerns about how to move the proceeds of the sale of their Canadian house to the U.S. (see "Income Tax Planning" below). They were concerned about the "loss" when exchanging Canadian loonies for U.S. dollars. We empathized but educated them on currency exchange and emphasized that their retirement investments should remain in Canadian dollars where appropriate investment vehicles existed. Since they intended to move back to Canada for their financial independence, their future needs would be in Canadian dollars, so converting everything into U.S. dollars and subjecting it to currency exchange fluctuations needed to be considered carefully. We also analyzed the cost-of-living differences between Canada and the U.S. for the Movers' desired lifestyle. They tracked their expenses for six months in the U.S. and found that they weren't significantly different. We helped get them a discounted currency exchange firm rate through NBCN that allowed them to conveniently move their cash to the U.S., saving significant currency exchange costs in the process.

Another issue the Movers had to face was qualifying for a mortgage in the U.S. since they had no U.S. credit rating. We worked with their lending institution to educate it on how to "pull" a Canadian credit report and ensure it was valued in the loan application process. With the support of John's employer and the "can do" attitude of their lender, the Movers succeeded in getting a mortgage to buy a house (using the house proceeds from Canada as a down payment). Through the credit union John's employer has in the U.S., the Movers were able to get a credit card issued in their names as well. We also advised John to pay off the Home Buyer's Plan on his RRSP before exiting Canada; otherwise, it would be considered a distribution and fully taxable in Canada on his exit return.

INCOME TAX PLANNING

Key Assumptions
- John's salary: U$140,000
- Capital gains jointly: U$35,000 (U$10,000 short term)
- Interest jointly: U$7,500
- Dividends jointly: U$12,500 (U$10,000 qualified/eligible dividends)
- Standard deduction used for U.S. scenario
- No exchange rates used (to show the net tax effect of the move)
- No tax planning included

TABLE E.2

2014 TAX COMPARISON

Canada	John	Jenny	C$	United States	U$
Federal	$32,392	$253	$32,645	Federal	$31,888
Ontario	$19,169	$39	$19,208	Arizona	$6,254
Subtotal	$51,562	$292	$51,853		$38,142
Payroll taxes	$3,339	$0	$3,339		$9,284
Total	**$54,901**	**$292**	**$55,192**		**$47,426**
% of income			28.3%		24.3%
Health insurance			$0		$6,000
Grand total			**$55,192**		**$53,426**
			28.3%		27.4%

In the Movers' situation, the move resulted in a tax benefit of $7,766 in 2014. When factoring in health insurance premiums (pre-tax), the playing field is leveled a bit more (U$1,766). However, if the Movers have a mortgage and property taxes, move to a state with no income tax, and take into account the exchange rates and Canada's sales taxes versus those in the U.S., the table tilts further toward the U.S. As this analysis clearly reveals, it is not a black-and-white decision to move to the U.S. for strictly tax reasons.

CANADIAN FILING REQUIREMENTS

John and Jenny would each need to file a Canadian "exit" return by April 30th following the year they left Canada. On this return, they are subject to the "departure tax" that CRA imposes on expatriates on "taxable Canadian property." Since the stock options and RRSPs are not considered taxable Canadian property by CRA (attachable in some way to ensure payment of any tax), the only items subject to the departure tax are the employee stock purchase plan and their brokerage account. Our analysis indicated there are embedded gains of C$70,000 in the employer's stock and C$250,000 in the brokerage account, leading to a departure tax of C$26,105 for John and C$13,188 for Jenny. To mitigate this departure tax, we were able to equip John with this information to negotiate higher moving expenses and signing bonus from his employer, delay his employment start date in the U.S. (and ensuing exit date from Canada), net some gains and losses together, and make RRSP contributions to offset some of the income. Despite the departure tax, the Movers decided to move to the U.S. because of the opportunity to reduce their income tax through planning, an increased signing bonus, the payment of moving expenses, better career opportunities, and a desired lifestyle.

To clearly demonstrate that they were severing their ties with Canada, the Movers canceled their Ontario driver's licenses, canceled OHIP, consolidated their banking to one account for convenience, sold their home, sold their vehicles, and moved the bulk of their goods to Arizona. In addition, Jenny turned down an offer to remain an additional three months with her employer after John's departure because of the complications of remaining a tax resident of Canada while John took up tax residency in the U.S. At our prompting, the Movers also notified all Canadian financial institutions (brokerage firms, banks, life insurance companies, mutual fund firms, etc.) that they were now non-residents of Canada and residents of the U.S. As a result, they were now subject to the appropriate withholding on any Canadian source income, as outlined in the Canada-U.S. Tax Treaty. Failure by a couple of financial institutions to withhold the appropriate amount (and in one case over-withholding) required a Part XIII tax return to be filed in Canada to correct the withholding, further complicating the Movers' situation.

U.S. FILING REQUIREMENTS

The Movers were required to file a U.S. "start-up" return by April 15th following the year they took up tax residency. To do so, they took our advice and both applied for a Social Security number upon entering the U.S. Our analysis revealed there was U$240,000 of embedded gains in the RRSPs (using the appropriate exchange rates). We "stepped up" the cost basis for U.S. purposes in the Movers' RRSPs prior to departure to eliminate any potential gains and set them up for a long-term, tax efficient withdrawal strategy. In addition to filing the appropriate tax forms for the RRSPs and the LIRA, we also took a Canada-U.S. Tax Treaty election on the U.S. return to step up the gains in the employer's stock and brokerage account for U.S. purposes. Our analysis also revealed that it was in the Movers' best interest to take a specific U.S. income tax election and be declared U.S. residents for the entire year and file jointly. Our analysis further revealed that, after they became residents of the U.S., it was worthwhile to collapse some of their RRSPs in Canada and transfer them to the U.S. in a staged fashion (they can't be transferred to an Individual Retirement Account, or IRA, in the U.S.). John created foreign tax credits with the 25% withholding rate, and Jenny was able to get some of her RRSPs out tax free while ineligible to work in the U.S. Through our structuring of their investment portfolio in both Canada and the U.S., we were able to use up some of these foreign tax credits on their U.S. tax returns (see "Investment Planning" below). We also ran a tax projection in the U.S. to give insights about John's W-4 form, instructing his employer how much income tax to withhold from his pay to ensure he wasn't over- or under-withheld. Finally, we informed John that, if he took up tax residency in the U.S. and exercised his stock options, he would have to file a Canadian T1 tax return to declare the income, as well as declare that income on his U.S. return with offsetting foreign tax credits. As a result, he decided to exercise some stock options prior to taking up tax residency in the U.S.

INDEPENDENCE PLANNING

In reviewing the Movers' financial projections, we determined that a move to the U.S. would enable them to achieve independence from work at John's age 59. If they were to remain in Canada the entire time, John would have to work until age 63 because of the higher income taxes, the fewer career advancement opportunities, and the lost tax benefits when reentering Canada. It appeared they would need a net worth of approximately C$3 million to live their desired lifestyle for the balance of their lives, so a disciplined savings plan was put in place but balanced with their desired lifestyle in Arizona to accumulate another U$500,000 before moving back to Canada.

In reviewing the different alternatives available for retirement savings, John began contributing to his employer's 401(k) plan only (no IRAs), with any surpluses going into their joint taxable portfolio. This approach set them up well for their pending move back to Canada.

Because both John and Jenny will contribute to the U.S. Social Security system while in the U.S., they will qualify for a Social Security retirement benefit at age 62 even if they move back to Canada. This is due to the Canada-U.S. Totalization Agreement, which allows both John and Jenny to use their working years in Canada to qualify for a retirement benefit in the U.S. as well. Further, since Jenny's working visa was delayed, she will pay less into the system and therefore can collect the greater of her benefit or half of John's at her age 62.

Both John and Jenny qualified for a Canada Pension Plan benefit before moving to the U.S. Although they will lose some contribution years during their absence from Canada, their current benefit will not diminish, and if they elect to stay in the U.S. after John's age 60 he could begin collecting his CPP benefit early (if doing so fits into their overall financial plan). The Movers will both qualify for Old Age Security when they return to Canada because they will have fulfilled the 40-year residency requirement after age 18.

RISK MANAGEMENT PLANNING

Besides a valid visa, the other item that is a "must have" before considering a move to the U.S. is some form of health insurance. The Movers' OHIP coverage ceased when they left Canada, but John is eligible for U.S. health benefits through his employer, and Jenny is included without any waiting period. This includes vision and dental care. Since John is the primary breadwinner, he has a C$500,000 term life insurance policy. The problem is that, if he dies in the U.S., the death benefit is only U$400,000 (at an 80¢ exchange rate). Based on our analysis and the Movers' new financial situation in the U.S., the death benefit is not sufficient for Jenny, so John is underwritten for a new 10-year term insurance policy in the amount of U$750,000 to replace his old policy. He has long-term disability insurance through his employer so that risk exposure is covered there.

We pointed out to the Movers that, with each year they work in the U.S., they accumulate credits toward Medicare. If they returned to Canada after just five years, they would have accumulated only 20 quarters of eligibility, so they would have to pay the full amount for Medicare Part A if they ever wanted to retire back in the U.S. However, if they stayed the full seven years as they desired and delayed resigning from John's employer until the start of the next year, they could accumulate 32 quarters of eligibility, enabling them to qualify for a discount of approximately 45% on Medicare Part A premiums should they return to the U.S. in the future. If they elected to remain in the U.S. for 10 years, they would be eligible for free Medicare Part A.

ESTATE PLANNING

In preparation for moving to the U.S., John and Jenny went to their local estate planning attorney in Ontario and had their wills updated. However, we pointed out the flaws of their current estate plan and the fact that their Canadian wills would not avoid the probate process in both Arizona and Ontario. To gain the greatest control in the event of death while in the U.S., John and Jenny elected to get a full trust-centered estate plan prepared in the U.S. after attending an estate planning seminar from a local attorney. We cautioned them on naming Canadian beneficiaries and being caught in the Canadian non-resident trust rules. They elected to change their estate plan to accommodate that by using testamentary trusts, and we encouraged them to contact us before moving back to Canada so the requisite pre-entry planning could be done with their living trust in place. After implementing their estate plan, they took more comfort with John's travels through work because, in the event of death, incapacity, or disability, their wishes would be implemented.

Using the information and titling provided in Table E.1, the Movers' U.S. estate tax liability was calculated as zero because they would be eligible for the unlimited marital deduction at the first spouse's death and, given the size of their estate, face no U.S. estate taxes since Congress increased the exemption to U$5.43 million.

If the Movers had stayed in Canada, the deemed disposition at death tax is estimated at C$474,319, including the RRSPs, LIRA, and brokerage account at the second spouse's death. Once they moved to the U.S., their Canadian deemed disposition at death was reduced to C$212,500 on the RRSPs and LIRA because of the 25% withholding (they had to move their brokerage account to the U.S. because their Canadian custodian told them to move it once they had a U.S. address on the account).

INVESTMENT PLANNING

As the collapsed RRSPs and brokerage accounts were transferred to the U.S., they were invested in a low-cost, tax-efficient, well-diversified investment portfolio with ample foreign exposure (outside the U.S. and Canada). The foreign exposure creates the right type of income to begin using up the foreign tax credits on the U.S. tax returns through the collapse of John's RRSPs, as well as hedges the Canadian loonie for their future retirement expenses in Canada. Further, the asset allocation we developed took advantage of the limited investment choices in John's 401(k) plan while maximizing the consumption of the foreign tax credits, all the while preparing the Movers for a potential move back to Canada.

APPENDIX F

Ed and Nettie Canuck hired Transition Financial Advisors to assist them in making a smooth transition to the U.S. (this case is based on a real-life fact pattern, but all names and numbers have been changed). Following are the financial planning issues, obstacles, and opportunities our planning process revealed for the Canucks. This is intended not to be blanket advice applicable to all situations but to increase your understanding of the many things that must be taken into account when considering a move to the U.S. Each person's situation is unique and requires a custom analysis to determine the best course of action. As any good transition planner should, we review the following eight areas of planning: customs, immigration, cash management, income tax, financial independence, risk management, estates, and investments; each is part of a comprehensive transition plan.

BACKGROUND
After many years of "snowbirding" in the U.S., Ed and Nettie decided to move permanently from Alberta to Florida to spend the rest of their lives. They were tired of watching the calendar, counting the days, and filing IRS form 8840 to show their closer tax connection to Canada. They

334

had some reservations about leaving their children, grandchildren, and friends but decided that visiting Canada rather than living there year round was more appealing. They recently wound up and sold their business for C$3.5 million and thought it was time to seize the opportunity to move to the U.S. Aged 65 and 62 respectively, married with three grown children and four grandchildren, both Ed and Nettie are Canadian citizens, with Nettie being an American citizen as well. The Canucks have a net worth of approximately C$8,833,333, comprised as follows.

TABLE F.1
CANUCKS' NET WORTH

Asset	Fair Market Value (C$)	Cost Basis (C$)	Titling
Canadian brokerage account	4,000,000	3,750,000	Joint
RRSP	600,000	—	Ed
RRSP	900,000	—	Nettie
IRA — U.S. (U$100,000)	111,111	—	Nettie
Checking/savings accounts	150,000	150,000	Joint
Principal residence (Alberta)	2,000,000	775,000	Joint
Florida home (C$650,000)	722,222	450,000	Joint
Autos (x2)	100,000	100,000	Joint
Personal/household/ jewelry	250,000	500,000	Joint
Total	8,833,333		
	600,000		Ed
	1,011,111		Nettie
	7,222,222		Joint

LIFE PLANNING

We started by determining where Ed and Nettie were "going," where they "were" now, and how they were going to get "there." The "plan" allowed individual financial decisions to be placed in context and ensure that limited resources were channeled toward achieving their plan. Following is a summary of their intentions.

- Ed and Nettie want to move permanently to Florida, severing their tax ties with Canada but spending summer months in Alberta close to their family.
- Now independent of work, they want to remain financially independent in the U.S.
- The Canucks want to pass their estate on prudently to their heirs in both Canada and the U.S., with a portion going to their church in Canada.

CUSTOMS PLANNING

The Canucks wanted to keep their home in Canada, along with a vehicle, for their visits in the summer months. We encouraged them to sell their home and take all of their personal goods with them to Florida, including their art collection, family heirlooms, and antiques, to ensure they properly severed their tax ties to Canada. Ed and Nettie elected to hire a reputable moving company to take care of all the details of moving their personal goods to the U.S., including development of a full inventory of goods to present to the U.S. Customs and Border Protection agent. To establish a defensible value for tax purposes, we advised them to get appraisals on their Florida and Alberta homes near the time they left Canada. We informed the Canucks that the vehicle they leave at their Florida residence would not be subject to the departure tax for CRA purposes.

Although "empty nesters," Ed and Nettie still had two babies: Dollar the collie and Loonie the yellow Lab. In preparation for their move, we suggested Ed and Nettie have both of their dogs examined by a vet and get a health certificate to assure their good health. At the same time, the veterinarian gave each dog a rabies shot and provided a letter confirming this treatment. When it came time to move to the U.S., the Canucks had no problems taking their dogs through U.S. Customs.

IMMIGRATION PLANNING

Since Nettie is an American citizen, she sponsored Ed for a green card. They had no set schedule for their move, so their plans accommodated the lengthy time it took to apply for his green card from Canada (versus the shorter period of time if they applied from within the U.S. during their winter vacation). We told Ed he should refrain from entering the U.S. while his green card application was being processed since he could jeopardize the entire filing. As a result, their immigration attorney applied for "advanced parole" at the same time the green card application went in so Ed and Nettie could come back to Canada in the summer after settling in Florida (while the green card application was still underway). Once he received his green card package from USCIS, we instructed him not to open it or he would delay his entry into the U.S. because he would have to wait for another one. The USCIS agent at the border must open the green card package when Ed crosses into the U.S. to take up residency there. In addition, Ed and Nettie were able to complete all of the pre-entry planning to mitigate their tax liability before Ed executed his green card package and took up tax residency in the U.S. After holding his green card for three years, Ed reviewed the pros and cons of U.S. citizenship with us and based on our conversation with him, he decided to become a U.S. citizen. They also used their citizenship to sponsor one of their grown children for a green card so she could realize her dream of moving to the U.S. as well.

CASH MANAGEMENT PLANNING

To expediently move their financial assets to the U.S., we helped the Canucks with currency exchange by pooling all of their available Canadian loonies at National Bank Correspondent Network Institutional. We had already moved the bulk of their investment portfolio into U.S. dollars once they made the decision to move to the U.S. and now exchanged the rest of their cash at our preferred rates with NBCN. These funds were wired into the Canucks' investment account in the U.S., so we were able to begin investing them the next day. This approach also avoided the required government paperwork surrounding the transfer of large amounts of cash to the U.S.

Ed and Nettie wondered about getting a U.S.-based credit card since they believed their Canadian U.S.-dollar credit card might be considered a tie to Canada. We advised them that a bank such as RBC Bank in the U.S. was comfortable with obtaining their Canadian credit report and based on it would issue them a U.S.-based credit card. To ease their move, the Canucks closed all of their checking and savings accounts except the one they would use for convenience when back in Canada during the summers, and to pay the bills related to their Canadian home. They also filed the necessary paperwork to have their CPP and OAS checks deposited directly into their checking account so their automated bill payments would be covered for their Canadian home.

INCOME TAX PLANNING

Key Assumptions
- CPP: C$12,780, Nettie C$7,300
- OAS: Ed C$6,765 (clawed back)
- Capital gains joint: C$75,000 (C$25,000 short term)
- Interest joint: C$42,000
- Dividends joint: C$83,000 (C$70,000 qualified/eligible dividends)
- Standard deduction used for U.S. scenario
- No exchange rates used (to show the net tax effect of the move)
- No tax planning included

TABLE F.2
2014 TAX COMPARISON

Canada	Ed	Nettie	C$	United States	US$
Federal	$11,672	$10,247	$21,919	Federal	$30,044
Alberta	$3,923	$3,375	$7,298	Florida	$0
Total	**$15,594**	**$13,622**	**$29,217**		**$30,044**
% of income			13.3%		13.5%
Health insurance			$0		$6,000
Grand total			**$29,217**		**$36,044**
			13.3%		16.4%

In the Canucks' situation, the move resulted in a tax differential that was nominal but the additional costs for health care in the U.S. caused more of a difference. Both Ed and Nettie were thrilled to find out that Ed would no longer be subject to the OAS clawback (nor would Nettie in the future), increasing their income every year in the U.S. by an inflation-adjusted C$13,530! Further, since OAS and CPP are taxed a maximum of 85% in the U.S., the Canucks had an even larger windfall. We were able to increase this differential by structuring their portfolio to integrate with their overall tax and financial plan. Through proper foreign tax credit planning and the use of other tax preference items, we were able to mitigate their U.S. tax liability even further and still meet their U.S. income requirements while maintaining their investment risk tolerance objectives.

CANADIAN FILING REQUIREMENTS

Ed and Nettie each needed to file a Canadian "exit" return by April 30th following the year they left Canada. On this return, the Canucks were subject to the "departure tax" that CRA imposes on expatriates. Included in this calculation, to the Canucks' surprise, were their Canadian brokerage account and their Florida residence. Our analysis indicated there were embedded gains of C$250,000 in the brokerage account and C$272,222 in their Florida home, leading to a departure tax of C$40,454 for Ed and C$40,454 for Nettie. To mitigate their departure tax, we delayed the Canucks' exit date from Canada to early in the year, netted some gains and losses together, and made RRSP contributions (plus some carry over amounts) to offset over C$20,000 of the departure tax. We also coordinated Ed and Nettie's charitable intentions with their tax situation so that a large charitable contribution could be made to their church before leaving Canada (we used this for tax purposes in both countries). These strategies, coupled with the reduced taxes outlined above, were more than satisfactory for the Canucks to realize their desired lifestyle and offset the departure tax they faced upon exit.

To clearly demonstrate that they were severing their ties with Canada, the Canucks canceled their Alberta driver's licenses, canceled their Alberta health care, consolidated their banking to one account for convenience, ensured their Florida address was on everything, and moved the bulk of their personal goods to Florida. They also canceled all but one of their Canadian credit cards and established a credit card in the

U.S. Further, they discontinued all of their subscriptions and memberships in Canada and reestablished them in Florida, including buying a membership at their local golf club.

U.S. FILING REQUIREMENTS

Since Nettie is a U.S. citizen, both she and Ed were shocked to find out that she was required to file U.S. federal tax returns (married filing separately) since moving to Canada in 1972, declaring her worldwide income (including that in Canada) on her U.S. return. We took advantage of the IRS' new streamlined ODVP filing procedures to file the required past three years' tax returns along with six years of FBARs to bring Nettie into compliance with the IRS. Given the offsetting foreign tax credits, there was no tax owing in the U.S. and, because they were filing from outside of the U.S. prior to their entry, no penalties would apply. Further, these tax returns were needed as part of her sponsorship of Ed's green card. Based on our analysis, we pointed out that Ed was required to file IRS Form 8840 — A Closer Connection Exception Statement with the IRS because he had exceeded 121 days in the U.S. for the previous three years. We filed this form to bring Ed into compliance with the IRS as well. Both he and Nettie were pleased to learn that Florida has no state income tax, so they would have no filing obligation with the state to contend with when they moved there.

When the Canucks moved to the U.S., Ed would simply be added to Nettie's tax return (married filing jointly) filed by April 15th. Our analysis revealed filing jointly with the specific income tax election to declare Ed a resident for the entire year was in their best interest to mitigate their U.S. tax obligation. Nettie had an existing Social Security number, but Ed had only an ITIN because of the previous sale of a U.S. property. We advised him that upon executing his green card package at the border, he would apply for a Social Security number that would replace his ITIN at that time.

Our analysis revealed there was U$75,000 of embedded gains inside Ed's RRSP (using the appropriate exchange rates), which we "stepped up" for U.S. tax purposes prior to executing his green card package. However, for Nettie, the embedded gains were more difficult to determine in her RRSP because she is a U.S. citizen. She began working with her brokerage firm while in Canada to establish a history in the account so we could determine the tax implications upon withdrawal.

INDEPENDENCE PLANNING

In reviewing the Canucks' projections, we determined that a move to the U.S. would not hamper them from maintaining their desired lifestyle for the balance of their lives (even with the departure tax and additional Medicare expenses they faced). Further analysis revealed they have a high probability of success in their projections; in fact, they'd have surplus funds that would allow for some lifetime gifting to heirs, philanthropy to their church, or enhancing their lifestyle. Furthermore, their projections revealed that they didn't need to take much risk in their investment portfolio to achieve their financial objectives.

They were thrilled to find out they would retain their current CPP benefits if they moved to the U.S. in addition to both of them being able to collect OAS. An even greater surprise came when Nettie found out she could double-dip into both Canadian and U.S. government pensions because she is eligible to collect her Social Security benefits at age 62 (U$6,000 annually after the windfall elimination provision is applied). Of even greater surprise was that Ed would automatically get half of her benefits or U$3,000 annually without having contributed a nickel to the system. We advised Nettie to contact the Social Security Administration to arrange for her and Ed's benefits to commence.

Nettie had concerns about her IRA in the U.S. From a tax standpoint, we advised her that it retained its tax-deferred status in the U.S. and in Canada. She would have to commence the required minimum distributions when she turned 70 1/2, and they would be fully taxable to her. We encouraged her to change the beneficiary on the IRA from her estate to Ed so he could maintain the tax-deferred status of the account in the event she predeceased him.

RISK MANAGEMENT PLANNING

One of the primary reservations Ed and Nettie had in moving to the U.S. was leaving the socialized medical system in Canada. We alleviated their concerns by showing them that through Obamacare, they were guaranteed insurable with a private policy. They could not be denied for Ed's high blood pressure and past basal cell removal. There was also the option of getting a catastrophic policy where they paid the first U$25,000 out of pocket with everything being covered after that. This policy would cost approximately U$3,000 per year for each of them. We further assured them that if something went very bad they could relocate back to Alberta for medical care because there is no waiting period there to obtain health care. Finally, because Nettie was a U.S. citizen and had established 40 quarters of coverage before getting married and moving to Canada, she would qualify for free Medicare Part A when she turned 65. After Ed had resided in the U.S. for five years, he would automatically qualify for free Medicare Part A as well, saving them U$9,768 in premiums in 2015. Part B would still cost them U$5,035 annually, and they would get on a basic Part D prescription plan for $144 annually.

ESTATE PLANNING

Given the size of Ed and Nettie's estate and because Ed — at the time of our initial planning — was not a U.S. citizen, comprehensive estate planning integrated with their financial plan was critical. Under the current estate exemption (U$5.43 million, for a total of U$10.86 million), the Canucks did not have a U.S. estate tax issue at this time. Given the size of their estate, and the potential for it to grow and exceed the exemption, Ed made substantial gifts to his children and grandchildren to reduce the size of the estate before taking up tax residency in the U.S. However, they needed a new U.S. estate plan as their health-care directives and powers of attorney would not be valid according to Florida statutes.

An additional complication was the fact that Ed and Nettie had heirs remaining in Canada who would receive a substantial inheritance at their passing. In most cases, a U.S. trust-centered estate plan is appropriate for a couple like Ed and Nettie. However, given that they have heirs in Canada, the establishment of a U.S. trust could be caught under Canada's non-resident trust rules. In this case, we looked at the role of wills (as opposed to living trusts) with specific U.S. tax language

If the Canucks had stayed in Canada, the deemed disposition at death tax is estimated at C$901,374, including the RRSPs, brokerage account, and Florida home at the second spouse's death. Once they moved to the U.S., their Canadian deemed disposition at death was reduced to

C$375,000 on the RRSPs because of the 25% withholding (they moved their brokerage account to the U.S. when they put a U.S. address on the account and immediately received notice from their custodian that they could no longer keep their account with them).

INVESTMENT PLANNING

As the collapsed RRSPs and brokerage accounts were transferred to the U.S., they were invested in a low-cost, tax-efficient, well-diversified investment portfolio with ample foreign exposure (outside the U.S. and Canada). The foreign exposure created the right type of income to begin using up the foreign tax credits in the U.S. generated with the collapse of their RRSPs (they have a "shelf life" of the current year plus 10 years in the U.S.). Further, the asset allocation we developed while they were still in Canada generated U.S.-dollar income to meet the Canucks' living expenses in the U.S. while further reducing their income tax liability (see "Income Tax Planning" above). We left a portion in Canadian dollars in Canada to meet their Canadian-dollar obligations for their home in Canada, etc. Their Canadian investment manager, unfamiliar with the Canada-U.S. transition planning issues, was eager to get the proceeds from the sale of their business working for them. She wanted to invest in a number of Canadian mutual funds. After consulting with us, the Canucks decided to leave their current investment manager, and some investments were made in Canada but in investment assets that were easily transferable to their U.S. brokerage account. The rest was left in cash and wired through NBCN where our clients get exceptional currency exchange rates. Shortly thereafter, we were able to finish implementing their investment policy statement.

INDEX

DISCLAIMER

This book presents general information including the author's investment philosophy. This information is not intended as personalized investment advice and should not be relied upon by any individual as the basis for investment decision making. Readers are encouraged to discuss their specific investment needs, goals, and objectives with a qualified investment professional.

Additionally, this book contains legal and tax information related to relocating from Canada to the United States. While the information contained in the books is deemed to be reliable, the author does not intend to provide comprehensive legal or tax advice. Readers are encouraged to seek the assistance of qualified legal and tax professionals regarding their specific legal and tax needs.